Baptismal
Ecclesiology

and the *Order of*
Christian Funerals

To Mark +
Susie —
May the Lord
guide your
baptismal journey!

Stephen S. Wilbricht, csc

Stephen S. Wilbricht, csc

FOREWORD BY **H. Richard Rutherford**, csc

LTP

LITURGY
TRAINING
PUBLICATIONS

Nihil Obstat
Rev. Mr. Daniel G. Welter, JD
Chancellor
Archdiocese of Chicago
September 18, 2018

Imprimatur
Most Rev. Ronald A. Hicks
Vicar General
Archdiocese of Chicago
September 18, 2018

BAPTISMAL ECCLESIOLOGY AND THE ORDER OF CHRISTIAN FUNERALS © 2019 Archdiocese of Chicago: Liturgy Training Publications, 3949 South Racine Avenue, Chicago, IL 60609; 800-933-1800; fax 800-933-7094; email: orders@ltp.org; website: www.LTP.org. All rights reserved.

This book was edited by Mary G. Fox. Michael A. Dodd was the production editor, and Kari Nicholls was the designer and production artist.

Cover art image from a stained glass window at St. Pius X Catholic Church, San Antonio, TX.

Interior art by Miloji/Shutterstock.com

23 22 21 20 19   1 2 3 4 5

Printed in the United States of America

Library of Congress Control Number: 2018949298

ISBN 978-1-61671-443-7

BECF

For Aaron Klippert and James Donahoe,
two hometown friends
for whom life here on earth was too short.
Be assured, my dear brothers,
that the ties of friendship and affection
which knitted us together as one
have not unraveled with your passing from our sight.

CONTENTS

FOREWORD

After more than five decades of pondering the complexity of Christian funeral liturgy, I read these pages with both nostalgia and trembling. Nostalgia, for the fresh challenge early post–Vatican II students of the liturgy faced seeking to interpret the theology of traditional funeral rites preserved in both literary and archaeological evidence across two millennia; trembling, because the years since have taught me the impossibility of ever apprehending fully the mystery embodied by the liturgy surrounding death for a Christian. With *Baptismal Ecclesiology and the* Order of Christian Funerals, Stephen S. Wilbricht, CSC, confrère and colleague, whom I have known for about half of these decades, corroborates the first and assuages the latter. By probing the rites of the *Order of Christian Funerals* through the lens of baptismal ecclesiology, Steve gives new life to Tertullian's adage "Christians are made, not born" (Apology 18, 4) and casts timely new light on today's challenges facing liturgical theology.

The book's conviction rests on the faith claim that, for the Christian, death—as we all must experience it—cannot have the last word before the God of the living. Preface I for Masses for the Dead professes, "for your faithful, Lord, life is changed not ended." While harsh reality teaches that our mortal life, the life lived between birth and death, indeed comes to an end, baptismal life in relationship with God established through the Paschal Mystery of Christ, enlivened by the enduring gift of the Paraclete, and sustained through the ministry of the Church, does not. Indeed, there is more to this claim than simply asserting the immortality of the soul. Mindful that there could be no Resurrection of the Christ without his very real "death, even death on a cross" (Philippians 2:8) and no baptismal ecclesiology without the death to self required of a vital Christian community, Wilbricht challenges the Church to be authentically Church when one of her own dies.

In this he intends that the ecclesiology of Church as Body of Christ and a constituent in the Communion of Saints invites us to rethink and reenvision the way the liturgy of the *Order of Christian Funerals* marks a death in the community. Death, perceived as a corporate event, forces a reordering in the Church. By acknowledging the death as a loss to the earthly Body and a change to the Communion of Saints, Wilbricht argues, genuine baptismal ecclesiology inherent to the *Order of Christian Funerals* does not leave the bereaved alone in their grief and, at once, serves as antidote to the Catholic funeral falling into the current cultural trap of denying or disguising the genuine human experience of death.

From the introduction, establishing theologies of Christian initiation and of death for a Christian as the unified point of departure, through five chapters that take up specifics of each, to the conclusion with its real-world pastoral emphasis, *Baptismal Ecclesiology and the* Order of Christian Funerals is liturgical theology at its best. A proven master of this discipline, Steve is a tribute to his doctoral alma mater the Catholic University of America and to the tireless commitment of emeritus professor Kevin W. Irwin and colleagues to instill in today's liturgical theologians the conviction that liturgy, such as Christian initiation and the *Order of Christian Funerals*, shapes "what the liturgy itself is and does." In so doing, Wilbricht brings into dialogue Bible and Tradition, church history and the magisterium past and present, the impact of culture in East and West, a wide range of authors, old and new—a who's who of voices that have shaped the discussion for over a century. More importantly, he accesses the rites and prayers of both the *Order of Christian Funerals* and the funeral Masses of *The Roman Missal* as well as the rituals and euchology of other Christian communions, particularly the Episcopal Church. Altogether, these resources are essential partners in his search to understand the link between Christian initiation and death—not just any death, but the death of a Christian. This all-inclusive approach to funeral liturgy as *locus theologicus* through the lens of baptismal ecclesiology is welcome and promises to keep readers broadly engaged throughout.

In developing this juxtaposition thoroughly for the first time, this is a work waiting to be written ever since *Sacrosanctum Concilium* established "the paschal character of Christian death" and "the community of the Church" as pillars on which to build the proposed revision of the Catholic funeral liturgy. A timely pastoral work, *Baptismal Ecclesiology and the Order of Christian Funerals* in the hands of skilled ministers has its work cut out for it. Changing cultural patterns bring with them trends, such as "do-it-yourself" funerals anywhere but at church and the "death is cool" or "death café" movements, and new language, where, for example, "passed" replaces "died," and cremated mortal remains or even ashes become "cremains." From the two-millennium-long history of wrapping the death of a Christian in the faith of the Church, nothing has been more pervasive than the give and take between Church and culture. Through it all, past and present, nothing likewise has been more effective than for the Church to be Church—doing what we do because we are who we are.

To this end, Steve Wilbricht has given us two master keys. Both invite pastoral sensitivity toward the dying and toward the bereaved. Regarding death for the baptized as a corporate event that touches the Body of Christ as a whole and revitalizing our appreciation for the mystery of the Communion of Saints speak a language both familiar and accessible to modern Christians. This is particularly true as well among contemporary bereavement theorists, secular as well as believers. Indeed, we have a long way to go in meeting the challenge, but every chapter of *Baptismal Ecclesiology and the* Order of Christian Funerals offers fresh nourishment for pastoral care in the cultural paradigm shift of our time, particularly for Sunday and funeral homilies. With the faith of baptized Christians, even before the open grave, we continue to make our song, *alleluia.*

H. Richard Rutherford, csc
Professor Emeritus
University of Portland

ACKNOWLEDGMENTS

The construction of this project largely developed during the summer months of 2017 and continued to fruition in the fall semester. It was during this time that I was graced with a sabbatical to relieve me of teaching duties in order to concentrate more fully upon research and writing. Thus, I am grateful for my colleagues in the Department of Religious Studies at Stonehill College in Easton, Massachusetts, who shouldered the bulk of my academic responsibilities. Likewise, I want to thank my local community of Holy Cross religious who graciously supported my decision to spend several months apart from them.

Of all the gifts that this sabbatical has provided, the greatest is the opportunity to spend the bulk of my time in Phoenix, Arizona. I spent the first five years of ordained ministry serving the people of two parishes in this part of the country: St. John Vianney Parish in Goodyear and St. Gregory the Great in downtown Phoenix. For those with whom I was able to reconnect, please know how much I cherish your friendship. The Southwest will always be home to me.

Among those who must be mentioned by name for their participation in this work are the seven Holy Cross priests with whom I prayed, ate, and socialized on a daily basis: John Pearson, csc; Jim Blantz, csc; Bill Faiella, csc; Duane Balcerski, csc; Joe O'Donnell, csc; Steve Sedlock, csc; and Jim Thornton, csc. I owe so much thanks to these brothers who exhibited such wonderful hospitality and provided me with friendship and support. A word of thanks to the house cook, Eric Howard, whose nourishing dinners were always valued!

I also wish to acknowledge the contribution that my brother in Holy Cross, Richard Rutherford, csc, played in the composition of this text. Not only am I indebted for the helpful suggestions he made in scrutinizing the text, but I am particularly grateful for his labor in writing the foreword.

For anyone wishing to research the topic of Christian funeral liturgy, the writing and thought of "Father/Doctor Death" is indispensable! Thanks as well to my fellow members of the Christian Initiation Seminar of the North American Academy of Liturgy, who provided input into the first chapter and overall shape of this book. Likewise, a great deal of gratitude must be expressed to Mary G. Fox and the entire editorial team at Liturgy Training Publications, who demonstrated great interest in this book from its conception through its publication. The same can be said for my parents, David and Sue Wilbricht, who have always shown an interest in my work and ministry and who continue to teach me about living fully the commitment of Baptism. Thanks, Mom and Dad.

Finally, I wish to thank my dear friend, Dixie Miller, who crossed over the waters of death on her way to the fullness of the Kingdom just hours after my arrival in Phoenix (October 7, 2017). A few short days before she died, she was planning a joyful reunion at her home; now she makes plans for that same reunion in the banquet halls of heaven. Dixie, I have felt your loving presence with me every step of the way in writing the pages that follow.

> *May the angels lead you into paradise;*
> *may the martyrs come to welcome you*
> *and take you to the holy city,*
> *the new and eternal Jerusalem.*

Introduction

At the death of a Christian, whose life of faith was begun in the waters of baptism and strengthened at the Eucharistic table, the Church intercedes on behalf of the deceased because of its confident belief that death is not the end nor does it break the bonds forged in life.[1]

Francis was a fisherman. Francis discovered his life's passion upon the waters of the Atlantic Ocean. A native of Provincetown, Massachusetts, at the tip of Cape Cod, Francis was a strong and rugged man whose years upon the sea had made him tough and resilient in his bodily frame and in his outlook toward life. Francis told stories of his days as a fisherman as though they were mystical experiences, times of beholding the wonder and power of creation; he looked at the ocean as a living being, as something to be cherished and respected. Although he no longer was capable of climbing into a fishing rig, Francis' heart was still somewhere out on the mighty seas.

I first encountered Francis not in a captain's chair but in a wheelchair, not with a fishing pole in his hands but with an oxygen tube in his nose. Although still exhibiting the look of strength, Francis was tired and weary. His loving and loyal wife, Rita, to whom Francis had been married for more than fifty-five years, was likewise a robust and sturdy woman. As a person of great faith, Rita labored to make her beloved Francis comfortable day and night. For while he still barked orders as though he were behind the wheel of his fishing boat, Rita could only hear the inherent gentleness that came forth from within.

Together with a minister of care from the local parish, I was fortunate to visit Francis' home several times and to sit at Rita's kitchen table. There she never missed the opportunity to place before us a bounty of fresh oysters on the half shell and mini lobster rolls, both well-known Provincetown delicacies. With Joe leading us in prayer, we gathered around Francis as he received Holy Communion and then prayed in thanksgiving for all who cared for him in an array of roles. We always made certain that Francis

---

1. *Order of Christian Funerals* (OCF), 4. From the General Introduction.

understood his oneness with the Body of Christ, even though he had physically been unable to be present at the Eucharist.

After this brief time of prayer, our attention naturally turned to conversation and enjoying the wonderful hors d'oeuvres that Rita had put before us. I relished the time of listening to Francis tell stories of his days as a fisherman. He talked about harrowing moments of surviving torrential storms, of the long hours that would pass between opportunities to catch a few moments of rest, of the incredible weight of some of the tuna that were bigger than a typical car. He was proud of his days as a fisherman. Francis had come ashore many years ago, but he was still one with the sea. It was an honor and a privilege to listen to his marvelous stories.

I had not heard enough of his tales of the mighty ocean before Francis would be called to make another journey over the waters, not those of the Atlantic Ocean but those that lead to eternal life. On the day of his Christian burial, fellow fishermen who had watched over Francis as passengers on his fishing vessel carried his body into the church that he had helped to build. For Francis' casket, the family chose a simple wooden box, which in many ways resembled a small rowboat. This fisherman was at home once again.

As Rita, her three children, and her grandchildren followed Francis' body into the church, the casket was placed near the small baptismal font at the entrance of the narthex. Friends and family were invited to crowd into the small space and to honor Francis' earthly remains with a gesture of welcome. The presider invited me, as a concelebrant, to sprinkle the casket before the white pall would be placed upon it. I cupped my hands and dipped them into the font, literally pouring the water upon the wooden box. Meanwhile, the presider loosely paraphrased words found in the 1970 *Rite of Funerals*: "We bless the body of Francis with the holy water that recalls his baptism of which Saint Paul writes: All of us who were baptized into Christ Jesus were baptized into his death. By baptism into his death we were buried together with him, so that just as Christ was raised from the dead by the glory of the Father, we too might live a new life."[2]

Rita and her three children were then invited to unfold the pall over Francis' casket. The care with which Rita led this liturgical gesture undoubtedly corresponded to the care she exhibited for Francis' clothing throughout

---

2. *Rite of Funerals*, 38.

his life. The clothes that were placed into her arms after a fishing expedition were certainly dirty and soiled. But this cloth that she now placed upon his body was one that would be forever unstained. Once again, the pastor employed words from the 1970 ritual: "On the day of his baptism, Francis put on Christ. In the day of Christ's coming, may he be clothed with glory."[3] Rita's hands worked to smooth out every possible wrinkle in the pall; the dedication of a loving wife was visible to all.

As those assembled in the narthex followed Francis' body into the worship space at the presider's invitation to "accompany the body of our brother into the church," everyone joined in a song known well to the people of this parish. "Pescador de Hombres" is sung each year at the blessing of the fishermen's fleet on the Sunday closest to the Solemnity of Sts. Peter and Paul, Apostles. The image of the Lord calling disciples at the water's edge resonates well with the parishioners. They know the verses by heart and sing them with gusto:

> Lord, you have come to the seashore
> neither searching for the rich nor the wise,
> desiring only that I should follow.
>
> O Lord, with your eyes set upon me,
> gently smiling, you have spoken my name;
> all I longed for I have found by the water,
> at your side, I will seek other shores.[4]

As the procession of ministers, casket, loved ones, and friends made its way down the aisle, the architecture of the worship space spoke as well. The windows along both sides of the church contain biblical scenes as well as contemporary events that occur on the water or at the beach, and directly behind the stone altar (literally an enormous rock) is a floor-to-ceiling stained glass window depicting Jesus pulling Peter out of the sea and saving him from his lack of faith. In addition to the water-themed windows, the wooden ceiling of the entire worship space, from the portals to the sanctuary, is designed to resemble the bottom of a ship. Once again, Francis was at home.

---

3. *Rite of Funerals*, 38.

4. "Pescador de hombres" © 1977, Cesáreo Gabaráin. Published by OCP, 5536 NE Hassalo, Portland, OR 97213. All rights reserved. Used with permission.

During the homily that followed the Gospel passage of the Risen Lord inviting the disciples to have breakfast with him at the shore of Lake Tiberias (John 21:1–19), the presider concentrated on the last two words of that passage in which Jesus tells Peter: "Follow me." The presider talked about Francis as responding fully to the Lord's call to follow him, not only in this life but in the next. He assured the assembly that a man who had spent his life navigating waters, sometimes calm and sometimes turbulent, was well equipped to follow the Risen Lord into the fullness of life. He suggested that the adventure for Francis was truly just beginning, that his Baptism was leading him to its true realization. Then, he stated with eloquence: "Baptism is not simply the assurance of eternal life; Baptism is a way of life, a way of following which does not end in death. Baptism is about the Church being one, of those living and those deceased together as one people making their passage over the waters into the waiting arms of God."

The celebration of Francis' life at the hour of his death was not about Francis, it was about the Church. Yes, stories of Francis in his young days as a rugged fisherman, in his role as a loving husband and a faithful father, and in his ability to portray an attitude of strength as death drew near were told so that the merit of this man was honored and would be remembered, but the emphasis of this funeral was that Francis is one with us in the boat. We were not truly leaving Francis, nor was he truly leaving us. Francis' Baptism made him a member of the Body of Christ, and as such, his gifts and talents were given to build up that Body and help it navigate the waters of life and death. Francis' funeral was a continuation of his Baptism, reminding the Church that he has a role to play even at, or perhaps more accurately, especially at, the end of his life on earth. The homily, the liturgical gestures, the music, and the prayers of Francis' funeral reminded all in the assembly that we continue to make our pilgrimage to God in our death. While his role in the Church has changed, Francis is still at home with us in the Church. Our common journey over the waters continues.

Funerals as a Christian "Order"

In August 1969, the work of the post–Vatican II's Consilium for the Implementation of the Constitution on the Liturgy led to the promulgation of the *Ordo exsequiarum*, which would subsequently be translated into English and published in 1971. The English translation for the title of this ritual was *Rite of Funerals*. Interestingly enough, after the revision of the Latin original edition of the *Ordo exsequiarum*, the 1989 English translation of the ritual book was changed to the *Order of Christian Funerals*. This change is not insignificant, as the word "order" is particularly important in our understanding of the death of a Christian. "Orders" are not simply the official outlines or patterns for liturgical prayer, they are also a way in which the Church establishes a certain portion of the Body of Christ as having a ministry to provide for the Church as a whole.

For example, catechumens in the early Church, just as they are understood today in the *Rite of Christian Initiation of Adults*, were pronounced to be members of a Church "order." Their ministry was, and continues to be, the embodiment of the spirit of conversion. The members of the Body of Christ as a whole look upon the catechumens and scrutinize their desire to abandon a way of life to fully respond to the Lord's call, "Follow me." Likewise, in the early Church, widows were considered to be a part of a Church order. Their ministry was prayer as well as giving the Church an object of pastoral care and support. This order did not separate them from the Body of Christ, but rather, it served to clarify the unique gifts that these individuals provided for the good of the whole. Yet another order in the early Church was the order of penitents. When men and women presented themselves for reconciliation with the Church for sins that could not be absolved by participation in the Eucharist (usually the three sins of adultery, idolatry, and murder), the Church would pronounce them to be public sinners. The penitents would humble themselves at the doors of the church in sackcloth and ashes and often receive the ridicule of onlookers. Nevertheless, in this order they were assisting the Church as a whole, reminding the Body of Christ of the need to refrain from sin and to help those who had sinned to be fully reconciled with the Body.

At the outset of this work, the important role that Christian death plays as the carrying out of a particular ministry for the Body of Christ is considered. Death provides the opportunity for the Church to work together to provide a ministry of consolation, and at the very same time, death allows the Christian community to strengthen its hope in the resurrection. As in all the other orders of the Church, death helps to put the members of the Body of Christ back together in a new relationship; after the Body of Christ has experienced a crisis, its members must be fitted together with a renewed outlook on the world. Paragraph 8 from the General Introduction to the *Order of Christian Funerals* explains:

> "If one member suffers in the body of Christ which is the Church, all the members suffer with that member" (1 Corinthians 12:26). For this reason, those who are baptized into Christ and nourished at the same table of the Lord are responsible for one another. When Christians are sick, their brothers and sisters share a ministry of mutual charity and "do all that they can to help the sick return to health, by showing love for the sick, and by celebrating the sacraments with them." So too when a member of Christ's Body dies, the faithful are called to a ministry of consolation to those who have suffered the loss of one whom they love. Christian consolation is rooted in that hope that comes from faith in the saving Death and Resurrection of the Lord Jesus Christ. Christian hope faces the reality of death and the anguish of grief but trusts confidently that the power of sin and death has been vanquished by the risen Lord. The Church calls each member of Christ's Body—Priest, Deacon, layperson—to participate in the ministry of consolation: to care for the dying, to pray for the dead, to comfort those who mourn.[5]

The General Introduction is clear that the three-pronged ministry of caring for the dying, praying for the dead, and comforting those who mourn is the work of all the baptized. With Baptism comes the duty to be "responsible for one another" in life and in death. This responsibility of baptized Christians does not end with the death of the physical body. For the Church "recognizes the spiritual bond that still exists between the living and the dead and proclaims its belief that all the faithful will be raised up and reunited in the new heavens and a new earth, where death will be no more."[6]

Baptism and Death

One of the many tasks of the Consilium, which labored extensively to renew the rites of the Church beginning in the mid-to-late 1960s, was to make funerals more paschal. The Council Fathers mandated, "The rite of funerals should express more clearly the paschal character of Christian death and should correspond more closely to the circumstances and traditions of

---

5. OCF, 8.
6. OCF, 6.

various regions. This also applies to the liturgical color to be used."[7] Thus, a theology of Baptism must undergird the renewal of funerals. This is not simply a matter of restoring the paschal symbols used in funerals but also is a restoration of a particular way of thinking about death. In Baptism, one dies to self in order to be raised in Christ (Romans 6:1–11). However, this dying to self is an ongoing process that encompasses the entirety of one's life and is only accomplished in the sharing of eternal life with God. This is what it means to profess one's baptismal commitment on a daily basis.

Likewise, one of the major aspects of post-conciliar reform concerning the Sacrament of Baptism is the recapturing of its communal character. This is most obvious with the restoration of the *Rite of Christian Initiation of Adults*, in which virtually every aspect of the process of conversion is celebrated publicly. Even with infant Baptism, most parishes make the attempt to regularly celebrate the Baptism of several children within the context of the Sunday assembly. At the very least, there has been a gradual shift away from seeking Baptism for fear-based reasons to that of desiring real participation in the life of a Christian community. When a life, either that of a mature adult or that of a swaddling infant, is grafted onto Christ through Baptism, the Body of Christ changes, it cannot remain the same. "Making entrance into the Christian community a choice between a Way of Life and a Way of Death suggests that in the process of becoming a Christian one leaves something behind and takes on something new."[8] The Body of Christ is fashioned anew, as Baptism involves the whole household of God.

At the same time, Baptism is eschatological;[9] it is always looking forward to the completion that will come in the final resurrection of the dead. The eschatological nature of Baptism is lived out as the Christian community experiences the journey through life as living into a new creation. Thus, every member of the baptized has the responsibility to work to build up the Body of Christ (Ephesians 4:12); Baptism is about death to self in order to live for others. Joann Crowley writes:

> Baptism is a time for the whole community to re-experience the transition (of death to life), and to move to a new deeper place of

---

7. *Sacrosanctum Concilium* (SC), 81.

8. Christian B. Scharen, "Baptismal Practices and the Formation of Christians: A Critical Liturgical Ethics," *Worship* 76 (2002): 49.

9. See Joann Crowley, "Baptism as Eschatological Event," *Worship* 62 (1988): 290–298.

realizing the cosmic unity of the reign of God. It is a sacrament *for the community*, not only adding to the body a new member with access to the Spirit, but also offering a moment of potency for radical new life and change to be incorporated into a newly structured way of existence. . . . Clearly, the impact of baptism cannot be grasped if it is viewed as a private effect on an individual. Christians are members of a corporate personality from which they derive life, and to which they contribute in such a way that the existence of the body depends on their existence (1 Corinthians 12:12–27).[10]

What is said here of Baptism also must be said of death. A Christian may die physically alone in his or her body, but membership in the Body of Christ does not cease, it is merely reordered. Just as the living are called to build up the Body of Christ through corporate worship and acts of charity, so too do the dead continue to build up the Body until that day when the entire Church will be ushered into heaven's light. Just as Baptism is not a sacrament about finality, but rather one of process and becoming, so too is death. While the rite of commendation and farewell at the funeral of a Christian acknowledges the reality of separation, it is not a moment of finality as much as a recognition of the Church becoming something new, progressing *together* a bit closer to the gates of paradise.

About this Book

The argument that is waged in the pages ahead is not simply that work needs to be done to make the funeral rites more baptismal, but that an understanding needs to be restored within the Church of our common Baptism in which the equality of all the members of Christ extends beyond the horizon that separates life from death. In other words, the contention is made here that a greater appreciation of baptismal dignity, in which all of the members of Christ play a valuable role in contributing to the functioning of the Body, will serve the Church well in the crisis moment of Christian death. For then, all of the members baptized into Christ will see their obligation to attend the dead with prayer, and to accompany the grieving with support, and they will help to preserve the ongoing memory of the dead as a truly active presence within the Church of the living.

---

10. Crowley, 295.

To this end, chapter 1, "What Is Baptismal Ecclesiology?" explores a term that will largely be foreign to most Roman Catholics. While many Reformed communities and much of the Eastern Church have a deep appreciation for the mystery of the Church based on fellowship, the Catholic West is slow to develop and embrace the ecclesiology articulated so well in the Second Vatican Council: "As all the members of the human body, though they are many, form one body so also do the faithful in Christ (see 1 Cor 12:12). A diversity of members and functions is engaged in the building up of Christ's body, too."[11] Consequently, chapter 1 will explore a wide range of literature on the concept of baptismal ecclesiology, beginning with those believed to be the originators of the term and continuing with various Catholic theologians who define the nature of the Church in conjunction with our common baptismal commitment.

Chapter 2, "The Ecclesial Nature of Death in Ancient Christianity," explores many of the known funeral practices of the early Christians and demonstrates their hope forged upon baptismal bonds. Christian thought around the topic of death and burial developed in the milieu of a Jewish patrimony and a pagan culture. How Christians adopted various customs and overtly challenged others helped to create a uniquely Christian approach to its theology of death. At the outset, a positive outlook toward death was accompanied with rituals of "refreshment" designed to help the dead in their transition to new life.[12] At the same time, the Church had to wrestle with the concept of God's judgment. It would be impossible for them to deny the scriptural references to a God who will at the end of time sit in judgment over all the tribes of earth. Thus, chapter 3, "The Turn to the Individual in Christian Funerals," explores how a sense of fear came to dominate Christian thinking around death, with the subsequent articulation of a theology of the afterlife based upon human unworthiness and sin. As a result, death became more individualistic and less ecclesial. The funeral itself would now be celebrated more as a rite of absolution for the dead than as the community's common transitus into divine life.

Chapter 4, "Restoring the Ecclesial Spirit in the *Order of Christian Funerals*," focuses on the work of the Vatican II Consilium charged with redrafting the funeral liturgy as well as the largely successful revisions that

---

11. *Lumen gentium* (LG), 7.

12. See Richard Rutherford with Tony Barr, *The Death of a Christian: The Order of Christian Funerals*, rev. ed. (Collegeville, MN: Liturgical Press, 1990), 6.

have been made to renew both the paschal and the ecclesial nature of Christian burial rites. Within this chapter will occur some comparison of the first English translation of the *Ordo exsequiarum, Rite of Funerals* (1970), to the second edition, *Order of Christian Funerals* (1989). The primary intent of this exploration will be to show how the revision process as a whole eliminated much of the fear-based elements of God's judgment found in the previous generations of rituals for celebrating a Christian's funeral. However, the chapter also will suggest that the renewal of the funeral liturgy is still incomplete and that various components of the funeral liturgy fail to develop an understanding of the Body of Christ along the lines of baptismal ecclesiology. The renewed liturgy may have succeeded in making the rituals surrounding death more paschal, but do they not continue to allow for an exaggerated emphasis to be placed upon the uniqueness of the individual celebrated in death so that the ongoing pilgrimage of the Body of Christ is left in the background?

This leads to the final chapter of the book, "Contemporary Conundrums and Pastoral Possibilities," which explores contemporary problems to be tackled in the celebration of Christian burial as well as pastoral suggestions on how baptismal identity may once again be at the center of our funeral liturgy. Several of the modern-day issues that impact our celebration of the death of a Christian are the general denial of death in society, the lack of participation of the community in the bereavement process, the planning of a funeral according to the needs and convenience of the family rather than the worshipping community, and finally, the ritualizing of Christian values in a society colored by individualism and commercialism. This chapter explores how a local Christian community might work together to ensure that it is allowed to fully take on its baptismal commitment to care for the grieving and to bury the dead. Some pastoral suggestions might seem impractical to the reader, given the way in which our society and culture are constructed. However, we must ask ourselves to what degree are we willing to challenge cultural norms and outlooks to maintain and to publicly profess our hope in the Resurrection. The issue of belonging is inherently tied to the way death is celebrated. For if we cannot publicly honor the dead as continuing to be members of the Body of Christ, or if the dead seem to no longer play a vital role (an "order") within the Church, then Christians will continue to be misled into thinking that their participation within the Body of Christ is nonessential to the makeup of the Church.

CHAPTER ONE

What Is Baptismal Ecclesiology?

The one mediator, Christ, established and constantly sustains here on earth his holy church, the community of faith, hope and charity, as a visible structure through which he communicates truth and grace to everyone. But, the society equipped with hierarchical structures and the mystical body of Christ, the visible society and the spiritual community, the earthly church and the church endowed with heavenly riches, are not to be thought of as two realities. On the contrary, they form one complex reality comprising a human and divine element.[1]

The theological study of the Church, *ecclesiology*, attempts to define the nature of the Church in terms of its foundation, its adherence to both Scripture and Tradition, and its mission to the world at large. One of the greatest tensions within ecclesiology is whether the Church is best defined by the structures of an institution or by the way of life set up by the disciples of Christ. In 1974, Avery Dulles offered what was then considered a revolutionary contribution to ecclesiology by contending that the Church is best understood through a variety of models that, when seen in relationship to one another, provide a well-rounded description of the mystery that is the Church.[2] Thus, Dulles put forth five models—Church as institution, Church as mystical communion, Church as sacrament, Church as herald, Church as servant—which he believed covered the broad and elusive landscape of the Church. Because the Church is a mystery, none of these models will succeed in and of themselves to exhaust the need for ongoing contemplation of the character of the Church. Ecclesiology must be approached anew in every age and culture.

As is the case with Dulles' *Models of the Church*, the event of the Second Vatican Council (1962–1965) in response to Pope John XXIII's call for *aggiornamento* (a "springtime" for the Church) opened the door for a

---

1. LG, 8.
2. See Avery Dulles, *Models of the Church* (New York: Doubleday, 1974).

radically new, or perhaps better stated, a restoration of ancient outlooks on the Church. Ecclesiology in the second half of the twentieth century was now free to move away from an insular method that kept the Church inwardly focused. As the Church came to understand its mission as one of empathy with (not separation from) the world, it would need to drop the fortress mentality that had prospered hand in hand with the spread of Christendom.[3] No longer would ecclesiology be limited to a hierarchical model, whereby the *ecclesia docens* ("the teaching Church," that is, the hierarchy) ruled over the *ecclesia discens* ("the learning Church," that is, the laity). The belief that the Church is a "perfect society," a description that came to the fore at the time of the Counter Reformation and continued to flourish through the first half of the twentieth century, no longer made sense in a world of burgeoning cultures that existed apart from the Church's domain.[4]

Thus, one of the primary fruits of the Second Vatican Council is the variety of images the Council Fathers use to describe the Church. For instance, the Council's Constitution on the Church, *Lumen gentium* (November 21, 1964), begins by calling the Church a sacrament:

> Since the church, in Christ, is a sacrament—a sign and instrument, that is, of communion with God and of the unity of the entire human race—it here proposes, for the benefit of the faithful and of the entire world, to describe more clearly, and in the tradition laid down by earlier council, its own nature and universal mission.[5]

By declaring the Church to be a sacrament, the Council rejected the idea that the Church is cut off from the world, isolated from the joys and sufferings of all humanity; rather, the Church "desires to bring to all humanity that light of Christ which is resplendent on the face of the church."[6]

A second image that emanates from the work of the Council is the very title of the second chapter of *Lumen gentium*, "The People of God." Paragraph 4 of the Constitution on the Church offers the following instruction: "Hence the universal church is seen to be 'a people made one by the

---

3. See Dennis M. Doyle, *The Church Emerging from Vatican II: A Popular Approach to Contemporary Catholicism* (Mystic, CT: Twenty-Third Publications, 1992), 9–15.

4. See Michael A. Fahey, "Church," in *Systematic Theology: Roman Catholic Perspectives*, vol. 2, ed. Francis Schüssler Fiorenza and John Galvin (Minneapolis, MN: Fortress Press, 1991), 32.

5. LG, 1.

6. LG, 1.

unity of the Father, the Son and the holy Spirit.'"[7] Furthermore, paragraph 9 states that God has "willed to make women and men holy and to save them, not as individuals without any body between them, but rather to make them into a people who might acknowledge him and serve him in holiness."[8] The Church is, by its very nature a communion (*koinonia*), a sharing, a participation, in the unity of divine life. As Michael Lawler and Thomas Shanahan comment: "In an ecclesiology in which a constitutive role is assigned to the Spirit, the Church is never an absolute *fait-accompli*, an institution. It is always an eschatological reality, a people-in-communion . . . making its pilgrim way to God who is Trinity."[9] Thus, *Lumen gentium* devotes an entire chapter to describing the People of God as a pilgrim Church. The Council Fathers write in paragraph 49:

> When the Lord will come in glory, and all his angels with him (see Mt 25:31), death will be no more and all things will be subject to him (see 1 Cor 15:26–27). But at the present time some of his disciples are pilgrims on earth, others have died and are being purified, while others are in glory, contemplating "in full light, God himself triune and one, exactly as he is." All of us, however, in varying degrees and in different ways share in the same love of God and our neighbor, and we all sing the same hymn of glory to our God. All, indeed, who are of Christ and who have his Spirit form one church and in Christ are joined together (Eph 4:16). So it is that the union of the wayfarers with the brothers and sisters who sleep in the peace of Christ is in no way interrupted, but on the contrary, according to the constant faith of the church this union is reinforced by an exchange of spiritual goods.[10]

The Church is not simply comprised of the earthly realm of disciples, but rather, it is made up of the dead who continue the journey into the fullness of divine life. "In the lives of those companions of ours in the human condition who are more perfectly transformed into the image of Christ (see

---

7. LG, 4.

8. LG, 9.

9. Michael G. Lawler and Thomas Shanahan, "The Church Is a Graced Communion," *Worship* 67 (1993): 489. Earlier in the article the authors write: "The transition from the preparatory document to *Lumen Gentium* is a transition from a juridical vision that sees Church as institution and structure to a theological one that sees it as mystery and graced communion. It is a transition from a fixation on hierarchical office and power to an appreciation of coresponsibility and service, from an exclusive focus on Roman primacy to an inclusive ecclesial communion" (486).

10. LG, 49.

2 Cor 3:18) God shows, vividly, to humanity his presence and his face."[11] To contemplate the mystery of the Church, therefore, it is necessary to ponder the mystery of death in the framework of the Mystical Body of Christ, head and members united as one.

While there are many more images of the Church developed in the writings of the Second Vatican Council (such as the Church as a "sheepfold," "God's farm or field," the "spotless spouse of the spotless lamb"),[12] it is the Pauline image of the Body of Christ that most commonly occurs in the Constitution on the Church as well as in other documents of the Second Vatican Council, such as *Sacrosanctum Concilium* (the Constitution on the Sacred Liturgy) and *Gaudium et spes* (the Pastoral Constitution on the Church in the Modern World), and is the one that will occupy the center of attention in this work. Paragraph 7 of *Lumen gentium* explores this image in great detail:

> In the human nature united to himself, the son of God, by overcoming death through his own death and resurrection, redeemed humanity and changed it into a new creation (see Gal 6:15; 2 Cor 5:17). For by communicating his Spirit, Christ mystically constitutes as his body his brothers and sisters who are called together from every nation.
>
> In this body the life of Christ is communicated to those who believe and who, through the sacraments, are united in a hidden and real way to Christ in his passion and glorification. Through Baptism we are formed in the likeness of Christ: "For in one Spirit we were all baptized into one body" (1 Cor 12:13). In this sacred rite our union with Christ's death and resurrection is symbolized and effected: "For we were buried with him by Baptism into death"; and if "we have been united with him in the likeness of his death, we shall be so in the likeness of his resurrection also" (Rom 6:45). . . .
>
> As all the members of the human body, though they are many, form one body, so also do the faithful in Christ (see 1 Cor 12:12). A diversity of members and functions is engaged in the building up of Christ's body, too. There is only one Spirit who, out of his own richness and the needs of the ministries, gives his various gifts for the welfare of the church (see 1 Cor 12:1–11). . . . The same Spirit who of himself is

---

11. LG, 50.
12. See LG, 6.

the principle of unity in the body, by his own power and by the interior cohesion of the members produces and stimulates love among the faithful. From this it follows that if one member suffers in any way, all the members suffer, and if one member is honored, all the members together rejoice (see 1 Cor 12:26).

The head of this body is Christ. He is the image of the invisible God and in him all things came into being. He is before all creatures and in him all things hold together. He is the head of the body which is the church. He is the beginning, the firstborn from the dead, that in all things he might hold the primacy (see Col 1:15–18). . . .

All the members must be formed in his likeness, until Christ is formed in them (see Gal 4:19). For this reason we, who have been made like to him, who have died with him and risen with him, are taken up into the mysteries of his life, until we reign together with him (see Phil 3:21; 2 Tim 2:11; Eph 2:6; Col 2:12, etc.) On earth, still as pilgrims in a strange land, following in trial and in oppression the paths he trod, we are associated with his sufferings as the body with its head, suffering with him, that with him we may be glorified (see Rom 8:17).[13]

While the drafters of the Constitution on the Church would not have referred to this depiction of the Church as "baptismal ecclesiology," that is precisely what it is. Studying the mystery of the Church through the lens of Baptism means, first and foremost, seeing it as a unified body, comprised of diverse (but equal) members, each with unique gifts and functions for use for the good of the whole, so "that if one member suffers in any way, all the members suffer, and if one member is honored, all the members together rejoice." As Paul instructs the community at Galatia, because of a common Baptism, "There is neither Jew nor Greek, there is neither slave nor free person, there is not male and female; for you are all one in Christ Jesus" (Galatians 3:28). Simply stated, baptismal ecclesiology underscores the fundamental oneness of Christ's Body; how the Church sets up its institutional structures and how it ministers in the world are meant to bear witness to this principle of unity. Fahey comments: "The emphasis is not on the role of Christians taken as individuals but rather as members of the body of Christ. The faithful find their dignity rooted in the gift of baptism

---

13. LG, 7.

through which even as lay persons they share in the priestly and prophetic office of Christ."[14]

A United or Divided Church?

One could argue that the most identifiable characteristic of Christianity today is not unity but rather division. Since the time of the definitive break between Eastern Orthodoxy and Western Catholicism in the Great Schism of 1054, through the Protestant Reformation in the sixteenth century, until today with the appearance of numerous non-denominational congregations, Christianity must be seen as giving a counter-witness to the oneness of Trinitarian life. "The most obvious fact about the Christian church today is that it is divided. Not only are the churches of the East and the West existentially estranged and still living in mutual suspicion of one another after over a millennium, but the churches of the West themselves have been tragically fragmented since the sixteenth century."[15] Indeed, if the true nature of the Church is to mirror the undivided unity of the Trinity, living as members of one body in which the "least" matter as much as the "greatest," then the division of the followers of Christ is a paramount scandal. The Fathers of the Second Vatican Council acknowledge this scandal in the Decree on Ecumenism: "The restoration of unity among all Christians is one of the principal concerns of the Second Vatican Council. Christ the Lord founded one church and one church only."[16] In an attempt to validate the status of Christians separated from the Catholic Church, they would continue to write in paragraph 3 of this same document: "For those who believe in Christ and have been properly baptized are put in some, though imperfect, communion with the Catholic Church."[17]

Since the close of the Council in 1965, the topic of Christian ecclesial unity has been widely explored within and outside the Roman Catholic Church. Some of the primary issues brought to light that constitute ongoing division within Christianity are: the separation of ministerial orders according to bishop, presbyter, and deacon; the nature of apostolic succession and the fullness of ordained ministry in the person of the bishop; papal

---

14. Fahey, "Church," 44.

15. Fahey, 6.

16. *Unitatis redintegratio,* 1.

17. *Unitatis redintegratio,* 3.

primacy; opening ordained ministry to women; and the theological under-standing of the sacraments and certain moral issues.[18] While these challenges seem daunting to resolve, one of the major achievements in ecumenical dialogue over the last fifty years has been the recognition of Baptism as a true and common bond among Christians. As one member of a Reformed church writes: "The reformation of baptism, it now is becoming clear, has taken on a new importance as the combined efforts of churches to reclaim authentic Christian identity in a time when citizenship in the cities of God and humankind are intermingled and confused."[19]

The most widely recognized accomplishment in the area of restored communion based on a mutual recognition of Baptism is the 1982 paper *Baptism, Eucharist and Ministry*, in which a gathering of a worldwide team of theologians representing a variety of Christian traditions declared:

> Administered in obedience to our Lord, baptism is a sign and seal of our common discipleship. Through baptism, Christians are brought into union with Christ, with each other and with the Church of every time and place. Our common baptism, which unites us to Christ in faith, is thus a basic bond of unity. We are one people and are called to confess and serve one Lord in each place and in all the world. The union with Christ which we share through baptism has important implications for Christian unity. "There is . . . one baptism, one God and Father of us all . . . " (Eph 4:4–6). When baptismal unity is recognized in one holy, catholic, apostolic Church, a genuine Christian witness can be made to the healing and reconciling love of God. Therefore, our one baptism in Christ constitutes a call to the churches to overcome their divisions and visibly manifest their fellowship.[20]

The work of restoring unity within a divided Christianity has been less about mandating that all Christians return to Roman Catholicism and

---

18. See Fahey, "Church," 7.

19. Keith Watkins, "Baptism and Christian Identity: A Presbyterian Approach," *Worship* 60 (1986): 56. He continues later in the article: "Our battles are no longer Catholic against Protestant, Lutheran against Reformed, 'paedobaptists' against 'anabaptists.' Rather, we struggle against evil rulers who in Europe, Africa, Asia, and the Americas have engaged in genocide during the past half century, a genocide that has made all of our belief in progress a terrible illusion and lie. We struggle against the abuse of the natural world that threatens a long and bitter descent into a new primitive way of life in which we scarcely can survive. We live in a world of sin, a world that contributes life-threatening ill-ness and maiming to the not-yet-born, a sin that engages the life of the youngest and tiniest among us, and the wealthiest and most powerful as well" (63).

20. *Baptism, Eucharist and Ministry*, Faith and Order Paper No. 111 (Geneva: World Council of Churches, 1982), paragraph 6, page 2.

more about helping Christians to recognize and honor a diversity of ways for following Christ, for worshipping God, and therefore for forming one Christian Church. As Catholic theologian and ecumenist Walter Kasper writes: "Church and baptism belong together from the very beginning. . . . Hence the ecumenical movement from the start has sought to make our common baptism the point of departure and the basis for ecumenical efforts."[21]

Writing at the beginning of the third millennium, one Roman Catholic author discusses "baptismal ecclesiology" as a way of thinking about the Church that moves away from seeing communion as a local reality (that is, something celebrated in a community's Sunday Eucharist) toward viewing the universality of the Church.[22] Gerard Kelly emphasizes that, even before a community celebrates the Eucharist for the purpose of manifesting and strengthening communion, Baptism is primarily a sacrament of communion. He writes:

> This emerging ecclesiology can open up another avenue for reflection and questioning, namely, the ecumenical significance and role of the community of the baptized. When we say that baptism creates communion we can be more specific and, using language with a solid biblical foundation in both the Hebrew and Christian scriptures, say that baptism creates a priestly people. The significance of this language is that it designates the communion of the baptized as being at the service of the work of God. In other words, one of the effects of baptism is that the church participates in the renewing work of God for the communion of the whole of creation with God and among themselves.[23]

Kelly's understanding of the corporate nature of Baptism eliminates any notion of passivity around the sacrament; "Baptism thus establishes a communion of service among all who are baptized."[24] In this way, "Church" is outwardly focused; it is not simply about recognizing itself in the gathering of the baptized but in realizing God's grace active for the world in the unity of the baptized disciples of every denomination. Lutheran liturgical scholar Gordon Lathrop shares this ecclesiological outlook toward the communion that is established in Baptism when he writes: "Baptism constitutes the 'holy

---

21. Walter Kasper, "Ecclesiological and Ecumenical Implications of Baptism," *The Ecumenical Review* 52 (2000): 526.
22. See Gerard Kelly, "Baptismal Unity in the Divided Church," *Worship* 75 (2001): 511–527.
23. Kelly, 517.
24. Kelly, 517.

people,' who are naked and needy, being forgiven, being drawn from death. Baptism gathers an assembly into Christ and so into identification with the situation of all humanity, not into distinction and differentiation. Paradoxically, Baptism is the washing that makes us unclean, with all the unclean and profane ones of the world. In Christ, Baptism makes us part of humanity, witnesses to the grace of the triune God for us all."[25] Thus, while age-old disputes and deeply-rooted suspicions may serve as road-blocks for ecumenical dialogue, perhaps the truth is that our one Baptism in Christ is more enduring and capable of creating a unity that can only come from the love of perfect communion, namely from the heart of God.

Baptismal Ecclesiology: The Contribution from the Episcopal Church

Interestingly enough, much of the work that has been done to reclaim the oneness of the Church based upon the bond of common Baptism has come from the descendants of the Protestant Reformation, specifically from the Anglican Church, which evolved out of the liturgy and practices of the Church of England established by King Henry VIII in 1534. Even more narrowly, it can be asserted that the primary scholars responsible for pro-moting this type of ecclesiology come from the Episcopal Church. Their efforts to replace a hierarchical ecclesiology with a baptismal ecclesiology has served to challenge Christianity, summoning it to reexamine the seri-ousness of baptismal commitment and to see it as the great social leveler, uniting a plethora of diversity into the oneness that is Christ.[26]

An early example of what would soon be known as "baptismal ecclesi-ology," and one representing the Episcopal Church perspective, is the book-let, *Baptized into the One Church*, written in 1963 by C. Kilmer Myers.[27] In

25. Gordon Lathrop, *Holy People: A Liturgical Ecclesiology* (Minneapolis, MN: Fortress Press, 1999), 182. At the conclusion of the book, Lathrop offers these stirring words regarding the power of the assembly (that is, the Church): "So come into the assembly. Hear the word of forgiveness that recon-ciles you to God's purposes with this gathering of people. Help renew the strength of the meeting, participating anew in the power of its symbols. Help make the connection with other Christians in other places. Welcome to the way of Baptism those who wish to join us. Help open the door. And see how, in the heart of the meeting, a mantle is wrapped around all of naked humanity and the jaws of death are opened" (227).

26. See Colin Podmore, "The Baptismal Revolution in the American Episcopal Church: Baptismal Ecclesiology and the Baptismal Covenant," *Ecclesiology* 6 (2010): 8–38.

27. C. Kilmer Myers, *Baptized into the One Church* (New York: Seabury Press, 1963).

twenty pages, Myers challenges an individualistic understanding of Baptism, whereby the sacrament is received for one's personal salvation. Myers writes:

> When, by God's action, we are brought into the Church, we, with all Christians, are indeed *in*. We are inside her life; her vitality passes into us. Our life is merged with her communal life. Now it is no longer "I" alone: now it is "we." Now we are a people—the people of God. We say *our* Father now, and we say *our* Lord . . . The individualistic Christian is primarily concerned with the state of single souls: he says, "Jesus is my God," and he may ask, "Are you saved, Brother?" . . . When a Christian is excessively individualistic, he finds it hard to grasp the Biblical doctrine of the Body of Christ. He is likely to devalue the Church's sacramental life, relegating Baptism to the area of personal salvation and looking upon the Lord's Supper as a sacramental means of personal communion with the Lord.[28]

To be baptized is to be made a part of the corporate Body of Christ; a Christian cannot tout an attitude of self-sufficient individualism. Furthermore, Myers describes the responsibility for ministry that is entailed with Baptism, which no Christian can escape. The author states: "Everyone who has been baptized, whether archbishop or new-born baby, belongs to the servant people of God. Though we have different functions and ministries, Holy Baptism is the great leveler among us."[29] While Myers did not use the term "baptismal ecclesiology" in 1963, he leaves no doubt that, because of the communal nature of Baptism and its inherent ministerial responsibilities, "Baptism is the key to our understanding of the Church."[30]

The mid-1960s through the late 1970s, for the Episcopal Church, was an important period of reshaping its institutional structures and social engagement. Of this time, Colin Podmore writes: "In the Episcopal Church the period from 1967 to 1979 was one of revolutionary change. The staid church of the American establishment suddenly began to engage collectively in social activism, supporting the empowerment of racial and ethnic minorities."[31] It was in 1967, in fact, that the drafting process began for a new prayer book, namely that which would be released in 1979 as *The Book*

---

28. Myers, 12–13.
29. Myers, 19.
30. Myers, 15.
31. Podmore, "The Baptismal Revolution in the American Episcopal Church," 9.

of Common Prayer.[32] One of the drafters of the new rite for Baptism in the prayer book, Louis Weil, may be the first to consistently use the term "baptismal ecclesiology," as he states: "For several years I had been advocating both in my teaching and writing, what I called 'a baptismal ecclesiology.'"[33]

Regardless of who first coined the phrase "baptismal ecclesiology," the appearance of the 1979 *Book of Common Prayer* clearly provided the grounds for such outlook on the nature of the Church as it defined Baptism as "full initiation by water and the Holy Spirit into Christ's Body the Church."[34] According to liturgical scholar Ruth Meyers, this definition of Baptism as "full initiation" has produced a "revolution" within the Episcopal Church, as she writes: "During the past half century, a revolution has been quietly taking place in the Episcopal Church, a revolution in the way we celebrate baptism and a revolution in the way we understand baptism."[35] In her work *Continuing the Reformation*, Meyers contends: "A baptismal ecclesiology understands the Church to be rooted in baptism and nourished by the eucharist. Baptism forms the body of Christ, a community which is distinct from the surrounding culture and yet is called to participate in Christ's reconciling ministry to the world. As this ecclesiology develops, continuing reform and renewal of baptismal practice is needed, and aspects of the baptismal rite requiring revision becomes evident."[36]

Not only is the definition of Baptism as "full initiation by water and the Holy Spirit into Christ's Body the Church" revolutionary for the Anglican community, but so too is the Baptismal Covenant that is found in the renewed rite of Baptism itself.[37] This set of five questions follows the Presentation and Examination of Candidates and begins with an interrogatory form of the Apostles' Creed. The questions that comprise the Baptismal Covenant are as follows:

32. *The Book of Common Prayer and Administration of the Sacraments and Other Rites and Ceremonies of the Church . . . according to the use of the Episcopal Church* (New York: Seabury Press, 1979).

33. See Louis Weil, "Baptismal Ecclesiology: Uncovering a Paradigm," in *Equipping the Saints: Ordination in Anglicanism Today*, Ronald L Dowling and David R. Holeton, eds. (Dublin: Columba Press, 2006), 18. Weil is referring to a gathering of the Anglican Liturgical Consultation at Ripon College Cuddesdon, Oxford, in 2003.

34. *Book of Common Prayer*, 298.

35. Ruth A. Meyers, *Continuing the Reformation: Re-Visioning Baptism in the Episcopal Church* (New York: Church Publishing Incorporated, 1997), xv.

36. Meyers, 226.

37. See *Book of Common Prayer*, 304–305.

Celebrant   Will you continue in the apostles' teaching
and fellowship, in the breaking of bread,
and in the prayers?

People   I will, with God's help.

Celebrant   Will you persevere in resisting evil, and, whenever
you fall into sin, repent and return to the Lord?

People   I will, with God's help.

Celebrant   Will you proclaim by word and example the
Good News of God in Christ?

People   I will, with God's help.

Celebrant   Will you seek and serve Christ in all persons,
loving your neighbor as yourself?

People   I will, with God's help.

Celebrant   Will you strive for justice and peace among all people,
and respect the dignity of every human being?

People   I will, with God's help.[38]

The structure of the Baptismal Covenant is at the same time both innovative and traditional: profession of the Triune God is followed immediately by a statement of commitment to a particular way of life. David Batchelder, representing a Presbyterian perspective, assesses the powerful impact of professing such vows: "We agree with the way God sees humanity and all creation. We subscribe to God's evaluation of human inequity and injustice. We concur with God's diagnosis of human misery and suffering. We affirm that our salvation depends upon the love of God in Jesus Christ."[39] What we say yes to, "with God's help," is a lifestyle meant to mirror that perfect communion of Father, Son, and Spirit. Meyers comments: "More attention is needed to the relation between faith in the triune God and the radical consequences of this faith for Christian living. . . . Yet it is remarkable that in just two decades the baptismal covenant has become a significant

---

38. I owe thanks to Susan Marie Smith, who alerted me to the fact that the Episcopal Church is considering a sixth question: Will you cherish the wondrous works of God and protect the beauty and integrity of all creation?

39. David B. Batchelder, "Baptismal Renunciations: Making Promises We Do Not Intend to Keep," *Worship* 81 (2007): 424.

statement of the essence of the ministry to which Christians are called by their baptism."[40]

Several consequences of defining Baptism as "full initiation by water and the Holy Spirit into Christ's Body the Church" in relation to the Baptismal Covenant of the Anglican rite of Baptism deserve mention. The three identified here are (1) the debate that arises regarding the purpose of Confirmation, (2) the necessary broadening of a theology of ministry, and (3) the meaning of personal holiness and sanctity. First, how does this definition affect the status of Confirmation? If Baptism is full initiation that is supported by ongoing nourishment in the celebration of the Eucharist, then what purpose does Confirmation fulfill? Daniel Stevick writes: "It needs to be said clearly that *Confirmation has no independent meanings*. All the meanings that have been ascribed to it are drawn from Baptism, which says at the beginning all that can be said concerning Christ and ourselves as united in a single, divine-human life in a divine-human community."[41] While the 1979 *Book of Common Prayer* understands Confirmation as the occasion of "mature public affirmation" of one's baptismal commitment, it is not to be seen as a completion of initiation.[42] The problem here is that by calling Baptism "full initiation," it can be misunderstood that initiation is complete, when, in fact, our initiation into the Christ life is a journey that does not end in this life. In his article "Is Baptism 'Complete Sacramental Initiation'?" Paul Avis argues just so, namely, that Baptism must always be seen as an ongoing process. He writes:

> First, Christian initiation is a process, or an extended event. Second, confirmation is part of the process and, as a means of grace with the sign of the laying on of hands, is, at the least, a "sacramental action." Third, initiation cannot be complete until every Christian has had the opportunity to confess the faith for him- or herself in a liturgical setting, and in the case of those baptized in infancy, to make their baptism promises their own. Finally, initiation into the life and worship of the body of Christ comes to completion only at first communion, through participation in the Eucharist, when we are drawn into the movement of Christ's self-offering to the Father, and receive sacramentally his

40. Meyers, *Continuing the Reformation*, 229.

41. Daniel B. Stevick, *Baptismal Moments; Baptismal Meanings* (New York: Church Hymnal Corporation, 1987), 72.

42. *Book of Common Prayer*, 412.

Body and Blood, his divine life and strength. Therefore, we can confidently state the negative and say that baptism is not complete sacramental initiation or even, as some would have it, complete Christian initiation *tout court*.[43]

Avis decisively asserts that Confirmation continues to play a liturgical role in the unfolding of the initiation process in the life of the baptized. Others, such as Geoffrey Lampe, argue that the Spirit's bestowal of gifts cannot be separated in any way, liturgically or theologically, from Baptism in water, as the presence of the Spirit is "one aspect of the sharing of the resurrection life of Christ that is begun in baptism."[44] While Lampe endorses a sense of "completion" at Baptism, Anglicanism predominantly favors the interpretation that Baptism is a process that unfolds in time.[45] Nevertheless, the debate continues as to whether the ongoing celebration of the Sacrament of Confirmation apart from the waters of Baptism serves to weaken the baptismal commitment as well as to create a false notion of gradated status in the Body of Christ (that is, with members being either more or less initiated).

The second development that arises from defining Baptism as "full initiation by water and the Holy Spirit into Christ's Body the Church" concerns the ministry of the baptized. Ruth Meyers defines baptismal ecclesiology as "an understanding of the Church as a community formed by baptism and empowered by baptism and the eucharist to carry out the reconciling ministry of Christ in the world."[46] Furthermore, she contends that the 1979 *Book of Common Prayer* understands Baptism as "commissioning for ministry."[47] Even before the appearance of the prayer book, Massey Shepherd advocated the extreme position of equating Baptism with ministerial ordination. In his 1965 book *Liturgy and Education*, he writes: "The laity is the fundamental Holy Order in the Church, and all of us are made laymen in our Baptism. . . . Baptism is the layman's ordination."[48] Returning to the work of C. Kilmer Myers, the author prefers to link the

---

43. Paul Avis, "Is Baptism 'Complete Sacramental Initiation'?" *Theology* 111 (2008): 168–169.

44. Geoffrey W. H. Lampe, *The Seal of the Spirit: A Study in the Doctrine of Baptism and Confirmation in the New Testament and the Fathers* (London: Longmans, Green, 1951), 318.

45. See Podmore, "The Baptismal Revolution in the American Episcopal Church," 13–14.

46. Meyers, *Continuing the Reformation*, xvi.

47. Meyers, 187.

48. Quote found in Podmore, "The Baptismal Revolution in the American Episcopal Church," 18.

ministerial commitment of Baptism not to ordination but to social action. He writes:

> By being baptized into the indivisible Body of Christ, every Christian is called to participate in the one Church's united ministry to the one world. . . . Though we have different functions and ministries, Holy Baptism is the great leveler among us. Whether we are clergymen or laymen, child or adult, by our Baptism we are drawn into the ministry of Christ. And that ministry is in the world. . . . Baptism initiates us into the holy society of servants. The ministry to which our Baptism commits us is outside the Church in the one world for which Christ died.[49]

This way of thinking about the "priesthood of the baptized" is very much in keeping with how *Lumen gentium* describes the apostolate of the laity:

> The apostolate of the laity is a sharing in the church's saving mission. Through Baptism and Confirmation all are appointed to this apostolate by the Lord himself. . . . The laity, however, are given this special vocation: to make the church present and fruitful in those places and circumstances where it is only through them that it can become the salt of the earth. Thus, all lay people, through the gifts which they have received, are at once the witnesses and the living instruments of the mission of the church itself "according to the measure of Christ's gift" (Ephesians 4:7).[50]

The question for many supporters of baptismal ecclesiology is that, because Baptism is a social equalizer, should not all members of the Body of Christ be considered ministers, thereby calling into question the need for Holy Orders?[51] An affirmative answer to this question has undoubtedly led the Episcopal Church to a broad endorsement of women's ordination. Louis Weil states: "If discernment concerning suitability for holy orders is

---

49. Myers, *Baptized into the One Church*, 18–20.

50. LG, 33.

51. See, for example, Paul Gibson, "A Baptismal Ecclesiology—Some Questions," in *Equipping the Saints: Ordination in Anglicanism Today*, Ronald L. Dowling and David R. Holeton, eds. (Dublin: Columba Press, 2006), 35. Gibson writes: "I have no quarrel with the theological democracy on which this ecclesiology is based—with the principle that all members of the church are equally 'living stones' in the temple of Christ's spiritual house. Nor have I a quarrel with the principle that all are equally called to a gospel-filled life of service no matter what their role and function in the Christian community may be. The church's ministers are in the church, not over the church. However, I do find myself asking if the equality established by baptism can carry the full freight of a theology of ministry and order."

grounded in a baptismal ecclesiology, then the fundamental issue is not a person's gender or sexual orientation, but rather the evidence of the charisms that the church needs in its ordained leaders."[52] The debate surrounding the relationship between Baptism and public ministry continues to be a topic for discussion in the Anglican communion.[53]

Although there are undoubtedly other advancements that have resulted from the understanding of Baptism as "full initiation by water and the Holy Spirit into Christ's Body the Church," a third and final development discussed here is the view of holiness that is created when basing the liturgical sanctoral calendar upon baptismal ecclesiology.[54] In 2009, the General Convention of the Episcopal Church released the document *Holy Women, Holy Men*, which added over one hundred saintly figures to be commemorated in the liturgical calendar.[55] The Introduction to the "Principles of Revision" that guides the reformation states: "The Church is 'the communion of Saints,' that is, a people made holy through their mutual participation in the mystery of Christ."[56] Furthermore, the second principle "Christian Discipleship" roots the recognition of holiness in Baptism:

> The death of the saints, precious in God's sight, is the ultimate witness to the power of the Resurrection. What is being commemorated, therefore, is the completion in death of a particular Christian's living out of the promises of baptism. Baptism is, therefore, a necessary prerequisite for inclusion in the Calendar.[57]

Daniel E. Joslyn-Siemiatkoski and Ruth Meyers comment on the importance of Baptism as the foundation for sanctity: "The centrality of

---

52. Weil, "Baptismal Ecclesiology: Uncovering a Paradigm," 26. See also Suzanne G. Farnham, et. al., *Listening Hearts: Discerning Call in Community* (New York: Morehouse Publishing, 1991). The authors discuss here the value of community in discernment for ministry. They write: "Although God calls each of us personally, as individuals we see only partially. Individual perception, reasoning, and understanding are always limited. Even a person who feels absolutely certain that a specific revelation comes from God may be mistaken as to how it is to be applied. Because God often reveals part of the picture to one person and another part to another person, it is prudent to consult one another to discern God's counsel, guidance, and direction, even if there is no apparent reason to do so" (46–47).

53. See Myers, *Continuing the Reformation*, 238–240.

54. See Daniel E. Joslyn-Siemiatkoski and Ruth A. Meyers, "The Baptismal Ecclesiology of *Holy Women, Holy Men*: Developments in the Theology of Sainthood in the Episcopal Church," *Anglican Theological Review* 94:1 (2012): 27–36.

55. Joslyn-Siemiatkoski and Meyers, 27.

56. *Holy Women, Holy Men: Celebrating the Saints* (New York: Church Publishing Incorporated, 2010), 742.

57. *Holy Women, Holy Men*, 742.

baptism as the defining marker of a Christian, and not membership in a particular ecclesial community, explains the high frequency of non-Anglicans on the new calendar."[58] Furthermore, the fifth principle, "Range of Inclusion," states: "Attention should also be paid to gender and race, to the inclusion of lay people (witnessing in this way to our baptismal understanding of the Church), and to ecumenical representation."[59] Again, Joslyn-Siemiatkoski and Meyers comment: "The deliberate inclusion of laity representative of various professions is a clear articulation of the Episcopal Church's teaching that all Christians are empowered for ministry on the basis of their baptism alone."[60] Thus, the revision of the calendar of saints in the Episcopal Church demonstrates clearly the understanding that holiness is not a gift imparted by the Holy Spirit on a select few, but rather, it is bestowed upon the People of God who are made Christians at Baptism.

Again, it is important to emphasize that the three areas of reform and renewal just articulated (that is, Confirmation, the status of Holy Orders, and sainthood) are merely three of the ways in which a baptismal ecclesiology has led to a revolution[61] within the Episcopal Church. Certainly, those within the Episcopal Church who have witnessed the transition of Baptism as a private affair to a public celebration of what it means to be one in Christ have seen many other ways in which this ecclesiological shift has had a major impact upon Anglicanism as a whole and its relationship with the broader Christian Church. For instance, in *Christian Ritualizing and the Baptismal Process: Liturgical Explorations toward a Realized Baptismal Ecclesiology*, Episcopal priest and professor Susan Marie Smith suggests that the baptismal life is about the ongoing encounter with crisis and change:

> Thus, for a contemporary baptismal ecclesiology, we need to look at the whole life of the baptized person as a process of change. . . . In contra-distinction to Christendom, our longing at the beginning of the third millennium in this post-Christendom church is for a realized baptismal ecclesiology, for the full engagement and empowerment,

---

58. Joslyn-Siemiatkoski and Meyers, "The Baptismal Ecclesiology," 33–34. The authors continue: "If the goal is to remember those from across the body of Christ as exemplars, and not just predominantly clerical or monastic representatives of a specific tradition as in Roman Catholicism or Eastern Orthodoxy, then the calendar will include names that are not immediately recognizable and some that may come as surprises" (34).

59. *Holy Women, Holy Men*, 743.

60. Joslyn-Siemiatkoski and Meyers, "The Baptismal Ecclesiology," 35.

61. Meyers, *Continuing the Reformation*, xv.

authority and ministry of all the baptized. This implies change, not just for clerics and monastics, but for all the baptized. We need, therefore, to look at the whole of the Christian life as a process, as unfolding development and maturing into union with God-in-Christ through the active work of the Holy Spirit.[62]

Smith continues by arguing that the change that is part of baptismal life is really the essence of *theosis* or deification, whereby believers are gradually drawn deeper and deeper into divine life. "It is a process of each member of the Body of Christ and of all the whole Body together. It is a way of purification and kenosis. It is the way of the cross. And it is a way of beauty and *plerosis*; it is the way of joy and intimacy and transcendence."[63]

Bringing this into the liturgical realm, it would seem that such an understanding of a "realized baptismal ecclesiology" is very much what the Council Fathers had in mind when they wrote of the rights and responsibilities of all the baptized who are to enact "full, conscious, and active" participation in the liturgy: "In the restoration and development of the sacred liturgy the full and active participation by all the people is the paramount concern, for it is the primary, indeed the indispensable source from which the faithful are to derive the true Christian spirit."[64] We now turn to the Roman Catholic perspective in order to see how various theologians, while not referring precisely to baptismal ecclesiology, emphasize the united Body of Christ as an important starting point for defining the nature of the Church.

Baptismal Ecclesiology:
A Roman Catholic Perspective

The ecclesiological perspectives in the documents of the Second Vatican Council did not appear out of thin air. Not only was their formation the result of consultation and study by experts in various fields, but they flowed naturally from the work of theologians who were discovering ancient sources that revealed the makeup of a very different church than the one of the mid-twentieth century. Further, these thinkers were applying anthropological, sociological, and even psychological tools to the theological

---

62. Susan Marie Smith, *Christian Ritualizing and the Baptismal Process: Liturgical Explorations toward a Realized Baptismal Ecclesiology* (Eugene, OR: Pickwick, 2012), 109.

63. Smith, 123–124.

64. SC, 14.

enterprise. For example, Belgian theologian Edward Schillebeeckx, OP, in an environment of post-World War II European restoration, employed phenomenology in order to define the Church as a relationship, or an "encounter" between God and humanity.[65] On the one hand, Jesus is the primary encounter with God, the "primordial sacrament . . . intended by the Father to be in his humanity the only way to the actuality of redemption."[66] On the other hand, humanity is in need of a tangible, "bodily" encounter with Christ, which is the role the Church is to fulfill. Thus, very similar to Pope Leo the Great, who stated, "What was visible in Christ has now passed over into the sacraments of the Church,"[67] Schillebeeckx contends that the Church is the sacrament of the Risen Lord. He writes: "To receive the sacraments of the Church in faith is therefore the same thing as to encounter Christ himself. In this light the sacramentality of the seven sacraments is the same as the sacramentality of the whole Church."[68]

Three years after the publication of *Christ the Sacrament of Encounter with God*, German theologian Karl Rahner, SJ, likewise called the Church the "Fundamental Sacrament."[69] He writes: "As the people of God socially and juridically organized, the Church is not a mere eternal welfare institute, but the continuation, the perpetual presence of the task and function of Christ in the economy of redemption, his contemporaneous presence in history, his life, the Church in the full and proper sense."[70] In no way is this a triumphalist outlook; rather, Rahner sees the Church as the perpetuation of the offering of God's mercy for all of humanity. He states, "Now the Church is the continuance, the contemporary presence, of that real, eschatologically triumphant and irrevocably established presence in the world, in Christ, of God's salvific will."[71] Thus, theologians such as Schillebeeckx and Rahner helped pave the way for understanding the Church as the corporate Body of Christ that is sent in mission to represent the saving deeds of the Risen Lord to every corner of the world. They expanded the

---

65. See Edward Schillebeeckx, *Christ the Sacrament of the Encounter with God* (New York: Sheed and Ward, 1963). Originally published as *Christus, Sacrament van de Godsontmoeting* (Bilthoven: H. Nelissen, 1960).

66. Schillebeeckx, 15.

67. St. Leo the Great, *Sermo LXXIV*, 2 (Patrologia Latina, 54, col 398).

68. Schillebeeckx, *Christ the Sacrament of Encounter with God*, 54.

69. See Karl Rahner, *The Church and the Sacraments* (New York: Herder and Herder, 1963).

70. Rahner, 13.

71. Rahner, 18.

meaning of sacrament, so that by its very nature, the Church is seen as a sacrament, a tangible embodiment of God's grace in the world.

Even prior to the writings of these theologians, Virgil Michel, OSB, who is considered the founder of the liturgical movement in the United States, contributed greatly to the development of a theology of the Mystical Body. Influenced by Belgian monk Lambert Beauduin, OSB, whose central thought was that the liturgy *is* the life of the Church, Michel labored in a post-Depression era to extol the formation of the Body of Christ at prayer so that in turn the Church might infuse the world with the life of Christ. Thus, in a culture of unbridled individualism, the liturgy would immerse Christians into the oneness of Christ so that the Church might influence the world to embody this same unity. Michel's biographer Paul Marx writes:

> Undoubted one of Michel's greatest discoveries in Europe had been the reality of the Church as the Mystical Body of Christ—a doctrine little stressed in the United States at this time—and the official life and prayer of that Body, the liturgy, which he now saw as the indispensable means of instilling the true Christian spirit into society by first permeating the lives of Christians. He began to perceive that a properly worshipping people, realizing the oneness in the Mystical Christ and actively contacting the living realities of the liturgy, could in time transform a whole society.[72]

For Michel, the sacramental life of the Church was a social affair, meaning that all of the sacraments are meant for the building up of the Body of Christ for the good of the entire world. He states, "Every participation in a sacrament is a dying to self, so that Christians might live wholly for God, and for the greater service of love of God's children, actual or potential fellow members in the Mystical Body of Christ."[73] Thus, Michel wrote in 1936:

> There is only one answer I know of to the problem of the balanced harmony between the individual and the social: *The Mystical Body of Christ.* There the individual retains his full responsibility, the fullest possibility of greater realization of his dignity as a member of Christ; yet he is ever a member in the fellowship of Christ, knit closely with

---

72. Paul B. Marx, *Virgil Michel and the Liturgical Movement* (Collegeville, MN: Liturgical Press, 1957), 36.
73. Marx, 53.

his fellow members into a compact body by the indwelling of the Spirit of Christ: *There* is the pattern of all social life lived by individuals.[74]

Again, for Michel, the liturgy is primarily a social activity in which one learns how to be a member of Christ's Body. In an age when individualism was replicated in worship patterns of devotional prayers and spectator participation at Mass, Michel desired to restore active participation. His article "Natural and Supernatural Society" states, "Far from depreciating or suppressing the values of individuality and personality, the Mystical Body of Christ gives these their best possible realization. The responsibility that each member has, not only for his own self, but also for the good of the whole Body, is the highest personal responsibility that the individual can be privileged to share."[75] To state this in political terms: "The Church is not a political democracy, which emphasizes equal *individuals*. Neither is it a political monarchy, which emphasizes unequal *individuals*. It is a communion, which emphasizes the interpersonal communion of equal men and women in one people and one body."[76] Thus, even though the term "baptismal ecclesiology" would not have been part of Michel's vocabulary, he understood well the Church as a unified Body composed of many diverse members.

Just as the 1979 *Book of Common Prayer* and its definition of Baptism as "full initiation by water and the Holy Spirit into Christ's Body the Church" would influence ritual change in Baptism and would call into question the nature of Confirmation in the Episcopal Church, so too did the theology of initiation in the Roman Catholic Church witness a certain upheaval after the close of the Council. The praenotanda for *Christian Initiation* states that, in addition to being freedom from sin (1) and adoption as God's children (2) as well as the "door to life and to the kingdom of God" (3), Baptism is incorporation into the Church:

> Further, baptism is the sacrament by which its recipients are incorporated into the Church and are built up together in the Spirit into a house where God lives, into a holy nation and a royal priesthood. Baptism is a sacramental bond of unity linking all who have been signed by it. Because of that unchangeable effect (given expression in the Latin liturgy by the anointing of the baptized person with chrism

---

74. Virgil Michel, "Natural and Supernatural Society," *Orate Fratres* 10 (1936): 244–245.
75. Michel, 434–435.
76. Lawler and Shanahan, "The Church Is a Graced Communion," 496.

in the presence of God's people), the rite of baptism is held in highest honor by all Christians. Once it has been validly celebrated, even if by Christians with whom we are not in full communion, it may never lawfully be repeated.[77]

A watershed period for the Roman Catholic Church regarding a renewed understanding of initiation came with the restoration of the adult cate-chumenate promulgated by Pope Paul VI in 1972. Not only did the *Rite of Christian Initiation of Adults* (RCIA) embrace a conversion model for initiation,[78] whereby formation was interpreted as an ongoing immersion into the life of Christ over the course of an extensive period of time, but the RCIA also united in one liturgical celebration the reception of the three sacraments of initiation: Baptism, Confirmation, and Eucharist. As the RCIA began to spread throughout the world, Catholics began to see a disconnect between infant Baptism and adult initiation: is Baptism about washing away Original Sin or is it about the commitment to discipleship?[79]

One who advocated the need for a serious appraisal of the ecclesial significance of Baptism was Aidan Kavanagh, who throughout his career as an academic liturgist argued extensively that the ongoing practice of indiscriminately baptizing infants before they are able to make the decision to follow after Christ weakens the Church as a whole.[80] For him, the "nor-mative" form of initiation in the Catholic Church meant adult conversion. In 1974, Kavanagh wrote:

A Christian is a person of faith in Jesus Christ dead and risen among his faithful people. This faith is no mere poetic thing but a way of living together: it is the bond which establishes that reciprocal mutuality

---

77. *Christian Initiation*, General Introduction, 4.

78. See James B. Dunning, "The Rite of Christian Initiation of Adults: Model of Adult Growth," *Worship* 53 (1979): 142–153. Describing conversion as a process, Dunning writes: "There is no one-time conversion. Holding my dead child, losing my job, entering my marriage, watching my children grow up and leave home, choosing my vocation, beginning a new life at age 91, kissing for the last time the lips of my dead husband or wife—again and again I am summoned to ponder my story, struggle with my questions, listen to the journeys of others, and make my surrender of faith that there is Good News here, Good News that life is more powerful than death and that God gives life. That is why the RCIA is a model for all adult growth and conversion" (153).

79. See Paul F. X. Covino, "The Postconciliar Infant Baptism Debate in the American Catholic Church," *Worship* 56 (1982): 240–260. In this article, Covino identifies four schools of thought on initiation: (1) The Mature Adulthood School, (2) The Environmentalist School, (3) The Initiation Unity School, and (4) The Corresponding Practice School.

80. See Aidan Kavanagh, "Initiation: Baptism and Confirmation," *Worship* 46 (1972): 263–276.

of relationships we call communion, and it is this communion which constitutes the ecclesial presence of Jesus Christ in the world of grace, faith, hope, charity and character. This is what the eucharist celebrates, signifies and causes within the community of the faithful: it is the church. This is what initiation in the fullest sense disciplines one for: it is the church.[81]

Richard H. Guerrette holds a similar position in an article that appeared shortly before Kavanagh's articles. Guerrette's article opens with the statement: "The current practice of infant baptism is a symptom of the radical problematic in ecclesiology."[82] He continues by describing the dominant ecclesiology of the post–Vatican II Church:

> The church is conceived as a community of God's chosen people who, through their faith-response to his call in Christ, are making their way as a pilgrim people toward the kingdom. The church is described in pastoral terms and is translated at the local level by a community of Christians committed, precisely through their baptism, to the service of diakonia. . . . The continuance of initiating more and more children into the church with little or no faith-commitment to diakonia on the part of the parents becomes increasingly more difficult to reconcile with the ecclesiological significance of baptism.[83]

Guerrette does not call for the wholesale abandonment of infant Baptism, rather, he suggests reform of the community itself, whereby parishes are replaced with small base communities that can truly sustain the various levels of commitment and engagement. His contention is that the replacement of communities that allow for virtual anonymity with ones that exhibit true social connectedness will lead all the baptized, young and old, to real diakonia.[84] He writes: "With the existence of a genuine Christian community, the celebration of the sacrament (baptism) conveys its intended ecclesiology

---

81. Aidan Kavanagh, "Christian Initiation of Adults: The Rites," *Worship* 48 (1974): 333.

82. Richard H. Guerrette, "Ecclesiology and Infant Baptism," *Worship* 44 (1970): 433.

83. Guerrette, 434.

84. See Paul J. Philibert, "Human Development and Sacramental Transformation," *Worship* 65 (1991): 535–536. Here the author discusses the success of Christian base communities: "One of the most hopeful phenomena in our world today is the appearance and growth of communities where individualism has been replaced by strong corporate life, where narcissism has been confronted and channeled into ministerial service, and where privatism has been broken down to create common energies for Christ witness. . . . In the U.S. the most common example of this is the RCIA catechumenal community. When leadership and chemistry are right, the catechumenal culture reaches out to transform the whole parish. The RCIA grew out of a conviction that adult conversion requires not

significance; and the participants in the liturgy, namely, the community, the child, and the parents, retain their true ecclesial identity."[85]

Earlier, we examined the critical role that a theology of the Mystical Body of Christ played in Virgil Michel's work to revitalize participation in the liturgy with the goal of transforming the society at large, drawing it away from a prevailing attitude of individualism toward the achievement of community. A generation or more after Michel's beginning of the liturgical movement in the United States, the theology of French Dominican Yves Congar, OP, placed a supreme value on koinonia, upon which a proper understanding of the Body of Christ is formulated.[86] For Congar, a peritus at the Second Vatican Council, the link between the image of the People of God with the more ancient Mystical Body theology was indispensable; he believed in the need to assist the faithful in developing their self-understanding as a priestly people. Thus, he writes in 1967:

> The new People of God have become the Body of Christ by the action of the Holy Spirit: Romans 12:4–6; 1 Corinthians 12:4–13, 27. Christ is always still alive, and he is our high priest (cf. Hebrews), but the church, which is his Body, is as such the very place where he continues his life and manifests it here below, where he operates through his Spirit, and where he makes the Christian mystery actual; this is achieved especially in the celebration of baptism and Eucharist (1 Cor 10:16–17). There is a profound unity between the physical body of the Lord, crucified and risen, his sacramental body offered in the Eucharist, and his ecclesial Body which offers itself up and, by this very fact, becomes the spiritual temple of God. According to the New Testament, then, it follows that the whole church, as People of God and Body of Christ, celebrates the spiritual worship both personal and communal, inaugurated by Jesus Christ, of which he himself remains the chief celebrant.[87]

Therefore, Jesus is the only priest who offers; the People of God can only give of themselves as members of his Body. "It is he, first of all, who offers, and the church offers only because she is his body and because she

---

just reasonable assent to creeds, but a thorough reorientation of one's whole symbolic universe—beginning with the symbol of relation: belonging."

85. Guerrette, "Ecclesiology and Infant Baptism," 436.

86. See Yves Congar, *Diversity and Communion* (Mystic, CT: Twenty-Third Publications, 1985).

87. Yves Congar, "The *Ecclesia* or Christian Community as a Whole Celebrates the Liturgy," in *At the Heart of Christian Worship: Liturgical Essays of Yves Congar*, trans. and ed. Paul Philibert (Collegeville, MN: Liturgical Press, 2010), 18.

follows him faithfully in everything."[88] Clearly, Congar's theology of the Mystical Body of Christ as it is lived out in the action of the liturgy corresponds to the vision of the unity between the Head and members as found in *Sacrosanctum Concilium*: "The liturgy is considered as an exercise of the priestly office of Jesus Christ. In the liturgy, by means of signs perceptible to the senses, human sanctification is signified and brought about in ways proper to each of these signs; in the liturgy the whole public worship is performed by the Mystical Body of Jesus Christ, that is, by the Head and his members."[89]

Paul Philibert, OP, a disciple of Congar, has labored in recent years to overturn the vision of Christendom that sees the laity as "clients" of a clerical institution in order to promote an "ecclesiology of communion."[90] In his article, "Reclaiming the Vision of an Apostolic Church," Philibert contends that St. Augustine's notion of the *Totus Christus*—the whole Christ, head and members pervades the documents of the Second Vatican Council and demands that the ministerial priesthood be understood as a consecration for service to the priestly Body of Christ. Priests can only be priests by virtue of first being members of the *Totus Christus*. Philibert writes:

> The ministry of the presbyter—what is commonly called the ministerial priesthood—is described in the Catechism of the Catholic Church with clarity. Number 1547 says, "The ministerial priesthood is at the service of the common priesthood. It is directed at the unfolding of the baptismal grace of all Christians. The ministerial priest is a *means* by which Christ unceasingly builds up and leads his Church." This way of putting things in no way diminishes the reality or the importance of the ministry of presbyter. The presbyter receives the unique grace to stand in the midst of a community of the faithful as a sacramental sign of its Head, particularly by leading it in the celebration of the sacraments in the name of Christ's headship.[91]

Thus, the ministerial priesthood must always be seen in relationship to the priesthood of the faithful; the ministry of sacramentalizing the

---

88. Congar, 33.

89. SC, 7.

90. See Paul J. Philibert, "Reclaiming the Vision of an Apostolic Church," *Worship* 83 (2009): 484–485.

91. Philibert, 493.

Body's head is to "invite universal solidary."[92] This is very much the challenge that Pope John Paul II offers in his apostolic exhortation *Pastores dabo vobis*, namely, that the role of the ordained priesthood is to "promote the baptismal priesthood of the entire People of God, leading it to its full ecclesial realization."[93] In words that sound very much like baptismal ecclesiology, Philibert challenges the Church to probe deeper into its teaching on the common baptismal priesthood: "The fundamental consecration of every Christian, ordained or not, is baptism—the deepest ontological change that a person can experience. Baptism is the change from being ordered to death to being ordered to life eternal, the change from being linked to a destiny that ends in futility (cf. 1 Pet 1:18) to being integrated into the Body of Christ the Lord. Every other dignity and service in the Church arises out of this fundamental consecration."[94]

Clearly, just as theologians in the Episcopal Church have wrestled with the question of the relationship between baptismal ecclesiology and a theology of ministry, lay and ordained, so too has the Roman Church been faced with difficult theological dilemmas arising from a restoration of Baptism as the fundamental call to ministry. Although Pope John Paul II decisively closed the door to the debate on women's ordination in 1994, inclusive theologies for Christian ministry continue to occupy the attention of many Catholic scholars. For example, Richard Gaillardetz maintains that Christian ministry ought to be based on a "relational ontology of communion," as he writes:

[W]hen ministry is considered within the context of this relational ontology the minister is seen fundamentally as a servant of communion. This image of ministry is multi-dimensional but gives primacy to the affirmation and nurturance of authentic human relationships which are inclusive, mutual, reciprocal and generative, and the condemnation of relationships of manipulation, domination and subordination as sinful perversions of the call to human communion. It is a vision capable of

---

92. Philibert, 494.

93. John Paul II, *Pastores dabo vobis*, 17. See also David Orr, "Educating for the Priesthood of the Faithful," *Worship* 85 (2009): 431–457. By largely examining the Mass, Orr suggests the many ways in which the faithful are called upon to make a sacrifice of themselves for the good of the whole Church. He writes: "The individual contribution of each member enables the community to form—by contrast, if there be no members gathered, then the community cannot form. Community requires the presence of others. Thus each member who comes contributes to the community. We may take this contribution for granted but it is constitutive" (441).

94. Philibert, "Reclaiming the Vision of an Apostolic Church," 494–495.

realization in every concrete ministry, ordained and nonordained, professional and occasional. . . . Finally, the life of communion has its origins in the deepest yearnings of the human spirit for true communion with another and, ultimately, true communion with God. Therefore, the minister, as servant of communion, is at the same time, servant of the Church, servant of God and servant of humankind.[95]

The instruction *Christian Initiation, General Introduction* states that Baptism is incorporation into Trinitarian communion: "The blessed Trinity is invoked over those who are to be baptized, so that all who are signed in this name are consecrated to the Trinity and enter into communion with the Father, the Son, and the Holy Spirit."[96] The more that ministry is focused on the minister as "servant of communion," who serves to lead others into the oneness that is divine life, the more a sense of equality among all the members of the Body of Christ will be realized and fewer distinctions will be made between lay and ordained.

What is at stake here is a call to recognize Baptism as the sacrament of discipleship. It is more than the cleansing of Original Sin and the adoption by God of new members into his household; Baptism is a way of life. Kathleen Cahalan discusses discipleship as follows:

> Discipleship is not an achievement. It is an identity, a commitment, a way of life, and a response to a call. . . . To be a disciple means to be a follower of Christ, committed to learning his ways; to be a worshiper, joining Christ and the community in praise of God's wonders; to be a forgiver by practicing reconciliation, healing and peacemaking; to be a neighbor by living mindfully of others' needs and reaching out to them with compassion; to be a prophet willing to tell the truth about the injustices that harm neighbors; and to be stewards of the creation, the community, and the mysteries of faith.[97]

---

95. Richard R. Gaillardetz, "In Service of Communion: A Trinitarian Foundation for Christian Ministry," *Worship* 67 (1993): 432–433. Earlier in the article, Gaillardetz establishes the theological grounds on which to base ministry upon the communion of the Trinity. He writes: "As creatures made uniquely in the life of communion patterned on the triune life of God. Just as the personal, relationship being of God as communion is devoid of any relations characterized by domination, manipulation or subordination, so too is the human person called to reject these kinds of relationships and to realize his or her personal being in relationships which are fundamentally reciprocal, mutual and life-giving." Baptism in the name of the Trinity must entail a life process of developing these positive relationships of communion.

96. *Christian Initiation*, General Introduction, 5.

97. Kathleen A. Cahalan, "Toward a Fundamental Theology of Ministry," *Worship* 80 (2006): 115.

Cahalan concludes her thought with the assertion: "A fully developed understanding of discipleship is yet another way of understanding the church's mission."[98] Understanding the Church in terms of discipleship is at the heart of baptismal ecclesiology. Susan Wood, who has written extensively on Christian ministry, calls Baptism the "primary sacrament of ministry." She writes:

> Baptism initiates a person as member of the community, and ministry arises from the community. Through baptism we participate in the three-fold office of Christ as priest, prophet, and king. Thus, all the baptized share in the priesthood of Christ in diverse ways within the royal priesthood of the baptized. Baptism is the primary sacrament of ministry. Ordained ministry does not have a different source, but finds its source in baptism, as does lay ministry. All ordained ministry, as all discipleship, proceeds from baptism. Priests "are disciples of the Lord along with all the faithful" and "in common with all who have been reborn in the font of Baptism, are brothers among brothers and sisters as members of the same body of Christ which all are commanded to build." The priesthood of the sacrament of orders serves the priesthood of the people of God.[99]

Continuing, Wood states that all order in the Church is established in Baptism: "We assume our place in the order of the Church according to our state in life and the charisms we bring for the upbuilding of the community and Christian discipleship."[100] Once again, this is baptismal ecclesiology; the Church manifests the ordering of the members of the Body of Christ, who with their diverse gifts and charisms work together for the building up of the community for the salvation of the world. No ministry in the Church can supersede this fundamental objective of Baptism.

---

98. Cahalan, 115.

99. Susan K. Wood, "Conclusion: Convergence Points toward a Theology of Ordered Ministries," in *Ordering the Baptismal Priesthood: Theologies of Lay and Ordained Ministry*, ed. Susan K. Wood (Collegeville, MN: Liturgical Press, 2003), 257. The quoted material in Wood's quote is taken from paragraph 1 of the Second Vatican Council's Decree on the Ministry and Life of Priests, *Presbyterorum ordinis*.

100. Wood, 257.

Conclusion

Like the Triune God whom Christians adore, the Church is an awesome mystery that is revealed anew in every age. Unlike the Triune God, who is immutable, the Church—the Body of Christ—is always in dynamic transition. The Church never stops welcoming new members into her fold while simultaneously sending forth others to journey toward the fullness of communion in heaven. Such an understanding of the relational nature of the Church, living and dead, corresponds well with the need for ongoing reform and renewal. Popularized by theologian Hans Küng around the time of the Second Vatican Council, the Latin phrase *ecclesia semper reformanda est* ("the Church is always to be reformed") expresses this desire to see the Church as defying static boundaries.[101] Similarly, *Lumen gentium* echoes this outlook by stating: "The Church . . . at once holy and always in need of purification, follows constantly the path of penance and renewal."[102]

Baptismal ecclesiology is a way of describing the Church as a holy people always in transition. The Church embraces journey as its way of life. Through the waters of Baptism over the waters of death, Christians together embark on their communal voyage into God. Baptismal ecclesiology is an ecclesiology of *theosis* or divinization, in which the baptized Christian is drawn deeper and deeper into the heart of Love. "For I am convinced," writes Paul to the Romans, "that neither death, nor life, nor angels, nor principalities, nor present things, nor future things, nor powers, nor height, nor depth, nor any other creature, will be able to separate us from the love of God, which is in Christ Jesus our Lord" (Romans 8:38–39). Baptismal ecclesiology sees divine koinonia as the icon of what the Church is yet to be: perfect unity in seamless diversity.

Largely a term used by the Episcopal Church, baptismal ecclesiology is not foreign to the Roman Catholic Church, which grows more and more comfortable with the universal Christian communion that is established in Baptism. Several of the key aspects of baptismal ecclesiology explored in this chapter (and there may be others) that will be pertinent in the pages ahead are summed up as follows:

---

101. See Werner Klän, "Reformation Then and Now: Ecclesia Semper Reformanda," *Journal of Lutheran Mission* 3 (2016): 14.

102. LG, 8.

A United People

Baptism unites all Christians as one in the Body of Christ. No matter what the world might see, all members of Christ's Body are equal. No two members of the Church are the same; each Christian bears unique gifts and talents that are to benefit the Body as a whole. Baptism is the great equalizer that strips away artificial distinctions that human nature seeks to magnify. "There is neither Jew nor Greek, there is neither slave nor free person, there is neither male and female; for you are all one in Christ Jesus" (Galatians 3:28).

A Pilgrim People

Baptism is lived as a daily event. Viewing the Church as a pilgrim people demands a willingness to embrace process as a hallmark of Christianity. As disciples of the Risen Lord, we are all in the process of becoming something more than we already are. Such a process of becoming means bearing one another's sufferings along the way. The Church is not about comfort but about confrontation of sin and injustice. "Yet I live no longer I, but Christ lives in me; insofar as I live in the flesh, I live by faith in the Son of God who has loved me and given himself up for me" (Galatians 2:20).

A Self-Giving People

Baptism entails self-sacrifice. One must let go of the self to become part of Christ. An attitude of individualism and self-containment is incompatible with a theology of the Body of Christ in which each of the parts works for the good of the whole. Community is the life pattern to be lived by all Christians. "As a body is one though it has many parts, and all the parts of the body, though many, are one body, so also Christ. For in one Spirit we were all baptized into one body, whether Jews or Greeks, slaves or free persons, and we were all given to drink of one Spirit" (1 Corinthians 12:12–13).

A Priestly People

Baptism is rooted in discipleship. Those baptized into Christ are baptized into his royal priesthood. Baptism is a sacrament of service that calls forth disciples to preach the Good News and to work for the coming of God's Kingdom. All Christian ministry is a sharing in the priesthood of Christ. "You are 'a chosen people, a royal priesthood, a holy nation, a people of his own, so that you may announce the praises' of him who called you out of darkness into his wonderful light" (1 Peter 2:9).

A Holy People

Baptism imparts holiness. Sanctity for Christians is not an escape from the world but rather a commitment to probe deeper and deeper into the messiness that pervades all of life. The call to be members of the Communion of Saints invites Christians to discern the will of God in all things and to view the world as God does. This approach to life does not try to hide the ugly aspects of human weakness but instead seeks the support and trust of the Christian community. A baptismal life is one that leads with the gift of mercy. "So be perfect, just as your heavenly Father is perfect" (Matthew 5:48).

For far too long, Baptism has been a sacrament of insurance for Christians, one that provides social comfort and the assurance of heaven. Only very recently is there the rediscovery that the heart of Baptism is belonging, a dedicated belonging to the Body of Christ, and a responsible belonging to the Church's mission to work for the coming of God's Kingdom. Belonging, furthermore, comes down to relationship, and relationship demands difficult work. At Baptism, we belong to Christ forever, but we also belong to each member of the Church and are missioned to participate in the redemption of all creation.

It is difficult to nurture a sense of belonging in a culture where so many people shy away from inconvenience, are afraid of revealing their true selves, have difficulty relying on the help of others, and quickly discard what is no longer relevant. Death can easily be reflected on in light of this culture. Desire for convenience far outweighs the exercise of Christian responsibility when it comes to death. In fearing death, our culture attempts to do everything in its power to mask it and keep it at bay. Restoring a link between Baptism and death, between the Church of the living as one with the Church on its final approach to God, may help Christianity to provide a challenge to our disposable culture. Recapturing some of the ancient attitudes and ritual practices surrounding death may help us to better enact our baptismal commitment to care for the Body, both living and dead.

CHAPTER TWO

The Ecclesial Nature of Death in Ancient Christianity

©

With willing hands they raised the bodies of the saints to their bosoms;
they closed their eyes and mouths, carried them on their shoulders,
and laid them out; they clung to them, embraced them, washed them,
and wrapped them in grave-clothes.[1]

Studying the nature of the Church from the perspective of membership in the Body of Christ, whereby Baptism into the Lord serves as a social leveler and allows each part of the Body to contribute to the good of the whole, challenges us to view death as a corporate event. In other words, the death of a Christian involves the entire Body of Christ. The crisis of death brings about a transition period in which the Church must separate from a former way of being in order to be incorporated into a new reality, as membership in the Body of Christ is reordered.[2] Baptismal ecclesiology demands that we restore an ancient understanding of Baptism and death as part of the Christian community's becoming. The process of being refashioned into Christ does not come to an abrupt end in death, rather the process of growing deeper into Christ and of surrendering one's desire for differentiation and distinctiveness is magnified in death.

The early Christian understanding of death and the development of Christian ways of ritualizing death and burial testify to the belief that the

---

1. Eusebius, *Historica Ecclesiastica*, VII 22.9. These words were taken from a letter written by Dionysius of Alexandria in the mid-third century. Quote taken from Geoffrey Rowell, *The Liturgy of Christian Burial: An Introductory Survey of the Historical Development of Christian Burial Rites* (London: SPCK, 1977): 20.

2. See Arnold van Gennep, *The Rites of Passage* (Chicago: University of Chicago Press, 1960): 21. See also Paul Sheppy, "The Dance of Death: van Gennep and the Paschal Mystery," *Worship* 75 (2001): 554. He writes: "Van Gennep's seminal work on rites of passage described a ritual process which pictures the movement of those engaged in the rites as moving from one room (or status) to another through a doorway or threshold—the *limen*. He described three stages in the process: the *preliminal*—in which separation from an earlier status is effected; the *liminal*—during which transition occurs; and the *postliminal*—when incorporation into the new status transpires."

Church had a serious obligation to assist communally with prayer and pastoral support. Such care was not extended merely to aid a grieving family but rather to reorder the Church and to increase a corporate conviction in the resurrection of the dead on the last day. The quote from Dionysius of Alexander in the mid-third century, at the outset of this chapter, clearly demonstrates the care with which Christians honored the dead. Dionysius depicts those accompanying the body of the deceased as "clinging" and "embracing" the dead; there is a sense here that the community does not want to let the deceased depart from them. Such is the work of Christian burial: to honor the body of the deceased in such a way as to soften the pangs of death while revealing a faith that the deceased live on in the Church and are now exercising a new and different charism for the good of building up the Body of Christ. They are living out their baptismal life in a new state of being.

Among the fascinating aspects of the rituals and traditions surrounding Christian death and burial is their relationship to and dependency upon Jewish and pagan customs. "Christianity," writes Alfred Rush, "made no violent breaks with ancient culture, but preserved whatever was best in it."[3] Likewise, Richard Rutherford notes: "Optimistic interest in life hereafter and ritual care for the dead were thus something Christians shared with the world around them as part of their human cultural heritage."[4] For instance, Dionysius suggests that the body of the deceased was washed and clothed by fellow Christians. Christians largely adapted Jewish cleansing practices but changed the meaning to signify care for the sacredness of the human body (whereas Jewish thought portrayed the body as unclean; washing restored ritual purity). In the pages ahead, many of the customs of the early Church will be examined both in terms of how they came to be but also in terms of how they supported and nurtured belief in the Resurrection throughout the subsequent ages. We will notice that the imagery used to capture the Church's understanding of death in its formative years was communal in nature; Christians desired to express a deep sense of communion that could survive the death of one of their members. For the early followers of the Risen Christ, Baptism was death, and death was Baptism, and the process of life was the growth and maturation of Christ's Body.

3. Alfred C. Rush. *Death and Burial in Christian Antiquity* (Washington, DC: Catholic University of America Press, 1941), vii.

4. Rutherford, *The Death of a Christian*, 5.

Death and the Attitude of Early Christians
Death as Sleep

The most ancient understanding of death for Christians was that of a sleep.[5] The likening of death to sleep stems from the Lord's miracle of raising Jairus' daughter from the dead and his accompanying question: "Why all this commotion and crying? The child is not dead but asleep" (see Mark 5:35–43). The Church understood this notion of death as sleep in a positive light as Jesus himself guaranteed that those who have fallen asleep will surely wake. This stands in marked contrast to the pagan understanding of death as a sleep. Immortality, in the pagan world, was not the universal destiny of all; rather, it belonged to those who held divine status in the world and would be the equals of god. Rush writes:

> [T]he conclusion is unavoidable that their chief characteristic is a dreary outlook, an utter lack of prospect of anything beyond the grave; and once they venture to look beyond the grave, all is dark and gloomy. Death simply meant the end of life. This outlook on death as the final and irremediable episode of life is summed up in that pagan concept of death as an eternal sleep, a sleep that has no end and a sleep from which there will be no rising.[6]

It is common to find evidence of pagan graves bearing the inscription: AETERNA DOMVS HAEC EST ("This Is Eternal Home").[7] Indeed, in ancient paganism, there was a genuinely pessimistic attitude toward a death that ended in eternal sleep; there was no hope of waking.

The gloomy interpretation of death as an eternal sleep that circulated among pagans was replaced by a different understanding of sleep—namely, a "temporary rest." Rush states, "Death, instead of being an eternal sleep became a temporary sleep; the grave, instead of being the eternal home of the dead, became the temporary abode of the body until the resurrection."[8] For the pagans, death as sleep was full of doom and gloom, but for Christians, death as sleep was full of consolation. Paul testifies to the hopeful nature of this sleep when he writes to the Thessalonians: "We do not want you to be unaware, brothers, about those who have fallen asleep, so

---

5. Rush, *Death and Burial in Christian Antiquity*, 1.
6. Rush, 8.
7. Rush, 9.
8. Rush, 12.

that you may not grieve like the rest, who have no hope. For if we believe that Jesus died and rose, so too will God, through Jesus, bring with him those who have fallen asleep" (1 Thessalonians 4:13–14). Toward the end of the first century, St. Ignatius of Antioch, bishop and martyr, will speak of his death as a sleep: "Rather entice the wild beasts that they might become my tomb and leave no trace of me so that when I shall have fallen asleep I be not burdensome to any."[9]

Hope truly is the Christian contribution surrounding the outlook on death in the first century. This was a time when the Church witnessed the accumulation of martyrs in large numbers, and it was a period of relative instability for the Christian communities who had to be on the lookout for persecutors. Interestingly enough, even though Christians often feared to gather publicly, they did not refrain from burying the dead in public cemeteries.[10] In these places of burial, it is not uncommon to see Christian funerary images mixed among Jewish and pagan tombs, with the Christian decoration depicting meals of refreshment and peace. Just as natural sleep provides rejuvenation for the body, so too did Christians understand the sleep of death to be a time for refreshment. Commenting on the imagery found on ancient Christian tombs that depict the sharing of a meal, Rutherford explains:

> Such funerary decorations preserved for us the symbolic motifs in which those early Christians gave expression to their faith in face of death, a faith that speaks not of death but of life. Far from denying physical death, this proclaims the belief that the life entered at baptism and nourished at the eucharist is of a different order. . . . Its food is the body of the Lord Jesus, broken and given as the bread of life. For those reborn to this life in the waters of baptism and fed at the Lord's eucharistic banquet in union with his Church, the idea that physical death might terminate such life simply has no place in the categories of the faith. This is not to say that physical death itself, as well as its harsh consequences for bereaved survivors, was not real. But in the face of grief, of painful human loss and separation, Christians found consolation in the

---

9. Ignatius, *Epistula ad Romanos*, 4, 2. Quote found in Rush, *Death and Burial in Christian Antiquity*, 16.

10. See Rutherford, *The Death of a Christian*, 6.

promise of life. They had every hope that the life they once shared in the eucharist would be theirs again in the eschatological kingdom.[11]

The last sentence of the quote is particularly important. The hope that Christians fostered in the face of death was communal. The imagery of sharing in a banquet meal suggests that the Christian community of the early Church saw the sleep of death as a transitional period in expectation of a great eschatological unification; sleep meant true refreshment. For this reason, the tombs of martyrs were sacred places of devotion, because these were the men and women who were granted immediate refreshment as a reward for the blood of their self-sacrifice.

Several of the church orders that begin to appear in the patristic period suggest that the sleep of the departed be accompanied by prayer and the singing of psalms, which communicated a sense of contentment and rest. For example, the Syrian order called the *Didascalia*, which comes from roughly the middle of the third century and was written to catechize pagan converts, suggests that Christians were to accompany those who had fallen asleep by meeting at the place of burial, by reading Scripture, and by offering up prayers and the Eucharist.[12] Likewise, an Egyptian source from roughly the middle of the fourth century, the *Sacramentary of Serapion of Thmuis*, contains a burial prayer that asks "We pray Thee on account of the falling asleep and going to rest of this Thy servant and plead for the soul's refreshment with Abraham, Isaac and Jacob."[13] Finally, the *Apostolic Constitutions*, a Syrian source from the late fourth century instructs the faithful to assemble in the resting place of the dead, read Scripture, and sing psalms of joy for all the martyrs and saints who sleep in the Lord.[14] Rush comments on these sources: "These works constantly avoid the use of the term death. The constant use of such words as 'sleep' and 'rest' show that the predominant notion in their minds regarding death was that it was a temporary sleep."[15]

A distinct manifestation of the Christian hopefulness that attended death in the early Church is the restriction against public mourning. While

---

11. Rutherford, 6–7.
12. See Rush, *Death and Burial in Christian Antiquity*, 17.
13. Rush, 17–18.
14. Rush, 18.
15. Rush, 18.

pagan burials were often marked by exorbitant wailing and violent gestures of grief, Christians were instructed to maintain a posture of austerity around death and burial. Thus, Tertullian writes in his *De Patientia*: "We grieve Christ when we do not accept with equanimity the death of those who have been summoned by Him, acting as though they were to be pitied."[16] Likewise St. Cyprian writes in his *De Mortalitate*: "Let us show that this is what we believe, so that we may not mourn the death even of our dear ones, and when the day of our own summons comes, without hesitation but with gladness we may come to the Lord at His call."[17] Because death is seen as a summons by the Lord, signs of outward mourning are deemed inconsistent with Christian hope. Just as sleep only temporarily removes a person from direct participation in the lives of others, and deserves no pity, so too is death seen as a temporary state of being, one that is to be honored as true and lasting refreshment.

Death as Voyage

This brings us to the motif of journey that surrounds death. If, first and foremost, early Christians understood death as falling asleep for a time after which would come a summons by the Lord, then the summoning itself sets off a journey of the soul to yet another state of existence. Ancient Egyptians believed that it was the work of the sun god Re to carry the souls of the dead to an abode of happiness in the East, thereby avoiding descent into the kingdom of the dead located in the West.[18] However, who were the ones who would receive a voyage to the place of happiness? The Egyptians believed that this journey served to separate what existed side by side on earth; the rich and the powerful of this world were to be chosen for an afterlife of bliss, while the poor would dwell forever in the kingdom of the dead.[19] It was believed that the rich were closer to divinity, those who would be favored for an afterlife. Rush writes: "In the Egyptian mentality the heavens were regarded as a vast ocean on which the sun and stars travelled about in ships. Every morning the sun was born in the East and they imaged that the sun sailed across the heavens in his celestial bark."[20]

---

16. Rush, 25.
17. Rush, 25.
18. Rush, 27.
19. Rush, 45.
20. Rush, 46.

The Greeks and Romans also had developed lore about death as a voyage. By the sixth century BC, the myth of Charon, the ferryman of the dead, who came in his boat to escort the dead across a treacherous river to the kingdom of the dead, had sparked the imagination of the Greeks so much so that it became popular in literature.[21] The story is often associated with the custom of placing a coin in the mouth of the deceased, a coin that was then received by Charon who, as ferryman, was to guard against floods, guide the boat with his pole, tend to the sails, and carry the dead across the waters.[22] Rush writes:

> Among the Greeks and Romans, this voyage to the lower world did not have the same happy connotation as the Egyptian voyage which the dead made in the bark of Re and which brought them to the kingdom of the dead in the heavens. Descriptions of the lower world were often most lurid and terrifying. . . . However, among the Greeks and Romans the idea of a journey to the underworld became transformed into that of a journey to the heavens. . . . It was to the moon that the bark of salvation had to bear souls across the stormy waters of matter. The Styx had become a celestial river; Charon, with the help of winds, caused pious souls to pass not to the subterranean world, but to the heavenly dwelling of the heroes.[23]

While Charon's crossing was viewed as arduous, it is indeed more hopeful for the masses than the outlook of the ancient Egyptians. With such widespread popularity among the Greeks and Romans, it is no wonder that Christians likewise popularized the imagery of journey in their portrayal of death and resurrection. As Rush states, "From this it seems that at the time when Christianity began to spread among these people there was a widespread belief that the dead embarked on a voyage after death to a future life of happiness."[24]

Because the voyage motif entered so prominently into the eschatology of the Romans and the Greeks at the outset of the Church's formation, it is no wonder that the symbol of the ship comes to play a prominent role in Christian funerary images. This symbol also was easily popularized among

---

21. Rush, 50.
22. Rush, 52.
23. Rush, 54.
24. Rush, 54.

Christians since some of Jesus' disciples were fishermen; the ship became a natural way to represent the Christian Church, able to symbolize both journey and community. What comes to be known as the *Migratio ad Dominum* is generally depicted as a corporate crossing: "The Church is spoken of as a ship voyaging through the present world and carrying the faithful to the safe port of heaven."[25] St. Hippolytus renders a beautiful description of the Church as a ship at sea:

> The sea is the world in which the Church, like a ship at sea, is tossed about by the storm, without, however, sinking, because she has with her the experienced pilot, Christ. She carries aboard ship the trophy of victory over death, since she has with her the Cross of the Lord. The prow of the ship is the East; the stern, the West; the hull, the south. Her two rudders are the two Testaments and the ropes stretched about her are the love of Christ which binds the Church together. The water which she carries with her is the bath of regeneration which renews the faithful. The bright sail which she has is the Spirit and it is through Him that those are sealed who believe in God. She also has iron anchors on board, that is, the holy Commandments of Christ which are strong as iron. She likewise has sailors on her starboard and larboard, namely guardian angels who speed by her side and it is by these that the Church is always governed and guarded. The ladder leading aloft to the sailyard draws the faithful to the ascent of heaven like the image of the sign of Christ's passion. The riggings over the sailyard and leading to the tip of the mast are the orders of Prophets, Martyrs and Apostles who have come to rest in the kingdom of Christ.[26]

Hippolytus describes here, most likely near the beginning of the third century, life in Christ as a voyage to the East. There are different parts to the crew and the ship itself, but all are united in a common journey. Such ordering of the Church is reflected in the *Apostolic Constitutions*, which spells out the duties of the bishop as follows: "When you gather the faithful in the Church of God about you, act like a pilot of a great ship. See that the gathering takes place in perfect order, commanding the deacons like sailors, that they carefully and properly point out to the brethren embarking on

---

25. Rush, 59.

26. Hippolytus, *De Antichristo*, 59. Quote taken from Rush, *Death and Burial in Christian Antiquity*, 60–61.

this ship, their right places."[27] All of this suggests that the early Church understood salvation as a corporate affair; Christians are redeemed as a people. As Anne Tigan writes: "As difficult as it may be, building the holy city of Jerusalem requires that we do it together, turning to one another with love and, transformed by the strength of this love, lifting one another up towards our foundation confident the elders and angels will not resist."[28]

Death as Birth

A third description that the early Christians used to describe death is the day of birth. As the cult of martyrs spread in the late first and early second century, the day of death became the marker of one's true birth, celebrated annually as a day of remembrance and feasting. The account of the martyrdom of St. Polycarp in the middle of the second century states: "There the Lord will permit us to come together according to our power in gladness and joy, and celebrate the *birthday* of his martyrdom, both in memory of those who have already contested and for the practice and training of those whose fate it shall be."[29] To those Christians who honored the life of the martyr, the day of death was the true *dies natalis*. In pagan antiquity, it was customary to celebrate the deceased on the anniversary of their birth into this life; thus it seems as though Christians made a deliberate attempt to break with this custom by celebrating instead the anniversary of death.[30] Tertullian states precisely this when he offers the instruction: "We offer sacrifice for the dead on the anniversary (of their death) instead of on their birthday."[31] By the time of Tertullian's writing, it was becoming customary to apply the term *dies natalis* to the death of any Christian and not simply martyrs alone.

Certainly, this idea of death as birth had its origins in the teaching of the Lord himself, who said to Martha at the raising of her brother Lazarus: "I am the resurrection and the life. Anyone who believes in me, even though that person dies, will live, and whoever lives and believes in me will never

---

27. *Constitutiones Apostolorum*, II, 57, 2–3. Quote taken from Rush, *Death and Burial in Christian Antiquity*, 62.

28. Anne Tigan, "By the Rivers of Babylon: Reflections on Pilgrimage, Jerusalem and Funeral Liturgy," *Worship* 72 (1998): 337.

29. *Martyrium Polycarpi*, 18, 3. Quote taken from Rush, *Death and Burial in Christian Antiquity*, 72.

30. See Rush, *Death and Burial in Christian Antiquity*, 74.

31. Tertullian, *De Corona Militis* 3. Quote taken from Rush, *Death and Burial in Christian Antiquity*, 74–75.

die" (John 11:25–26). Interchangeable here with "life" is the symbol of "light." Jesus spoke to the crowds, saying, "I am the light of the world; anyone who follows me will not be walking in the dark but will have the light of life" (John 8:12). Regarding the connected images of birth and light, Rush states, "Just as birth means seeing the light of day, so, too, the attaining of heavenly light in death was a symbol indicating that death was a birthday for heaven."[32] The rising of the sun in the eastern sky was a sign of the newness of life and God's triumph over darkness. Writing in the fourth century to the deceased Valentinian, St. Ambrose contemplates death as birth into perpetual light:

> I seem to see you in splendor, I seem to hear you saying: The dawn is mine, O Father, the night on earth has passed, the day of heaven is at hand. Therefore, you look on us, O holy soul, looking back from a region above, as it were, on things below. You have gone forth from the darkness of this world, and you shine like the moon, you are resplendent like the sun. And rightly as the moon, because, before, although in the shadow of this earthly body, you shone and illumined the darkness of earth, yet now by borrowing light from the sun of justice you are beginning a new day, a clear day. Therefore, I seem to see you withdrawing, as it were, from the body, and, having thrust aside the darkness of night, rising at dawn like the sun, approaching God, and, in swift flight like an eagle, abandoning the things which are of earth.[33]

Clearly, Ambrose suggests that the going forth of a soul into the "sun of justice" involves a speedy transition to a state of "abandoning the things which are of earth." Light is seen here as freedom. For this reason, St. John Chrysostom instructs against mourning the death of Christians: "Therefore thou shouldst do this (i.e. mourn) at the birth of a child, for death is also a birth and a better birth than the birth into this life. For here (in death) the soul goes forth to a different kind of light."[34] It is important to note that likening death to a *dies natalis* is very much what Baptism is for a Christian. While the birth of a child in the flesh is the beginning of new life in this

---

32. Rush, *Death and Burial in Christian Antiquity*, 76.

33. Ambrose, *De Consolatione Valentiniani*, 64. Quote taken from Rush, *Death and Burial in Christian Antiquity*, 79.

34. Chrysostom, *Homilia* 21 in *Actus Apostolorum*, 4. Quote taken from Rush, *Death and Burial in Christian Antiquity*, 80.

world, Baptism in water and the Holy Spirit is new life in Christ. Death is the birth of the Christlife lived in the heavenly realm.

The three outlooks on death developed in early Christianity examined here—death as sleep, death as voyage, and death as one's birthday—certainly do not exhaust the Church's attempt to profess belief in the resurrection of the dead. However, they provide clear evidence of the overarching Christian attitude regarding death, namely, a communal hope in the life that is yet to come. As Paul writes to the Thessalonians:

> We do not want you to be unaware, brothers, about those who have fallen asleep, so that you may not grieve like the rest, who have no hope. For if we believe that Jesus died and rose, so too will God, through Jesus, bring with him those who have fallen asleep. Indeed, we tell you this, on the word of the Lord, that we who are alive, who are left until the coming of the Lord, will surely not precede those who have fallen asleep. For the Lord himself, with a word of command, with the voice of an archangel and with the trumpet of God will come down from heaven, and the dead in Christ will rise first. Then we who are alive, who are left, will be caught up together with them in the clouds to meet the Lord in the air. Thus we shall always be with the Lord. Therefore, console one another with these words. (1 Thessalonians 4:13–18)

The Christian community honored the memory of the dead because it believed that the one Church would one day "be caught up together in the clouds to meet the Lord in the air." This ecclesial unity was not simply a theological outlook for the Church, it was expressed in the ritual activities undertaken by the Church when a member of Christ's Body crossed the threshold of death to new life. To these Christian rituals we now turn.

Rituals of Corporate Care at Death and Burial

As stated at the outset of this chapter, the Christian understanding of death did not develop in a vacuum; instead, Christians were greatly influenced by pagan and Jewish attitudes regarding death. The same is true for rituals surrounding death and the disposal of the body. The Christian approach to caring for the body and disposing of it with prayer flowed decidedly from Jewish precedents. Just as Jesus' bodied was anointed, clothed, and laid in a tomb, his early followers believed that proper care of the dead was, in fact, proper care of the Lord himself. Also stated at the beginning of this chapter is the understanding of Christian death and burial in terms of ritual passage. Arnold van Gennep's simple concept of rites of passage entails rituals of separation from a former world, rituals of transition or liminality that help a community embrace change, and rituals of incorporation that serve to celebrate a new status or way of being in the world.[35] Early Christians developed their burial process very much along the lines of ritual passage. Thus, attention will be given to many of the customs that have fallen out of use in the Church of the twenty-first century. Many reveal much about a baptismal understanding of death, whereby the deceased member of Christ's Body continues to play a venerable role in the life of the Church.

Deathbed Care and Vigils: Rituals of Separation

Early Christian witness gives testimony to four rites that were enacted as the moment of death approached, namely, the stretching out of the feet, the celebration of Viaticum, the catching of the last breath, and the giving of a final kiss.[36] Both the stretching out of the feet and the administering of Viaticum were intended to aid the dying in their subsequent journey; stretching out the feet made for a swift release from this world, while Viaticum was given to nourish the dead on their way to eternal life. Viaticum has been likened to the pagan custom of placing a coin in the mouth of the dead to pay the ferryman for a successful voyage; however, the extension of the Eucharist to the dying has a distinctively Christian characteristic of continuing the nourishment that had guided the deceased throughout their journey through life. In other words, Viaticum had a greater ecclesial significance to Christians than payment for a safe voyage.[37] The catching of the last breath and the giving of a parting kiss were two related customs meant to assist in the soul's transition. The first was a means of connection with the dying person's soul, the second was a simple

---

35. See Arnold van Gennep, *The Rites of Passage*.

36. See Rush, *Death and Burial in Christian Antiquity*, 91.

37. Rush, 91. On page 101, the author comments: "In the light of what has been said above regarding the use of the word *viaticum* to signify money for a journey and money for Charon, and in the light of the ancient custom of supplying the dead with a coin, it is not improbable that the Christian practice of calling the Eucharist administered at death a Viaticum, and of insisting that it be in the mouth of the dying when the soul departed out of the body, and of placing it at times in the mouth of the dead, was a Christian substitution for a similar custom in antiquity. Here it is not intended to infer that the giving of the Eucharist was the same as supplying the dead with a coin. However, the desire to supply the deceased with some protection for this journey was prevalent in both pagan and Christian circles. To the Christians, the greatest safeguard was the Body and Blood of Christ which was their pledge of immortality. This, then, was their *Viaticum*."

act of tenderness. These two gestures will eventually be morphed into a ritual conducted at the time of burial. "The liturgical kiss is a sign of reverence signifying the supernatural charity existing among Christians. The
kiss of peace, therefore, in the burial service shows the intimate bond of
union and charity existing between the living and the dead."[38]

These four ritual gestures that took place as life in this world was coming to an end suggest a unique approach to the body that differed from
Jewish and pagan traditions. While the former took great pains to wash the
body at the moment of death, the corpse soon became a source of defile-
ment; thus, there was the need to dispose of the body as rapidly as possible.
In the Christian understanding, however, the body never loses its sacredness; Christians were unafraid of contact with it. Thus, "the kiss of peace
is given to the dead because everyone who has lived a godly life is dear and
worthy of praise in the mind of all who are god-like."[39] In addition to these
first four customs of attending to the body at the moment of death,
Christians also adopted the Greek and Roman tradition of closing the eyes
and the mouth of the corpse. Like the catching of the last breath, these gestures were intended to aid the smooth passage of the soul. While seemingly
insignificant actions, the closing of the eyes and of the mouth were to be
the duties of the closest relatives and thus became a way for them to physically express care for the body. What needs to be underscored here is that
the early Christians were unafraid of the dead body; they did not shy away
from touching it or continuing to look upon it with noble respect. In many
ways the presence of the dead body, with the memory of all that person
contributed to the community, was seen as a physical manifestation of
ecclesial unity.

In the Roman world, after the eyes and the mouth had been properly
closed, the *conclamatio* would follow.[40] This was a loud clamor shouted by
those who surrounded the body of the deceased that served the purpose of
making certain that the person was truly dead. The *conclamatio* could
range from calling out the name of the dead person to a violent display of
grief and anguish. Christians would supplant this custom with the singing
of psalms. Instead of filling the room with chaos and pandemonium,

---

38. Rush, 103.
39. Rush, 104.
40. Rush, 108.

Christians chose to sing psalms of praise to God, thereby expressing their belief that death is life. Rutherford suggests that the dominant theme that surrounded the care for the body at the time of death was one of *exitus* or departure.[41] Thus, a most suitable psalm to be sung is Psalm 114, which praises God for Israel's departure from Egypt:

> When Israel came forth from Egypt,
>   the House of Jacob from a people of foreign speech,
> Judah became God's sanctuary,
>   Israel, God's domain.
> The sea saw and fled;
>   the Jordan turned back.
> The mountains skipped like rams,
>   the hills like lambs.
> Why was it, sea, that you fled?
>   Jordan, that you turned back?
> Mountains, that you skipped like rams?
>   You hills, like lambs?
> Tremble, earth, before the Lord,
>   before the God of Jacob,
> Who turned the rock into pools of water,
>   flint into a flowing spring.[42]

This psalm of exitus wonderfully expresses God's power and strength in guiding a people to freedom; the individual soul is made a part of this communal exodus. In the development of a liturgy to be prayed at the moment of death, this psalm came to be accompanied by the "song of farewell":

> Saints of God, come to his (her) aid!
> Come to meet him (her), angels of the Lord!
>
> Receive his (her) soul and present it before
> the face of God the Most High.

---

41. Rutherford, *The Death of a Christian*, 43.
42. Psalm 114:1–8.

> May Christ, who called you, take you to himself;
> may angels lead you to Abraham's side (bosom).
>
> May the choirs of angels welcome you, and with
> Lazarus once poor may you have eternal rest.[43]

Soon more will be said of the Christian duty of singing psalms as a procession accompanies the transition of the body to its place of burial; however, it is most important here to see the attempt by Christians to turn the scene of death away from tragedy and uncleanliness to one of joy and sacredness. The community together rehearsed its faith around the body of the dead Christian.

Moreover, the duty of Christians to care for the body was physically communicated in the washing of the corpse. Both Jews and pagans had highly developed rituals surrounding the washing of dead bodies. For example, the Eyptians believed that washing the body served to make the deceased more like the gods, this done in imitation of the daily washing of the statues of gods in their shrines by priests.[44] On the other hand, the Romans washed the bodies of the dead with warm water to ensure that the person was indeed dead.[45] The Jewish practice of washing the dead body was a matter of religious obligations in order to restore purity to the household.[46] The Talmud provides a stringent list of activities to be avoided by a mourner who has not completed the prescribed burial obligations:

> He is forbidden to do work, to bathe, or anoint himself, to have
> (marital) intercourse, or don sandals; he is forbidden to read the
> Pentateuch, Prophets, or Hagiographa, or to recite the Mishnah,
> or Midrash and *halacoth*, or the Talmud or *aggadoth*.[47]

In adopting the tradition of washing the body, it was customary for Christians to follow the practices of the Romans and the Egyptians in anointing the body. Rush notes that "in anointing their dead, the Romans used salt, cedar resin, honey, myrrh, and balsam."[48] Anointing in the

---

43. See Rutherford, *The Death of a Christian*, 44.

44. Rush, *Death and Burial in Christian Antiquity*, 112.

45. Rush, 113.

46. Rowell, *The Liturgy of Christian Burial*, 3.

47. *Mo'ed Katan*, 21a. Quote taken from Rowell, *The Liturgy of Christian Burial*, 3.

48. Rush, *Death and Burial in Christian Antiquity*, 118.

Christian world tended to be less elaborate and was geared for a brief pres-
ervation while the body was laid out. However, just as Scripture testifies
that Joseph of Arimathea and Nicodemus went to great lengths to ensure
that the body of the Lord was anointed and cared for, anointing certainly
communicated a great deal of reverence for the body.

Interestingly enough, one source, namely that of the Pseudo-Dionysius,
a Greek Christian philosopher/theologian of the late fifth, early sixth century, mentions the custom that had grown up in his locale that involved
pouring oil on the deceased after the kiss of peace in the context of the
funeral liturgy.[49] Rush states:

> In the commentary on this rite, he (Pseudo-Dionysius) makes a
> comparison between the anointing at baptism and that which took
> place during the funeral service. The baptism anointing was a call and
> a challenge to take up the sacred warfare of life; the anointing at burial
> signified that the struggle of life was over and that the deceased had
> come off glorious and was perfected.[50]

While the West exhibits no ritual similar to this, it is likely that the entire
Christian Church interpreted the washing of the body and its subsequent
anointing through the lens of Baptism. If death is considered through the
perspective of the real day of birth, then it would be logical for Christians
to contemplate the ritual washing as a symbol of Baptism. This form of
ecclesial care represented belief in the enduring sacredness of the body.

A final responsibility that Christians undertook regarding care for the
body is the clothing of the deceased. While the Egyptians predominantly
wrapped the dead in linen, the Greeks and Romans dressed their dead in ways
meant to reflect social status. For Christians, clothing in linen seems to have
been typical, while they also buried the dead in the ordinary clothes of everyday life or sometimes in special garments. The tendency to clothe Christians
in distinctive or extravagant garments proved to be problematic:

> Certain Fathers denounced this and it is from these denunciations that
> the Christian practice of attempting to procure special and costly burial
> garments can be seen to a greater advantage. . . . St. John Chrysostom
> bitterly inveighed against the extravagance of Christians who clothed

---

49. Rush, 124.
50. Rush, 124.

their dead in precious apparel and often in silks and gold. After showing that Christ rose naked from the tomb, he refers to the extravagances of Christians as a madness and urges them to cease from such excess. . . . In opposition to the gold and silken clothing with which the Christians were adorning their dead, Chrysostom sets before their minds the garment of immortality which the body is to put on, and which is more glorious than garments of silk and gold. St. Jerome with equal vehemence attacked the rich who lavished luxurious attire on their dead. . . . St. Augustine speaks against the foolishness of some who give no thought to the manner in which they live, but think only of the splendor in which they will be buried. The desire to be buried in precious garments and to lie in a costly sepulchre is, according to Augustine, nothing but vanity.[51]

Thus, in the debate that took place between officials of the Church and the Christian community at large, it can be seen that the Christian ideal in clothing the dead was to represent an equality, in which no one was marked with signs of privilege. In the end, to die with Christ and to rise with him meant that one was identified solely by attachment to him.

Similarly, another mark of distinction to be avoided in the Christian world was the pagan custom of crowning the dead.[52] The act of crowning was interpreted as idolatry, and thus, both Christians and Jews were apt to avoid such a ritual. As one writer spoke in defense of not crowning the dead: "We arrange our funerals as simply as our lives; we twine no fading crown but await from God a crown blossoming with eternal flowers."[53] For Christians, the crown of discipleship was awarded only by the Lord himself as an imperishable prize. As St. Paul writes to Timothy: "I have competed well; I have finished the race; I have kept the faith. From now on the crown of righteousness awaits me, which the Lord, the just judge, will award to me on that day, and not only to me, but to all who have longed for

---

51. Rush, 131–132.

52. Rush, 133–137. Concerning the crowning of the dead in ancient Egypt, Rush writes: "Crowns were given to the dead in ancient times on account of the close connection between the cult of the dead and the cult of the gods. The crown was a mark of divinity. The crown was bestowed upon the dead, therefore, because they were regarded as being deified after death and taking on a higher sanctity" (135). Later, he explains the Roman significance of crowning: "Among the Romans, a religious interpretation was given to the funeral crown. The souls of the elect were crowned like athletes and soldiers; their wreath was the crown of life symbolizing their immortality and their triumph over the forces of evil, the most implacable of which was death" (137).

53. Rush, 140. In his work *Octavius*, Marcus Minucius Felix, a renowned Christian apologist of the late second century, rejects crowning with these words.

his appearance" (2 Timothy 4:7–8). Once again, to suggest that one member of the Body of Christ has run the race faster and has been singled out for the prize of a crown lessens the notion that the Church is running the race together.

The Church attempted to guide these household rituals performed by family members and close friends in a way that countered pagan superstitions with acts of hope and faith. As with the celebration of Viaticum as death was approaching, the Christian community expressed the enduring power of the Eucharist to guide the pilgrim's journey. It was as much an expression of the person's unity with the Church as it was a gesture of farewell. Likewise, the washing of the corpse in the Christian household served to emphasize the lasting sacredness of the body, as for a Christian, the human body was always to be the temple of the Holy Spirit. Finally, early Church leaders are outspoken about the need for following a principle of noble simplicity in clothing the dead. Marks of wealth and distinction were to be avoided, since in the Body of Christ, the Church, there is neither rich nor poor.

As suggested earlier, Christians maintained a positive respect for the dead from the very beginning of the formation of the Church. They surrounded the dying with prayer and with Viaticum, they worked to assist the soul's transition, and they washed and prepared the body for burial with reverence and care. While these necessary steps in the process of caring for the dead were usually attended to by the immediate family and friends of the deceased, the wider Christian community was actively involved in the next part of the process, namely, that of keeping watch around the body with song and prayer. The act of preparing the body for some form of public viewing and the subsequent time spent in vigilant prayer can be likened to van Gennep's understanding of rites of separation. Touching the body, washing it, clothing it, and then spending time with it are all ways in which the mourners are able to accept the reality of death and ready themselves to transition successfully to a new way of life in the physical absence of the deceased. Thus, they needed time to contemplate the new way in which the deceased would continue to be present, albeit in a non-physical state.

Time for contemplating this change was of great importance. Thus, in the Greek world, the general custom was to have the body of the deceased laid out for viewing for three days before it was to be buried.[54] The length of the wake for Romans varied according to status in the empire, with the more solemn occasions lasting up to seven days.[55] As it was the practice of Jews to bury the dead on the day of death, it is likely that Christians brought the body to be buried very shortly after it was prepared.[56] Therefore, the earliest form of the Christian wake would most likely have been a vigil held at the grave. Jewish mourners believed that it was necessary to keep watch over the grave for three days, as this was the time period during which the soul hovered over the body.[57] Thus, it is very likely that Christians gathered at the graveside for three days of attending to the dead with prayer and the singing of psalms. Rush writes:

> Hence, in Christianity, the practice was continued of holding a vigil at the grave; and very often a three day vigil or wake is mentioned . . . The Martrydom of Polycarp speaks of the brethren coming together at his grave and celebrating the *dies natalis* of his martyrdom according to their power in gladness and joy . . . In the *Apostolic Constitutions*, the faithful are enjoined to gather in the cemeteries and read the Sacred Scriptures and sing psalms over the martyrs who have gone to rest and also over all the saints and all the brethren who have died in the Lord. In North Africa, where the practice was to bury on the day of death, they had the custom of keeping a vigil at the grave for three days. Thus bishop Evodius, writing to St. Augustine about the death of a pious youth, says that for three days they praised the Lord at his grave and that they offered the sacrifice of the Eucharist, the sacrifice of the Redemption, on the third day.[58]

Therefore, it can be largely surmised that Christians adopted the Jewish practice of burying the dead on the day of death itself and then continued to keep vigil with the body after it had entered the grave. The funeral meal or Eucharist would then take place in the subsequent days after the burial of the body.

---

54. Rush, 150–151.

55. Rush, 153.

56. Rush, 157. Rush states: "This was necessitated by law as well as by the warm climate of the country which did not permit the bodies to be held over for any length of time."

57. Rush, 158.

58. Rush, 159–160.

With the bestowal of peace upon the Church in the early fourth century, it became possible for Christians to wake the bodies of the dead publicly in the church building.[59] Now the three days of waking the body would be transferred to the church.[60] Thus, the development of the Christian wake progresses from a short time of vigiling with the body at the home of the deceased, to an extended time of keeping watch over the dead at the grave, to a formalized time of prayer around the body of the deceased at the church building, which shifted the celebration of the Eucharist to a position before burial. According to Rutherford:

> Their faith and its liturgical expression made the funeral of Christians different from that of their cultural neighbors. Faith saw to the preparation of the corpse in a setting of prayer; faith expressed itself in psalms during the procession with the body; and faith rendered the church and its immediate surroundings the Christian place of burial par excellence.

> This pattern was characterized by two principal locations of liturgical action: home and church. Here we must think of "church" as church compound, including churchyard, cloisters, and the like—a broader architectural notion than the church edifice of today. The two liturgical services were joined by the traditional funeral procession. The church compound functioned symbolically as the heavenly Jerusalem, which the deceased drew near and entered to remain. And in the Christian community, it functioned as the place where prayer was offered for the deceased and the body laid to rest. There does not appear to be have been any separate liturgy in the church apart from the service of burial, consisting of a solemn entrance, prayers for the deceased, and interment.[61]

What needs to be underscored in the ritual activity surrounding the movement of the prepared body to the place of burial through the time of keeping vigil with the body is the general Christian characteristic of visibly

---

59. Rush, 160.

60. Rush, 161. Rush writes: "According to St. Jerome, it seems that it was the custom in the Church at Palestine to bring the body to the Church and hold a vigil over it for three days. In this account of the death of Paula he mentions that she was brought to the Church of the Savior. Then he says: 'Psalms were chanted in Greek, Latin and Syriac not only for the three days which elapsed until she was buried beneath the church and close to the cave of the Lord, but through the entire week.' St. Jerome mentions that the burial of Paula was an exception to the general rule in so far as her funerals solemnities lasted not only for three days, but for an entire week."

61. Rutherford, *The Death of a Christian*, 40–41.

displaying hope in the resurrection. For pagans, the time of preparing to bury the body called for mostly violent manifestations of mourning, such as "rolling on the ground, tearing the hair, plucking the cheeks, tearing the clothing, striking the breast, and extending the hand to the corpse."[62] For Christians, however, the time of waking the body was a manifestation of prayer; it was the duty of the Christian community to support the dead with their prayers and to care for those who were entrenched in mourning. The singing of psalms and hymns at the home, the graveside, or the church became standard Christian practice as a direct correlative to the pagan dirges and songs of lament.[63]

Processions: Rituals of Transition

Therefore, while the wake was certainly more public in places where Christianity prospered, even as its location and duration varied from place to place, the funeral procession (at first from the house to the place of burial and subsequently from the church to the place of burial) became the most public means for displaying the Christian virtue of hope. In the language of van Gennep, the procession is the ritual enactment of liminality, of the time that is "betwixt and between" two worlds.[64] Christians processed with their dead to the place of burial in order to experience the movement of the Church as one into the Communion of Saints. In the pagan world, the funeral procession was often the occasion for grand pageantry in which masks were worn by members of the family, horns and trumpets were sounded, and the cries of mourners filled the streets.[65] These were certainly grand displays used for ritualizing liminality. Furthermore, it was believed that the gods "demanded this vociferous wailing," and that "they welcomed the deceased all the more cordially, the louder the mourning display" at burial.[66] In contrast, the Christian funeral procession was much simpler

---

62. Rush, *Death and Burial in Christian Antiquity*, 165.

63. Rush, 184. Rush writes: "To assure the triumph of Christianity in this regard, it was the desire of the Church that the teachings of Christianity should permeate the lives of the faithful so that everything out of harmony with this might disappear. St. Cyprian says that the fear of death will depart when the thought of immortality takes root, and he recommends to his flock that they should show that this is what they believe so that they should not mourn. St. Ambrose says that tears and mourning will cease when the soul heeds salutary remedies. St. John Chrysostom admonishes his flock to devise what consolation they can for the departed, but instead of seeking it in tears and lamentations, they should rather seek it in the Christian substitutions of alms, prayers, and oblations for the dead."

64. See van Gennep, *The Rites of Passage*, 20–21.

65. Rush, *Death and Burial in Christian Antiquity*, 190–191.

66. Rush, 231.

and deliberately more austere. Rutherford outlines the details of the Christian funeral procession as follows:

> When all was ready, the body was carried in solemn procession to the grave or tomb. . . . The body was preceded by wax tapers and incense. Lighted tapers or candles continued earlier pagan usage, which Christians had given their own meaning. Incense at the funeral was something Christians likewise retained from pagan custom. Gradually, the use of incense as a sign of honor was applied to the deceased, undoubtedly by analogy to its use in honor of the relics of the martyrs. . . . The singing of psalms and antiphons accompanied the procession.[67]

Three psalms in particular were popular for the funeral procession: Psalm 25 "To you, I lift up my soul," Psalm 118 "Give thanks to the Lord, for he is good," and Psalm 42 "Like the deer longs for running water."[68] Rutherford comments on the symbolic nature of singing and processing: "For while the Christian community carried the body of a dead member to its earthly grave, the liturgy saw the community of saints and angels accompanying the deceased into the eschatological kingdom."[69] As St. John Chrysostom writes: "What is the reason for the hymns? Is it not that we praise God and thank Him that He has crowned the departed and freed him from suffering, and that God has the deceased, now freed from fear, with Himself? Is this not the reason for the singing of hymns and psalms? All this is a sign of joy, for it is said: 'Is anyone cheerful, let him sing.'"[70]

The role of pallbearers in the funeral procession, which was the common means of transporting the dead for the Greeks and the Romans, became a way in which the Christian community expressed its oneness, as great care was taken to ensure that the poorest of members would be delivered gracefully to the grave.[71] Using the closest of kin as pallbearers for the deceased visibly witnesses to the maintenance of relationship, so providing pallbearers for the poor who had no immediate family likewise became a way in which the Church expressed an enduring connectedness with the dead. Rush writes:

---

67. Rutherford, *The Death of a Christian*, 49.
68. Rutherford, 49–51.
69. Rutherford, 50.
70. Chrysostom, Homilia 4 in Hebraeos, 5. Quote taken from Rush, *Death and Burial in Christian Antiquity*, 233.
71. Rush, *Death and Burial in Christian Antiquity*, 203.

Tertullian refers to the special trustfund of piety that was set aside for the burial of the poor. The Canons of Athanasius prescribed that if the deceased were poor the Church would provide for his burial. In these cases it is probable that the Church in providing for the burial would likewise provide pallbearers for the carrying of the corpse to the grave. It is known that Constantine at Constantinople set aside a group of *lectiarii,* whose office it was to take over the entire charge of the burial and carry the dead to the grave. They were likewise to provide for the burial of the poor, gratuitously, and to carry them to the grave, at least where there were endowments for this purpose.[72]

In addition to those who led the procession (the light and incense bearers) and those who carried or escorted the body in procession (the pallbearers), those who comprised the ranks of mourners played a significant symbolic role as well. On the one hand, they symbolized the Church on its pilgrim journey (as it engaged in singing psalms of hope and joy), and on the other hand, they represented the human reality of suffering that called for the community's ongoing outreach of pastoral care. The Greeks and the Romans dressed in black and red to outwardly communicate their mourning. Christianity attempted to challenge this by mandating that mourners wear white, the color of joy or immortality.[73] Even though St. Cyprian would contend that "dark garments should not be worn here in as much as they (the dead) already assumed white garments there,"[74] Christianity did not succeed in overturning the practice of wearing dark-colored clothes to suggest mourning.

One final element of early Christian funeral processions is the symbol of light. The use of candles in the solemn nighttime procession of the dead was particularly popular in pagan Rome.[75] In fact, Servius suggests that the word *funalia* comes from the word *funis,* which was rope set on fire for illumination purposes.[76] When burial at night became uncommon in the Roman world, torchbearers continued to be an integral part of the processional pageantry. Because of the pagan fascination with fire and light, it

---

72. Rush, 204.

73. Rush, 219. Rush writes: "That wearing clothing specific to mourning was one of those remnants of paganism that came to be regarded more as a convention of society and as the separation from paganism became great, the opposition to it became less pronounced."

74. Rush, 216.

75. Rush, 221.

76. Rush, 221.

should not be surprising that Christianity was opposed initially to the use of candles in the funeral procession.[77] However, by the middle of the third century, and especially after the peace of the Church, Christianity largely adopted the use of candles in the funeral procession. The reason for their use was not to dispel the shadows of darkness but to reveal a sense of joy in Christ who is the light of the world. Rush writes:

> Thus it is seen that the candles were given a spiritual symbolism by the Christians. The candle became a symbol of Christ who was the light of the world. It symbolized the Christians who were the "children of light." The torch, too, was a symbol of life. . . . Death to the Christian was a *dies natalis*. The light of the candles was a symbol of life. It represented the eternal light or the eternal life to which the soul had gone forth. It is this for which the Church prays when it says: *Lux perpetua luceat eis.*[78]

Once again, even though the carrying of candles in the daylight may be likened to superstition, the Christian symbolism of light standing for Christ's victory over sin and darkness won the day. Christians would continue to include torchbearers in their processions to materially symbolize the hope that death contains.

Clearly, the procession with the body to its place of rest along with the time given over to keeping vigil at the grave or the church demonstrate the Christian understanding that the burial of the dead required the work of the community. It may have been difficult for Christian mourners to exude a sense of joy, yet such an expression seems to have been a clear way that they rehearsed their attitude of hope in the face of death. An excerpt from the *Ecclesiastical Hierarchy*, a work attributed to Psuedo-Dionysius the Areopagite in the fifth century, depicts the triumphal demeanor of a throng of Christian mourners:

---

77. Rush, 224. Regarding the use of candles and torches, Rush writes: "It is probable that up to about 200, their use was forbidden in Rome and Africa, and that in some places the opposition to the ceremonial use of lights lasted even longer. The use of candles is something indifferent in itself and it draws its significance from the purpose for which they are employed. By reason of their association in the pagan cult of the dead, the Church forbade the use of candles. It was only when the practice lost its pagan connotation that it was adopted by the Christians, and then it was given a definite spiritual symbolism."

78. Rush, 227–228.

The just man is full of holy gladness when he comes to the end of his warfare, and it is with great joy that he advances towards his new life. His acquaintance, his neighbours in God, whose lives resemble his own, congratulate him on having attained the victory and goal of his desires. They sing hymns of thanksgiving in honour of him who is the author of this victory, asking him to grant them also the grace of such a repose. Then they take the body of the dead and carry it to the bishop as if for the award of the crown of victory. The latter receives it with joy and, in accordance with the rules, performs the second rites instituted for those who have died a holy death.[79]

The ritual acts of processing with the body and keeping vigil with prayer and song not only provided the dead with dignity as means of Christian congratulations, but it also allowed the community to understand itself as newly reordered. Tigan sums up this ritual movement as follows: "With the deceased we move from the home, or place of death, to the church. Here the deceased remains with us as part of the community at prayer in the face of death. The deceased, baptized into this community and nourished, nurtured and formed with it through its life and prayer, henceforth remains in the community's prayer as 'one who has gone before us marked with the sign of faith.'"[80]

As has been seen repeatedly, not only did the heritage of Jewish belief influence the Christian outlook on death, but so too did the interaction with Egyptian, Greek, and Roman cultures. While Christians often adapted customs for their approach to death, they also directly challenged the ways of the surrounding world. In what has been examined thus far, we see that Christians wished to treat the body as sacred, attending to it with physical care, the singing of psalms and hymns, the utterance of prayers, and a reverent transferal to its final place of rest. The Christian community believed that it had a responsibility and an obligation to assist in the reordering of the Body of Christ when one of its members moved to a new state of being in the Church. Nowhere is the obligation clearer than in the act of burying the body and in commemorating the dead.

---

79. Pseudo-Dionysius, *Ecclesiastical Hierarchy*. Quote taken from Rowell, *The Liturgy of Christian Burial*, 28.
80. Tigan, "By the Rivers of Babylon," 341–342.

Burial and Feasting: Rituals of Incorporation

While the Church witnesses to a longstanding tradition of celebrating a funeral liturgy prior to burial, with the presence of the body in the midst of the assembly, the early Christians buried the body first and then remembered the dead in subsequent celebrations at the graveside. Post-burial, it was necessary to perform rituals of incorporation, which van Gennep argues serve the purpose of sealing the new worldview that has been established in the rearranging of relationships.[81] Christians observed two very distinct models (one Jewish and one Roman) upon which to develop their rites of incorporation: Jews celebrated a funeral feast in the home after the burial of the body, while Romans deemed it necessary to gather at the graves of the deceased for the celebration of a commemorative meal. As Rowell writes:

> In Roman religion the funeral feast was clearly connected with the belief that the dead required nourishment in some way, and that the tedium of their existence in the tomb could be relieved by participation in a feast held by their relatives and friends at their place of burial. There are a number of Roman tombs in existence with holes in their outer coverings to permit libations to be poured on to the corpse or ashes of the dead, and other tombs which consist, not only of a burial chamber, but also of a dining-room (triclinium) and sometimes a kitchen. These graveside funeral feasts were often riotous and drunken occasions, and the church disliked them both for this reason and because of their implications concerning the state of the departed.[82]

The Church found it difficult to control the *refrigerium* (a meal of "refreshment"), which had great popularity as familial celebration. However, the attempt was made to temper these feasts by substituting a funeral Eucharist and by insisting that the purpose of the funeral feast was to feed the poor and the hungry, not an excuse for lewd and drunken carousing.[83] At first, the refrigerium was celebrated over the graves of martyrs alone, but it was quickly appropriated for dead Christians in general.

In addition to the celebration of a graveside funeral feast, it became customary to celebrate this meal not simply once, but three times in the

---

81. See van Gennep, *The Rites of Passage*, 20–21.
82. Rowell, *The Liturgy of Christian Burial*, 10.
83. Rowell, 11.

days subsequent to burial. In the Eastern Church, the threefold pattern arose of gathering for this commemoration on the third, the ninth, and the fortieth day after death; in the West, the meals were celebrated generally on the third, the seventh, and the thirtieth day. Rowell explains the nature of the festival days:

> When these pagan commemoration days passed into Christian observance, they were, of course, given an explanation in Christian terms. The third day was clearly justified by the Resurrection of Christ on the third day, and, where the seventh day was observed, which again was the Jewish custom, the Genesis creation narrative provided a basis for the practice. The fortieth was more difficult. The *Apostolic Constitutions* cite the mourning for Moses as the justification, but the relevant text in Deuteronomy in fact refers to thirty days, which some manuscripts give as an alternative reading.[84]

Note that these three days marked for commemoration, based largely on a Jewish schema, are all about passage or transition: the third day is likened to the pascha of Christ; the seventh day represents the completion of creation; the thirtieth day completes the mourning for Moses that allowed the Israelites to move into and take possession of the Promised Land. Each of these days is seen as containing a marvelous act of God's grand power to recreate and sustain his holy people.

Besides the days for commemorating the deceased, a great deal of significance was attached to the final farewell. Whether this was ritualized at the graveside with the burial of the dead or whether it was celebrated at the close of the eucharistic liturgy, this was seen as the moment of articulating a confident faith in the Resurrection of the Dead. Christians were very familiar with the pagan "vale" in which words of final farewell meant a total severing of the dead from the living. Rush writes:

> Because the Christians had a different outlook on death and the future life than the pagans, their farewell prayers to the dead were likewise different. All that the pagan belief in the future life would warrant them to say was a simple *Vale*, a *Vale* uttered to those whom they were never to see again.

---

84. Rowell, 12.

The farewell prayers of the Christians manifest a vivid belief in the fact that death, instead of being the end of life, is in reality the beginning of true life. It is on this account that the Christian acclamations constantly repeat the theme of Life. Hence, in opposition to the pagan *Vale* there arose the Christian formula *Vivas*. Time and again the inscriptions reecho with prayers indicating the new life that the soul has entered upon. At times the simple prayer is addressed to the deceased: "May you live."[85]

The *Apostolic Constitutions* contains several prayers that constitute the final farewell of the burial liturgy. They are thoroughly hopeful, refer to God as the creator of life and the giver of mercy for the forgiveness of sins, and ask that the deceased Christian may enjoy the peace of paradise with the patriarchs and all the saints. First, the deacon prays:

> Let us pray for our brethren that are at rest in Christ, that God, the lover of mankind, who has received his soul, may forgive him every sin, voluntary and involuntary, and may be merciful and gracious to him, and give him his lot in the land of the pious that are sent into the bosom of Abraham, and Isaac, and Jacob, with all those that have pleased him and done his will from the beginning of the world, whence all sorrow, grief, and lamentation are banished.[86]

Then the bishop offers a second prayer:

> O thou who are by nature immortal, and hast no end of thy being, from whom every creature, whether immortal or mortal, is derived; who didst make man a rational creature, the citizen of this world, in his constitution mortal, and didst add the promise of a resurrection; who didst not suffer Enoch and Elias to taste of death; 'the God of Abraham, the God of Isaac, and the God of Jacob, who are the God of them, not as of dead, but as of living persons: for the souls of all men live with thee, and the spirits of the righteous are in thy hand, which no torment can touch'; for they are all sanctified under thy hand: do thou now also look upon this thy servant, whom thou has selected and received into another state, and forgive him if voluntarily or involuntarily he has sinned, and afford him merciful angels, and place him in the bosom of the patriarchs, and prophets, and apostles, and of all those that have

---

85. Rush, *Death and Burial in Christian Antiquity*, 256.
86. Rowell, *The Liturgy of Christian Burial*, 27.

pleased thee from the beginning of the world, where there is no grief, sorrow, nor lamentation; but the peaceable region of the godly, and the undisturbed land of the upright, and of those that therein see the glory of thy Christ; by whom glory, honour and worship, thanksgiving and adoration be to thee, in the Holy Spirit, for ever. Amen.[87]

This prayer is followed by the final blessing, which again is prayed by the bishop:

O Lord, save thy people, and bless thine inheritance, which thou has purchased with the precious blood of thy Christ. Feed them under thy right hand, and cover them under thy wings, and grant that they may "fight the good fight and finish their course, and keep the faith" immutably, unblamably, and unreprovably, through Jesus Christ, thy beloved Son, with whom glory, honour, and worship be to thee and to the Holy Spirit for ever. Amen.[88]

All three of these prayers are composed with a tone of true thanksgiving. There is almost a sense that the Christian community is presenting the soul of the deceased as an offering to God: "do thou now also look upon this thy servant, whom thou has selected and received into another state." The grave of the ancient Christian could indeed be likened to an altar itself, whereby God would continue to receive the offering of a people united to Christ.

While it is clear that Christians believed they had a duty to commemorate the new life of the deceased with prayer and with a festive meal, it is unclear as to when the Eucharist came to be the acceptable and preferred form of commemoration for the dead. With the widespread building of churches after the Peace of Constantine in the fourth century, and as Christians dedicated their altars over the bones of martrys and saints, the development of a funeral Eucharist within the church building rather than at the graveside became a natural transition for communities. One of the earliest references to celebrating the Eucharist as a funeral liturgy comes from the *Didascalia Apostolorum*, written in the first half of the third century. Here the author writes:

Do you according to the Gospel, and according to the power of the Holy Spirit, come together even in the cemeteries, and read the holy Scriptures,

---

87. Rowell, 27.
88. Rowell, 27.

and without demur perform your ministry and your supplication to
God; and offer an acceptable eucharist, the likeness of the royal body
of Christ, both in your congregations and in your cemeteries, and on
the departures of them that sleep—pure bread that is made with fire
and sanctified with invocations—and without doubting pray and offer
for them that are fallen asleep.[89]

As the church becomes the locus for celebrating the funeral liturgy, the
grave gradually loses its sense as a place of "refreshment" in the Christian
imagination. As the funeral Eucharist develops as an offering for the souls
of the departed, it becomes more closely associated with the ideas of "deliverance" from sin and the forgiveness of human transgressions. Rutherford
points to the change in artwork and epitaphs at cemeteries that begin to
appear after the peace of the Church, namely, former images of shepherd,
banquet, fisherman, and ship are replaced with images of Christ and "deliverance motifs."[90]

A very significant change in the ritual process is this shift to celebrating a funeral liturgy (that is, the Eucharist) prior to burial. The Eucharist
and the subsequent procession to the grave now become the central rituals
for transition, with the burial taking on the role of ritual incorporation.
While Christians will mark the new state of life with the funeral meal after
burial as well as in celebrations of the Eucharist on the anniversaries of
death, there is less celebration of the corporate Church and its eschatological destiny when the grave loses its symbolic role as a place of feasting. The
grave as a place of "refreshment" very soon becomes associated with the
site of judgment in the Christian imagination. All of this goes hand in hand
with the development of a recognized funeral liturgy that becomes standard practice in the Roman West. As will be seen in the next chapter, the
funeral liturgy very quickly loses the sense of reordering the Body of Christ
as it becomes the principle offering for the cleansing of one's individual

---

89. *Didascalia Apostolorum*, xxvi. Quote taken from Rowell, *The Liturgy of Christian Burial*, 25–26.

90. See Rutherford, *The Death of a Christian*, 13–14. He writes: "Among the miracles of Jesus, the
healing of the blind man and the raising of Lazarus from the dead, both symbols of baptism, continue
the theme of 'life' that death cannot destroy. Peter's denial 'at the crowing of the cock' was seen as the
dawn of new life after the forgiveness of sins. Nearly all known Christian cemeteries dating from after
AD 313 show the continued practice of decorating the resting places of the dead with Old Testaments
scenes of divine deliverance: the sacrifice of Isaac, Daniel among the lions, Jonah freed from the sea
monster, the three young men in the furnace, Susanna rescued from the 'dirty old men,' and Job
delivered from misery."

soul and for the deliverance from the debt of personal sin. Death becomes a matter of the individual.

Conclusion

This chapter has tried to uncover many of the ancient sources that suggest both a hopeful faith in the afterlife and an ecclesial understanding of the resurrection. From the outset, the Christian people manifested belief in a God who promised to restore them to the fullness of life in Christ Jesus. At the same time, the early Church would have to combat cultural forces that denied life after death as well as the fear from within that God would impart justice for sin and evil. Thus, the conviction that the Church was composed of both the living and the dead moving as one people toward the eschaton did not go unopposed.

Nevertheless, the Church began with a very positive outlook on death. Death was imaged as a temporary sleep from which one would be called by the Lord into eternal life. It was also symbolized as a voyage whereby the Church as a whole was traversing cosmic waters toward divine life. Death was also called the *dies natalis*, or one's birthday, for it was on this day that Christians believed life truly began. These hopeful ways of describing death served to underscore the ecclesial nature of death. One does not truly die alone, because one simply enters into the company of others who have gone before. Death is baptismal since it is the moment when a disciple surrenders fully to the call to follow Christ.

Likewise, the rituals used to assist the passage of the Church from one ordered state to another, most of which were adapted from the Jewish and pagan worlds, demonstrated the great care Christians took to exercise their responsibility to support mourners and to bury the dead. From the rituals of preparing the body in the home and keeping watch over it with prayer and song, to the transition of moving the body from the house to the place of burial, to the final act of farewell, the Church enacted gestures that demonstrated true reverence for the dead. The dead were not to be disposed as something to be rid of but rather as something sacred that continues on in being.

The five characteristics of baptismal ecclesiology mentioned at the close of chapter one are all applicable to the early Church's portrayal of death. Christians did not allow death to break apart their oneness in Christ (*A*

Unified People). Just as Paul said there is a grand equality in life with Christ, the same continued in death. For example, Christians resisted crowning the dead or adorning them in special clothing since life in Christ means shedding the desire for distinction. Furthermore, the early Christians saw death as a voyage, the *Migratio ad Dominum* (*A Pilgrim People*). They understood Christ to be at the helm of the sailing ship that is the Church, as she makes its passage to eternity. All Christians, living and dead, sinner and saint, played a role in this voyage. Christians also understood the obligations of care and prayer at the time of death to flow from their identity of shedding the self in order to live in Christ (*A Self-Giving People*). They saw death as an opportunity to redistribute the wealth of the community so that the poor were honored and the hungry were fed. The early Church wished to be deliberately public in the celebration of its rites in order to evangelize others on the power of faith in the resurrection of the dead (*A Priestly People*). Christians gathered at the graves of the dead on particular anniversaries and uttered prayers of thanksgiving for the lives of the deceased, and they looked after the widows and orphans of the dead. Finally, the early Christians were very much devoted to preserving the memory of the martyrs and striving to embody their holiness (*A Holy People*). The early Church trusted in the mercy of God and believed that death invited them to see the world as God sees it, with death upheld as God's "refreshment" rather than his "judgment."

CHAPTER THREE

The Turn to the Individual in Christian Funerals

Deliver me, Lord, from everlasting death in that awful day, when the heavens and the earth shall be moved, when you will come to judge the world by fire. Dread and trembling have laid hold upon me, and I fear exceedingly because of the judgment and the wrath to come. O that day, that day of wrath, of sore distress and of all wretchedness, that great and exceeding bitter day, when you will come to judge the world by fire.[1]

Death impacts the Church. When one person dies and is no longer physically present to the Body of Christ, the Holy Spirit takes up the task of reordering the Church. Members are brought into wholeness once again. In fact, the wholeness achieved here could be termed a "mystical" or "cosmic" unity, as death constitutes a new state of membership in the Church. The dead are not cut off from the Body. The early Church provides solid witness to an understanding of death that was corporate. Whether the dead were envisioned as having "fallen asleep," or whether they were understood as undertaking a "voyage" into another state of being, or whether they were seen as being "born" into eternal life, those who lived on in this world clearly understood themselves as integrally grafted onto those who had preceded them on the way to eternity.

Because death did not destroy the sacredness of life for the early Christians, they understood that they had ecclesial duties to perform in caring for the dead and in supporting the living. They surveyed the cultures around them and adapted burial customs in such a way as to make apparent their hope in the Resurrection. Their ritualizing the washing of the body was not about restoring purity but rather about honoring the dignity of the body itself. Their way of grieving was a direct challenge to the surrounding

---

1. A twelfth-century responsory prayer entitled "Deliver Me, O Lord, from Eternal Death." Quote taken from Rutherford, *The Death of a Christian*, 62–63.

world that wailed at the face of death; instead, Christians sang hymns and psalms of thanksgiving and joy. In keeping vigil around the grave, Christians ate and drank as a sign of eschatological victory, imitating the heavenly banquet with all the angels and saints; the pagans, on the other hand, feasted at the grave because they believed that the dead required nourishment and satisfaction.

In his evaluation of the attitudes of early Christians regarding death and burial, Richard Rutherford uncovers two conflicting patterns that he suggests grew up in the Church side by side.[2] The first he calls the "pristine" attitude of hopefulness, while the second he labels "threatening" and "pessimistic."[3] The previous chapter was centered on the first of these attitudes, the hope that joined the Christian community together to turn the crisis of death into a moment of faith. Fledgling communities enacted rituals that provided for a smooth passage through the process of death to a new corporate life. However, as Paul's writings in the New Testament suggest, Christians were not immune to the anxiety and fear that came with death. As the delay of Christ's return became more and more pronounced, pessimism certainly could not be dismissed, as clearly evident in Paul's exhortation to the Thessalonians: "We ask you, brothers, with regard to the coming of our Lord Jesus Christ and our assembling with him, not to be shaken out of your minds suddenly, or to be alarmed either by a 'spirit,' or by an oral statement, or by a letter allegedly from us to the effect that the day of the Lord is at hand" (2 Thessalonians 2:1–2). Regarding such pessimism, Rutherford states:

> Optimistic faith began to tend toward pessimistic fate. Belief that
> "the just God is merciful and therefore forgiving" shifted to mean
> that "the merciful God is just and therefore demands expiation." . . .
> This prevailing pessimism about the living had its effect on the attitude
> toward the lot of the dead. With the advent of severe penitential discipline,
> being Christian became a preoccupation with sin; care for the dead
> became, in turn, a preoccupation with the wages of sin.[4]

While we may be quite certain that the early Church worked together to manifest both in teaching and action a hopeful faith in their

---

2. See Rutherford, *The Death of a Christian*, 28.

3. Rutherford, 28.

4. Rutherford, 24.

participation in Christ's Resurrection from the dead, it is also evident that they were unsuccessful in truly rooting out a sense of fear surrounding death. As much as they wanted to believe in the merciful care of a loving God who desired that "creation itself would be set free from slavery to corruption and share in the glorious freedom of the children of God" (Romans 8:21), they could not escape a detectable fear for the wrath of God's judgment. As Paul writes to the Corinthians: "For we must appear at the judgment seat of Christ, so that each one may receive recompense, according to what he did in the body, whether good or evil" (2 Corinthians 5:10).

As the Church continued to spread beyond the locale of the Mediterranean world, especially northward into the region of Gaul, and as its local communities grew larger and more sophisticated in their patterns of organized worship under the leadership of professional clergy, emphasis on the Church as the manifestation of the living Body of Christ began to dwindle. Rather than focusing concern on the welfare of the Body of Christ as a whole, Christian spirituality began to concentrate on individual prowess. Participation in the Eucharist was no longer a striving for oneness in Christ, but instead was a means of accumulating merit for one's personal salvation. Responsibility for the building up of the Church would be placed in the hands of clerics, and the laity would gradually lose sight of the connection between liturgy and life. Finally, Christian attitudes toward death would quickly shift from a spirit of joy to an overarching theme of fear for the fires of damnation. In the celebration of rites accompanying death and burial, the duty of Christians gathering as a community to celebrate the soul's "refreshment" in the next life was now overshadowed by the duty to pray for the protection of the soul that was in jeopardy of being cast into the fires of hell. Very clearly, an individualistic outlook on death, brought on by fear of God's punishment, would rule the day for many centuries to come.

Origins of the Turn to the Individual

One of the basic ways in which the living continue their ecclesial bonds with the dead is through prayer. The deceased, especially the saints and martyrs, could guide the Church on earth with their concern from beyond, while the living, through prayers of expiation, could assist the souls of the dead in their transition to a place of light and happiness. Prayers for the dead were meant to be simultaneously prayers for the living. This is demonstrated in a prayer in the fourth-century *Euchologion* of Bishop Serapion:

> [W]e beseech thee for the repose and rest of this thy servant or this thine handmaiden: give rest to his soul, his spirit, in green places (Ps. 22,2), in chambers of rest with Abraham and Isaac and Jacob and all thy Saints: and raise up his body in the day which thou hast ordained, according to thy promises which cannot lie (Titus 1, 2), that thou mayest render to it also the heritage of which it is worthy in thy holy pastures. Remember not his transgressions and sins: and cause his going forth to be peaceable and blessed. Heal the griefs of those who pertain to him with the spirit of consolation, and grant unto us all a good end through thy only-begotten Jesus Christ, through whom to thee (is) the glory and the strength in holy Spirit to the ages of the ages. Amen.[5]

While this is unarguably a prayer of expiation ("remember not his transgressions and sins"), it is hopeful in seeking a place of rest for the soul "in green places," and also asks for the "consolation" of those grieving. This prayer from the fourth-century Egyptian Church has not yet lost a sense of the ecclesial nature of death; its purpose is to ask God to unite the soul in "repose and rest" with "Abraham and Isaac and Jacob and all thy Saints" until the day when the body will be raised up.

It is proposed here that a major shift in thinking about the consequences of death, a movement from ecclesial joy to personal fear, begins with the influence of St. Augustine of Hippo, who lived between 354 and 430. Around 422, Augustine composed a short treatise to a fellow bishop named Paulinus on the subject of the Christian duty to care for the dead.[6] In this letter, Augustine suggests that while it is important that Christians make every effort to perform their duties to ensure the burial of the dead, in the end, God will care for things according to his will. Thus, he suggests that the rituals of the funeral liturgy are primarily for those left on this earth:

> So, then, all these things, care of funeral, bestowal in sepulture, pomp of obsequies, are more for comfort of the living, than for help to the dead. If it at all profit the ungodly to have costly sepulture, it shall harm the godly to have vile sepulture or none. Right handsome obsequies in

---

5. *Euchologion*, 18. Quote taken from Rutherford, *The Death of a Christian*, 17.

6. See St. Augustine, *On Care to Be Had for the Dead*, Philip Schaff, ed., H. Browne, trans. (CreateSpace Independent Publishing Platform, 2015).

sight of men did that rich man who was clad in purple receive of the crowd of his housefolk; but far more handsome did that poor man who was full of sores obtain of the ministry of Angels; who bore him not out into a marble tomb, but into Abraham's bosom bore him on high.[7]

With the intention of countering the movement of Pelagianism, which taught that humans are capable of achieving salvation by themselves, Augustine suggests that, in his judgment of the departed soul, God will not be fooled by lavish monuments or beautiful pageantry. Instead, God will know the good or the bad that the person exhibited while on this earth; God probes the intention of the individual human heart. Intentionally or not, Augustine moves the Church in the direction of thinking of death in terms of personal (individual) salvation; the individual soul has taken center stage.

It is important to add to this that, most likely in the last decade of the fourth century, St. Augustine had worked out a complicated philosophical teaching on the nature of Original Sin.[8] This understanding of God's withholding the fullness of his grace due to human disobedience not only had a major impact on the Sacrament of Baptism, which now became understood as the sacrament necessary for the removal of Original Sin, but it would also significantly influence subsequent interpretation of God's plan for salvation. Augustine developed his theory of Original Sin based on Romans 5:12: "Just as through one person sin entered the world, and through sin, death, and thus death came to all, inasmuch as all sinned." Once again, he wished to counter Pelagian thought that human beings could lead sinless lives and be saved through their merit. Augustine maintains humanity's absolute dependence upon the grace of God. Unfortunately, humanity's "concupiscence" becomes the centerpiece of the doctrine of Original Sin:

> Thus, the source of the true evil in a disorderly expression of a bodily desire is not the body; it is the soul. The body is of course a necessary condition for this particular brand of evil. A person could not perceive bodily satisfaction as a good if he did not have a body. Devils may be damned for many vices but they cannot be accused of having bodily

---

7. Augustine, 6–7.

8. See Ernesto Bonaiuti and Giorgio La Piana, "The Genesis of St. Augustine's Idea of Original Sin," *Harvard Theological Review* 10 (1917): 159–175.

lust. Any human desire, including sexual desire, can get out of control in our present condition. But Augustine is at pains to emphasize that this does not point to some tragic flaw in the way humans have been made. It is a wound or weakness that humans have made for themselves. It was not so in the beginning of the human race. Concupiscence in the sense of desire comes from being human. Disordered concupiscence comes from being wounded. The frenzy that sometimes drives humans comes only as a result of sin.[9]

Thus, what is seen here in the description of Augustine's thought is the "priority of the radical perversion of mankind before the idea of its inability to merit restoration and salvation."[10] Humanity is now seen as a "massa damnata," an imperiled lot that is trapped in the sinfulness of the body's desires; left to their own designs, men and women would always choose the evil over the good.

Such an understanding of Original Sin and its ongoing effects on human beings would open the door to the theological shift described above, namely, that death is something to fear as the moment for God to inflict his wrath. John Hick assesses Augustine's contribution to a theology of death as retribution as follows:

> [I]t was St. Augustine in the fifth century who, elaborating Paul's thought in his own way, definitively projected the picture that has informed the Christian imagination for 1,500 years. In the *City of God* he said that "the first men were so created, that if they had not sinned, they would not have experienced any kind of death; but that, having become sinners, they were so punished with death, that whatsoever sprang from their stock should also be punished with the same death." On this view our mortality is not an aspect of the divinely intended human situation, but is an evil, a state that ought never to have come about, a disastrous consequence of man's turning away from his Maker. Death is a punishment, and the emotions that appropriately reverberate around it are those of guilt and sorrow, remorse and fear.[11]

---

9. Donald X. Burt, *Augustine's World: An Introduction to His Speculative Philosophy* (Lanham, MD: University Press of America, 1996), 68–69.

10. Bonaiuti and La Piana, "The Genesis of St. Augustine's Idea of Original Sin," 164.

11. John Hick, "Towards a Christian Theology of Death," in *Dying, Death, and Disposal*, Gilbert Cope, ed. (London: SPCK, 1970), 17.

While Augustine would be remembered for his famous address to God—"You stir man to take pleasure in praising you, because you have made us for yourself, and our heart is restless until it rests in you"[12]—the attitude of death as a corporate pilgrimage would have no place in his theology. Because sin is experienced as a bodily desire, and because the human body is the source of individuality, death too is experienced individually. Matthew Levering summarizes Augustine's thought as follows: "To understand our origin and to attain our end, we must come to realize that we have been disordered by a profound rebellion. This rebellion manifests itself in disordered desire: we seek happiness not in eternal things but in ambition, sexual pleasure, and so forth."[13] With Augustine's writings, the fear of death expands broadly in the Christian imagination.[14] Consequently, from this period moving forward, the tone of the prayers surrounding death and burial would now accentuate the need for the soul's protection; the purifying flame of God's love now became something to be dreaded.

As protection of the dead became the major responsibility of the Christian community, certain aspects of burial practices begin to morph along superstitious lines. Rutherford points to these in his work *The Death of a Christian*. Principle among these superstitions was the custom of giving the Eucharistic bread to the already dead body. Whereas Viaticum had been understood as food for the journey that would serve to perpetuate the Eucharist in the next life, now it was viewed as a means of protecting the dead.[15] Similarly, altar cloths and other linens used in the celebration of the Eucharist were employed for magical purposes, while some went to great lengths to have their dead buried under or near a baptistery. "All these abuses," writes Rutherford, "shared a common motivation: securing protection for the soul of the deceased after death."[16]

Over the next two hundred years, the fear of death would continue to become more entrenched in the minds and hearts of Christians. At the end

---

12. Augustine, *Confessions*, 1.1.1, trans. Henry Chadwick (Oxford: Oxford University Press, 1991), 3.

13. Matthew Levering, *The Theology of Augustine: An Introductory Guide to His Most Important Works* (Grand Rapids, MI: Baker Academic, 2013), 110.

14. See Burt, *Augustine's World*, 65. He writes of Augustine's personal fear of death: "The pain of having a body that was falling apart caused him to fear death and illness for most of his life. In his early years this fear was close to panic, pleading for baptism when as a boy he thought he was close to death. Even in his later years as a believing Christian sure of his immortality, he admits that though he was truly dying to get to the city of God he would much prefer to get there without dying."

15. See Rutherford, *The Death of a Christian*, 23–24.

16. Rutherford, 23.

of the sixth and the beginning of the seventh centuries, Pope Gregory the Great's writings and implementation of liturgical reform fully exaggerated the theme of expiation in the rites of death and burial. The predominant focus of the prayers for the dead became one of liberation and purification, as though death produced an intolerable predicament of misery and woe. Rutherford explains:

> With Augustine as their most notable master, Gregory and others explained the earlier emphasis on the effectiveness of prayer for the dead. The prayer of the Church, they taught, brought about the liberation of the faithful dead from the purifying fire of expiation for sin. Before long, this fire would become localized as "purgatory" and the tradition of prayer for the release of the "poor souls" its complement in popular piety. . . . Thus, to Gregory and his contemporaries, even the faithful Christian was presumed a sinner whose immediate lot after death was at best one of purification. It was the exceptional saint who escaped.[17]

What a dramatic shift from the hope of eternal refreshment that all Christians looked forward to sharing to an outlook on death in which every effort was put forward to help souls escape the "purifying fire of expiation for sin." The development of a piety around the poor souls in purgatory thus has its beginnings in Gregory and would have major ramifications for the conservative nature of liturgical renewal in the future. Moreover, key among Gregory's contributions to sacramental theology, a contribution that would soon become a major detriment, is his understanding that performing a certain amount of prayers in just the right way would secure the release of souls from purgatory. Rutherford recounts a story told by St. Gregory that is believed to be the origin for Masses for the suffrages of the dead:

> The story goes that Justus, a monk of Gregory's monastery, fell ill. During his illness it was discovered that the monk had hidden three gold pieces in his cell, contrary to the *Rule*. In order to teach a lesson, Gregory was extremely severe. He ordered that no one offer consolation to the dying monk in his last moments, and furthermore, when he had died, the monks were to throw his gold pieces into the grave after him, crying, "May your money be with you in perdition." Brother Justus died

---

17. Rutherford, 24–25.

repentant. Nevertheless, for 30 days, Gregory refused to allow prayers to be offered for him. Finally, he took pity on the deceased monk, whom he described as suffering in the fire, and ordered that Mass be celebrated for Justus on 30 consecutive days. At the end of that time, Justus appeared to Gregory and told him that until then, he had been suffering, but now he was well because on that day he had been received into heaven. Gregory explains that his release coincided exactly with the Mass on the 30th day, clear proof that Justus had been freed through the offering of the Mass.[18]

In what approaches an almost quid pro quo relationship with God, Masses could be multiplied for the dead that would serve to make them more satisfactory to God. The system worked because it mattered not to God whether the individual soul paid the price for purgation or the living paid the time with their prayers. As Rutherford writes: "The attitude of those times, which Gregory thus shared and articulated in theology and liturgical practice, revealed the shift away from the ecclesial eschatology of the earlier tradition to an eschatology of the individual."[19]

The Evolution of Funeral Liturgies

The papacy of St. Gregory the Great (590–604) marks an important stage in the formation of Christian liturgical prayer, as it was around this time that Christians first began to write down and organize services for prayer. This corresponded with the advent and rapid growth of monasticism, which would be the primary means for copying and transmitting liturgical rites. The oldest forms of what might be called a "Roman" funeral liturgy are found in the Roman *Ordines*, specifically *Ordo XLIX*, that most likely comes from the seventh century.[20] Vincent Owusu offers a summary of the most ancient "Roman" liturgy as follows:

> The ancient Roman funeral liturgy began not with death but with the preparation for it. For this liturgy, the viaticum and the reading of the Lord's Passion were indispensable provisions for the journey into the beyond. Appropriate liturgical rites to mark the dying person's last

---

18. Rutherford, 25–26.

19. Rutherford, 26.

20. See Vincent Owusu, *The Roman Funeral Liturgy: History, Celebration and Theology*, (Nettetal: Steyler Verlag, 1993), 8.

living moments as well as those immediately after death, characterized this ritual. At death the ritual indicates a commendatio animae (Subvenite and the Suscipiat Christus with the psalm In exitu and antiphon Chorus angelorum and a prayer). There are also the preparation of the body in the home and a funeral procession with the body to the church during which time antiphons and psalms are sung. A prayer service follows in the church where the body is immediately buried or kept until the time of burial later within the church compound.[21]

Thus, the structure of the Christian funerary prayer (from the time of death through the time of burial) that comes from a seventh-century Roman source is very consistent with the information given us from the early patristic sources.[22] Owusu suggests that the development of this liturgy indicates three traditions regarding death.[23] The first tradition, the simplest pattern, calls for the preparation of the body in the home, the procession with the body to the church, and its subsequent burial there. The second tradition adds prayers and rituals for preparing for death, the moment of death itself, and the procession to the cemetery from the church. The third tradition witnesses to the procession to the cemetery at a distance from the church where prayer was conducted. Adding to the complexity of labeling a rite a pure example of Roman liturgy, Owusu acknowledges: "Obviously, the celebration of funerals would have followed varied traditions. One can well imagine that a funeral would have been more solemn in the city than in the countryside, and the funeral of a cleric more elaborate in general that that of a lay person."[24]

It is important to note that this early form of Roman liturgy does not yet exhibit signs of being influenced by a theology of death as something

---

21. Owusu , 19.

22. See Rowell, *The Liturgy of Christian Burial*, 57. The author writes: "The actions involved in the preparation of the body for burial, its removal to the church, a service in church, and then a further procession to the place of burial followed by the burial itself provided the pattern around which particular liturgical forms grew up, but there was always a certain fluidity in the distribution of the prayers and psalmody which came to be used."

23. See Vincent Owusu, "Funeral Rites in Rome and the Non-Roman West," in *Handbook for Liturgical Studies, Volume IV: Sacraments and Sacramentals*, ed. Anscar J. Chupungco (Collegeville, MN: Liturgical Press, 2000), 357.

24. Owusu, 358. Also see Rutherford, *The Death of a Christian*, 39–40. Rutherford writes: "[F]unerals varied greatly from place to place at that time. An urban funeral might have been a solemn affair with cathedral clerics and chanters on hand, whereas in the country, funerals were necessarily much simpler. Likewise, the funeral of a bishop, civil dignitary, priest, or monk was certainly much more elaborate in general than that of a simple peasant. Each local church followed its own customary liturgical usage; no universal set of formularies existed."

to be feared. Instead, it is very much focused on a positive transition of the soul. *In paradisum*, sung at the time of death, and the *Subvenite sancti Dei*, sung as the body is greeted at the church doors, both suggest a joyful movement of the deceased into the hands of God. The procession from home to cemetery is designed to mark a true "passover," a letting go of one's familial home in order to enter that place that is home to the Communion of Saints. Owusu comments:

> The hope of the resurrection gives a joyful tone to the whole ritual. Throughout the ritual the communal dimension comes to the fore. The liturgical reunion around the dying symbolizes the earthly community accompanying the dead in their migration, to be welcomed by the inhabitants of heaven, that is, their ancestors: the saints, martyrs, and patriarchs; by the messengers of God, the angels; and finally by the Lord of the house, who personally incorporates them into the great family of the saints. The Christian who dies therefore passes from one community to another.[25]

Furthermore, the ancient Roman prayer texts portray God as a loving and merciful God who desires the salvation of his people. The dead are destined for union with God rather than for destruction. "The elements in this most ancient Roman funeral ritual," writes Owusu, "give meaning to death as a paschal journey symbolized in triumphant processions. It is a transitus related to Christ's own passing from death to life, to the serenity of paschal hope. This is the basis of the Roman funeral liturgy."[26]

From the eighth through the thirteenth centuries, this primitive Roman funeral liturgy began to spread far and wide in Western Europe, especially over the Alps into Gallican territory.[27] In its migration, it would encounter and be mixed with other sources that exhibited greater superstitions and a more pessimistic approach to death. The sources that are called Gallican missals (from the seventh, eighth, and ninth centuries) include the *Missale Gothicum, Missale Gallicanum Vetus, Missale Francorum*,

---

25. Owusu, "Funeral Rites in Rome and the Non-Roman West," 359.

26. Owusu, 360.

27. See Rutherford, *The Death of a Christian*, 54. He writes: "Thus, these five centuries of gradual, spreading influence of the ordo tell a story of both fidelity to the Roman tradition behind the simple rite and further amalgamation with local Frankish practices. The earlier process of subtle amalgamation gave way during this period to explicit adaptation. The one force most responsible for adapting the rite of funerals and for giving direction to its future was the medieval monastery."

and the *Missale Bobbiense*.[28] The most important feature of these missals originating in Gaul is their pagan influence, as they tend to be more dramatic and expressive in language, symbolism and ritual in general, as well as more negative and gloomy in portraying death. For example, the prayers depict death as "a snare from which one is to be delivered: *quem Dominus de laqueo huius saeculi liberare dignatus est*," and include phrases such as "the gates of hell" and "the way of darkness."[29] Simply stated, the euchology of these Gallican missals is focused more on the terrors of God's judgment upon an individual soul. Owusu writes:

> From a paschal, sober, and peaceful vision of the Christian *transitus*, therefore, there is a passage to a dramatic vision of judgment and the need to ask for God's mercy for the dead. Preoccupied with the uncertain fate of the soul, the euchology asks God to receive the soul of the dead into the "bosom of Abraham." Surprisingly, neither the figure of Christ nor the paschal event plays much of a role in the Roman-Gallican funeral rituals. Death is not viewed as related to the paschal mystery of Christ, nor is the dead person presented as participating in Christ's resurrection.[30]

Probably the best example of euchology that takes on a gloomy tone is the responsory *Libera me, Domine* that developed during this time period and was expanded into the *Dies irae* of the Tridentine Requiem Mass. Quoted at the beginning of this chapter, this prayer reads:

> Deliver me, Lord, from everlasting death in that awful day, when the heavens and the earth shall be moved, when you will come to judge the world by fire. Dread and trembling have laid hold upon me, and I fear exceedingly because of the judgment and the wrath to come. O that day, that day of wrath, of sore distress and of all wretchedness, that great and exceeding bitter day, when you will come to judge the world by fire.[31]

There is no mistaking the pessimism expressed by the phrase "dread and trembling have laid hold upon me," as well as the personal nature of the prayer as a whole. The individual soul is left to face the wrath of God alone.

---

28. Owusu, "Funeral Rites in Rome and the Non-Roman West," 360.
29. Owusu, 361.
30. Owusu, 361–362.
31. See Rutherford, *The Death of a Christian*, quote taken from pages 62–63.

In addition to the influence that Gallican exuberance and superstition had in shifting the overall tone of burial from hope to anxiety, so too did the appearance of monastic rituals serve to sharpen the individualization of death. The event of death became a penitential act for the monastic community to perform: the dying monk was treated as a sinner in need of penance, and the community was left to perform a sort of penance after the monk had expired. The following lengthy description by Rowell of the tradition of Cluniac monks details the rigorous penitential prescriptions surrounding death:

The monk who feels the moment of his death approaching is bidden to summon the abbot or prior in order that he may confess his sins and receive the sacrament of unction. He is then brought into the presence of the assembled chapter, supported by two of the brethren, and publicly confesses his omissions in his duties towards God and his neighbour. The prior then absolves him, and the community respond 'Amen.' The sick man is then taken back to his bed, where he lies to receive Holy Unction. The sacrament is administered by the priest of the week, who comes in procession to the infirmary with servers, holy water, cross, and candles, and with the rest of the community following in attendance. Unction is given whilst psalms are recited, and the sick man then receives communion, after which the community withdraws, leaving the staff of the infirmary to watch over the sick man, lest he die unnoticed. A cross and lighted candles are placed at the head of the bed. When the moment of death approaches, the sick man is laid on a hair-shirt and is sprinkled with ashes, and the cloister door is beaten rapidly to summon the community. All brethren outside of choir must leave whatever they are doing immediately and go to the infirmary. When they are assembled, the creed is said and (should the moment of death be delayed) litanies, with the responses *Ora pro eo*, and psalmody. At the moment of death the prior commends the departing soul to God with the prayers *Pie recordationis affectu, Deus cui omnia vivunt*, and *Suscipe, Domine, animam servi tui*. The community then go to the Lady Chapel of the monastery to sing vespers of the dead followed by matins, at the end of which the collect *Omnipotens sempiterne Deus* is said. A little after this bells are rung, and a second cross, holy water, lights, and incense are brought, and the body is washed and placed on the bier by those of equal standing in the community. The body is clothed in a shirt and a habit with hood, and the hands are joined across the breast.

The bier is then carried into the church, where from that time there is continuous offices and mass. The night is divided into three watches, assigned to the two sides of the choir and the children with their masters respectively. Mass the next morning is offered for the dead, and the deacon is directed to cense the body after the censing of the altar. When mass is ended, the body is carried to a place of burial whilst the community in procession chant psalms. On arrival at the grave, it is censed by the priest and sprinkled with holy water, after which it is laid in the grave and earth is cast upon it. The procession returns after the burial to the tolling of bells.[32]

From this description of the customs of the Cluniac community, it is clear that the monks were united in a sense of duty, just as family members were united around the body in previous Christian centuries. However, what is drastically different is the tone of their gathering. Suggested here is an almost ominous encroachment of death, with the dying monk playing the role of a public sinner, making a public confession of sin and covered with ashes, while the community prays for his sins to be forgiven. The dying man's final moments on earth are seen as an enactment of Job's wrestling with God. Furthermore, the Office for the Dead, which was compiled at this time, did not exude a sense of joy and thanksgiving, rather it "emphasized the penal nature of death; the Gloria, Alleluias, blessings before the lessons, and other joyful responses were omitted."[33] Moreover, notice here the tolling of bells as the community resumes its former way of life; the symbols of death have turned to sadness.

However, nothing is more expressive of the shift in tone, from joy to fear, than the hymn *Dies irae*, which was composed in the early thirteenth century and eventually became the official Sequence of the Mass for the Dead. For many years, "The Day of Wrath" was considered the work of the Franciscan, Thomas of Celano (c. 1190–1260), but it is now believed that the authorship was much earlier, perhaps even written by the pen of Gregory the Great.[34] Rutherford writes regarding this popular medieval hymn: "Poetic descriptions of the last day, coupled with the theme of the worthlessness of human and worldly achievements, led to prayerful pleas

---

32. Rowell, *The Liturgy of Christian Burial*, 64–65.
33. Owusu, "Funeral Rites in Rome and the Non-Roman West," 263.
34. See Rowell, *The Liturgy of Christian Burial*, 67.

that the just would be preserved from eternal damnation."[35] To better understand just how far we have moved away from the Christian virtue of hope toward the expression of fear and trembling, the entire hymn is included below:

> That day of wrath, that dreadful day,
> shall heaven and earth in ashes lay,
> as David and the Sybil say.
>
> What horror must invade the mind
> when the approaching Judge shall find
> and sift the deeds of all mankind!
>
> The mighty trumpet's wondrous tone
> shall rend each tomb's sepulchral stone
> and summon all before the Throne.
>
> Now death and nature with surprise
> behold the trembling sinners rise
> to meet the Judge's searching eyes.
>
> Then shall with universal dread
> the Book of Consciences be read
> to judge the lives of all the dead.
>
> For now before the Judge severe
> all hidden things must plain appear;
> no crime can pass unpunished here.
>
> O what shall I, so guilty plead?
> and who for me will intercede?
> when even Saint shall comfort need?
>
> O King of dreadful majesty!
> grace and mercy you grant free;
> as Fount of Kindness, save me!
>
> Recall, dear Jesus, for my sake
> you did our suffering nature take
> then do not now my soul forsake!

---

35. Rutherford, *The Death of a Christian*, 63.

In weariness You sought for me,
and suffering upon the tree!
let not in vain such labor be.

O Judge of justice, hear, I pray,
for pity take my sins away
before the dreadful reckoning day.

Your gracious face, O Lord, I seek;
deep shame and grief are on my cheek;
in sighs and tears my sorrows speak.

You who did Mary's guilt unbind
and mercy for the robber find,
have filled with hope my anxious mind.

How worthless are my prayers I know,
yet, Lord forbid that I should go
into the fires of endless woe.

Divorced from the accursed band,
o make me with Your sheep to stand,
as child of grace at Your right Hand.

When the doomed can no more flee
from the fires of misery
with the chosen call me.

Before You, humbled, Lord, I lie,
my heart like ashes, crushed and dry,
assist me when I die.

Full of tears and full of dread
is that day that wakes the dead
calling all, with solemn blast
to be judged for all their past.

Lord, have mercy, Jesus blest,
grant them all Your Light and Rest. Amen.[36]

---

36. Translation from the 1962 Missal, based on the work of James Ambrose Dominic Aylward (1813–1872) and William F. Wingfield (1813–1874), http://www.preces-latinae.org/thesaurus/Hymni /DiesIrae.html.

There is no escaping the "day of wrath" here, nor is there any sense that salvation is a gift granted corporately to believers. This very personalized hymn categorically emphasizes the judgment of each individual soul: "Now death and nature with surprise behold the trembling sinners rise to meet the Judge's searching eyes." Individually, the Judge will search the eyes of sinners. Even worse is that, according to the seventh stanza, even the saint must fear God's wrath! As Philippe Ariès states in his work, *Western Attitudes toward Death*, "In the thirteenth century the apocalyptic inspiration and the evocation of the Second Coming were almost blotted out. The idea of judgment won out and the scene became a court of justice. . . . Each man is to be judged according to the balance sheet of his life. Good and bad deeds are scrupulously separated and placed on the appropriate side of the scales."[37]

Hand in hand with the victory of a theology of death that was penal and focused on a God who required adequate repayment (from the dead in purgatory or the living on earth) for the forgiveness of a soul's sins, was the growth in importance of the funeral Mass itself. The post-death ceremonies of preparing the body, the transfer of the body with a procession, and even the commendation of the body at the grave all fell into the background as the Mass was seen as the primary means of paying the debt of sin. Whereas in earlier times, the celebration of the Eucharist in honor of the deceased person often fell after burial on the third, the seventh, or the thirtieth day after death, now the Mass was central to the concept of Christian burial. Thus, in the thirteenth century, we see the formation of the Requiem Mass, which would become normative in the 1570 Tridentine *Missale Romanum* and would serve as the standard funeral liturgy until the Missal of Paul VI after the Second Vatican Council.[38] Not only was a special Mass designed for the dead, but the funeral liturgy came to be celebrated apart

---

37. Philippe Ariès, *Western Attitudes toward Death: From the Middle Ages to the Present*, trans. Patricia M. Ranum (Baltimore: John Hopkins University Press, 1974), 31–32. See also Rowell, *The Liturgy of Christian Burial*, 68. He writes, "One of the marks of medieval piety in general was its special concern for the welfare of the departed. The development of this can be traced in the burial rites and offices for the dead with the increase of prayer for delivery from the pains of hell, at the expense, very often, of more primitive elements with their paschal emphasis and prayer for entry into a place of refreshment, light, and peace. This changing mood was not, however, something confined to the burial offices, properly so called; it extended to the church's everyday worship in the multiplication of masses for the dead, the practice of obituary lists and the wide observance of the Commemoration of All Souls."

38. See Rutherford, *The Death of a Christian*, 59.

from the regularly scheduled Mass of the local parish.[39] Perhaps this development, more than the shift to a tone of desolation and despair that accompany death, demonstrates that burial had become about the individual soul, not about the community that continues on earth awaiting the fullness of life to come in the next.

One of the particular developments that blossoms with the introduction of the Requiem Mass is the *absolutio* (the absolution service) that took place at the end of the Mass prior to the procession to the place of burial. For this service the priest would remove his chasuble and return wearing a black cope. The prayer *Non intres in judicium cum servo* tuo asking for God's forgiveness upon the departed soul is uttered at the foot of the casket by the priest:

> Enter not into judgment with Thy servant, O Lord; for in Thy sight shall no man be justified, save Thou grant him remission of all his sins. Therefore let not, we beseech thee, the sentence Thou pronouncest in judgment fall heavily upon one whom the faithful prayer of Thy Christian people commend to Thee, but rather by the help of Thy grace, may be found worthy to escape the judgment of condemnation, who in his lifetime was signed with the seal of the holy Trinity. Who livest and reignest world without end. Amen.[40]

Notice that this prayer uses the word "judgment" three times. The brief mention of Baptism as being "signed with the seal of the holy Trinity" is no match for overturning the heavy weight of sin that a dead person accumulated during his or her lifetime. The *Non intres in judicium* is followed by the singing of the *Libera me Domine* and the Kyrie along with the recitation of the Our Father. In silence, the priest sprinkles the casket with holy water and encircles it with incense. It is important to note that the use of water and incense here is not as a reminder of Baptism and the sacredness of the body, but rather, these are meant to be tools for purification. Finally, the prayer of absolution is pronounced:

> O God, whose property is ever to have mercy and to spare, we humbly beseech Thee on behalf of the soul of Thy servant N., which Thou has this day called out of this world, that Thou wouldst not deliver him

---

39. Rutherford, 59.
40. *Saint Andrew Daily Missal* (St. Paul, MN: E. M. Lohmann, 1957), 1653.

(her) into the hands of the enemy, nor forget him (her) for ever, but command that he (she) be taken up by Thy holy angels and borne to our home in paradise, that having put his (her) hope and trust in Thee, he (she) may not suffer the pains of hell, but may come to the possession of eternal joys. Through Christ our Lord. Amen.[41]

The body is processed out of the Church accompanied by the singing of *In Paradisum*. The absolution service is clearly marked by medieval fear; notice how the translated text of the original Latin prayer refers to the soul as "it"—the deceased person has become an object needing deliverance. Rutherford comments that the *absolutio* "soon became the moment above all others in the funeral liturgy to ensure God's good favor and forgiveness of the deceased."[42] The absolution clearly witnesses to the turn toward the individual in the practice of Christian burial. The process of salvation is localized in the forgiveness of each individual soul, while the prayers lack any reference to the Christian community left behind. Preoccupation with being "delivered from the pains of hell" has completely overshadowed the role of the soul's ongoing participation in the Body of Christ. Christian burial is no longer about the unbroken oneness of the community, it is about "dreading the loss of heaven and the pains of hell."[43]

The Reformation and the Roman Ritual of 1614

As the drama of death, constituted by the pangs of terror and destruction, reached a high point in the late Middle Ages, the reformers of the sixteenth century set out to renew Christian burial practices. The most liberal reformers sought to detach burial from any religious significance at all, while the mainline advocates for renewal sought the simplification of rites, with the goal to eliminate references to purgatory and to make the subject of prayer the mourners rather than the dead. The major stumbling block for the reformers was the way in which they believed the Catholic Church employed the Eucharist as a ticket to get the dead to heaven. They believed thoroughly that only God's grace could accomplish such a feat; human

---

41. *Saint Andrew Daily Missal*, 1654.
42. Rutherford, *The Death of a Christian*, 62.
43. Words spoken in the standard Act of Contrition.

prayers could not jolt God into enacting a different sentence upon the dead. Similarly, Martin Luther worked to dismantle the Catholic notion that the saints could intercede for the dead. While he did not deny the existence of the Communion of Saints, he objected to their being useful for the salvation of one's soul. From Luther's perspective, personal faith was the only armor against sure damnation.

Consequently, one of the positive aspects of reformed theology regarding death was the return to an emphasis of a corporate resurrection on the last day. It was belief in purgatory as a place of transitional waiting that troubled the reformers and their understanding of God's plan for salvation. Thus, a seventeenth-century creed of the Westminster Confession of Faith states:

> The bodies of men, after death, return to dust, and see corruption; but their souls (which neither die nor sleep), having an immortal subsistence, immediately return to God who gave them. The souls of the righteous, being then made perfect in holiness, are received into the highest heavens, where they behold the face of God in light and glory, waiting for the full redemption of their bodies; and the souls of the wicked are cast into hell, where they remain in torment and utter darkness, reserved to the judgment of the great day. Besides these two places for souls separated from their bodies, the Scripture acknowledgeth none.[44]

There is no purgatory mentioned here. Although the creation of a doctrine on purgatory may have created a place in the Christian imagination that fulfilled the idea of the need for eschatological purification prior to the day of the resurrection of the dead, it resulted in an individualization of death. "For the Reformers," writes Thomas Long, "the whole idea of purgatory was not only a church scandal; it was also thoroughly unbiblical and unjustified theologically."[45]

Thus, while the tenor of the prayers of the Reformation Movement continues to exhibit the total unworthiness of the human lot, they also leaned toward restoring the concept of a corporate resurrection of the dead on the last day. An example of this shift can be found in the Lutheran services

---

44. The Westminster Confession of Faith, XXXIV.1, in *The Book of Confessions* (Louisville, KY: Presbyterian Church USA, 1999), 159. Quote taken from Thomas G. Long, *Accompany Them with Singing: The Christian Funeral* (Louisville, KY: Westminster John Knox Press, 2009), 48.

45. Long, 51.

composed by Olavus Petri in 1529.[46] The emphasis in this service is on Christian hope and consolation for the mourners:

> The heathen, that have no knowledge of the resurrection from the dead, are greatly troubled and grieved that they lose their friends, for they have not the hope that they will some time receive them again. But we Christians, who know that we shall receive them in better estate than when we lose them, have no such trouble; but rather do we meditate upon it, so that we too are in readiness, when God shall call us from this poor and wretched world, as he hath done with our friend.[47]

It is important to observe that it is this life on earth that is deemed "wretched;" gone is the concept that the life to come is filled with pain and suffering. Likewise, such positivity continues in the prayer that follows in Petri's Swedish service:

> Turn now thy fatherly countenance toward us thy poor children, and hear our prayer, that if this our departed brother (sister) whom thou through death has called from this miserable life, be in such an estate that our prayers can avail for his (her) good, thou wilt be gentle and merciful to him (her), O heavenly Father, preserve him (her) in Abraham's bosom, and at the last judgement raise him (her) up in the resurrection of the just.[48]

In their attempt to strip Christians of a "works righteous" mentality, whereby it was believed that an accumulation of prayers and Masses for the dead could ease the pains of the deceased's time in purgatory, the reformers returned to the ancient image of death as a sleep from which only God (and not the influence of prayers and Masses) could awaken the just. As Rowell writes, "The prayers are much more concerned with admonishing and exhorting the living than with commendation of the dead, and there is a striking emphasis on the hope of resurrection at the Last Day, in contrast to the immediate expectation of the joy of paradise or deliverance from purgatorial fires."[49]

---

46. See Rowell, *The Liturgy of Christian Burial*, 78.
47. Text taken from Rowell, 78.
48. Text taken from Rowell, 78–79.
49. Rowell, 80.

An unfortunate consequence of the paring down of the burial rites in the Reformed tradition was that many Christians were encouraged to abandon the religious significance of the custom of burying the dead. Many Christians began to be buried without any formal service at all. For example, the Calvinist Directory of 1644 mandates a public burial without any prayer:

> When any person departeth this life, let the dead body, upon the day of burial, be decently attended from the house to the place appointed for public burial, and there immediately interred, without any ceremony.

> And because the custom of kneeling down, and praying by or towards the dead corpse, and other such usages, in the place where it lies, before it be carried to burial, are superstitious; and for that praying, reading, and singing, both in going to and at the grave, have been grossly abused, are no way beneficial to the dead, and have proved many ways hurtful to the living; therefore, let all such things be laid aside.[50]

To suggest here that the traditional practices of processing with the body to the grave while singing hymn and psalms "have been grossly abused" and "have proved many ways hurtful to the living" demonstrates the seriousness by which many reformers wished to make death solely about the growth in faith of the living. Commending the dead to God with prayer and other forms of ritual contradicted the central belief of *sola fide*.[51] Indeed, the criticism that the Church came to profit from the granting of indulgences was just one of many abuses the reformers waged against Catholicism, with such others as lay men and women paying to be clothed as monks or nuns on their deathbeds, the exacting of heavy payments for the inscription of names on obituary rolls, and the giving of absolution to the dead on occasions of solemn remembrance.[52]

Clearly, the call for a restoration of earlier theological concepts surrounding death, as well as for the renewal of liturgical practices, was sounded loudly by the Protestant Reformers. The Roman Church needed to respond. Thus, the Council of Trent (1545–1563) inaugurated the

---

50. Text taken from Rowell, 83.

51. In commenting on the presence of a prayer of commendation in the 1549 prayer book, the German reformer Martin Bucer wrote: "I know that this custom of praying for the pious dead is most ancient (pervetustam) but, as it is our duty to prefer the divine to all human authority and since Scripture nowhere teaches us by word or example to pray for the departed. . . . I wish that this commendation of the dead and prayer for them be omitted." Text taken from Rowell, 87.

52. See Rowell, 69.

beginning of the Counter-Reformation, which was largely a reaction to the challenges posed by the reformers regarding Catholic sacramental practices and ecclesial structures. Simultaneous to this conservative response, the Church also began its most rigorous attempt to universalize the Roman liturgy. With the invention of the printing press well established, the Roman Ritual of 1614, promulgated by Pope Paul V, could be easily disseminated throughout the entire world. The objective for those who drafted the 1614 ritual was to expunge some of the monastic elements that had crept into and complicated the rite. As Rowell writes: "The Ritual of 1614 was an attempt to make the medieval services manageable, and, as far as possible, to bring order out of chaos, for, by the end of the Middle Ages, the early pattern of the burial rites had become swamped by a mass of psalmody, antiphons, and responses. . . ."[53] While the 1614 ritual witnesses to a somewhat simplified liturgy, it does not demonstrate the restoration of the paschal nature of the early vision of Christian death and burial. The individual soul on its journey in pursuit of a happy verdict in its trial before God continues to be the Catholic Church's *lex orandi*.

Nevertheless, it is necessary to observe some of the reform of the rite and its intersection with culture. Although it had already begun to fall out of the Gallican missals, the washing and preparation of the body is not mentioned in the 1614 ritual. The prayers that accompanied the preparation of the body were designed for the healing of mourners as they were forced to face death head on. Perhaps these prayers were deleted because the 1614 ritual was to be strictly a prayer for the dead, or maybe the decision was based on the need to simplify. For as Owusu states, "The ritual of 1614 tried to integrate the varied contributions of the centuries and to produce a rite marked by restraint and brevity."[54] Although the preparation of the body has been eliminated, the traditional stations of the funeral liturgy survive, as Owusu provides the following characteristics of the ritual:

> It provides for a procession from the home of the deceased to the church, preceded by the sprinkling of the dead body with holy water while Psalm 129 (*De profundis*), with its antiphon *Si iniquitates*, is sung. For the funeral procession to the church, the *Miserere*, with the antiphon *Exsultabunt Domino ossa humiliata*, is sung; this concludes

53. Rowell, 72.
54. Owusu, "Funeral Rites in Rome and the Non-Roman West," 364.

with *Requiem aeternam*; then the Office for the dead and the funeral Mass, followed by the absolution, are celebrated. The absolution concludes with the prayer *Deus, cui proprium est misereri*, which refers to the soul on a dangerous journey, yet protected by the angels. Then follows the procession from the church to the place of burial. The antiphons *In paradisum* and *Chorus angelorum* are sung.

On arrival at the grave, if it has not already been blessed, the priest blesses it, saying the prayer *Deus cuius miseratione*, the coffin is sprinkled and incensed again, and then it is placed in the grave. The canticle *Benedictus* is said, with *Ego sum resurrectio et vita* as the antiphon, followed by the Kyrie and the Lord's Prayer, during which the body is sprinkled and incensed. Then after the prayer *Fac quaesumus* has been said, the priest makes the sign of the cross over the grave, saying the response *Requiem aeternam*, followed by *Requiescat in pace*. On the return from the place of burial to the church, the *De profundis* is again said with the antiphon *Si iniquitates*, thus maintaining a prayerful unity in the funeral liturgy from beginning to end.[55]

While this outline for the funeral liturgy is slightly simpler than those found in the early medieval missals, the rite seems to be extremely silent on the sacredness of death. With the absence of any rubrics concerning care for the body at the moment of death, the funeral liturgy becomes a "meditation on death on the occasion of the obsequies of a particular individual."[56] Such focus on the departed individual can be seen in the final prayer *Fac quaesumus* spoken at the grave:

> Grant to Thy servant (handmaid) departed, O Lord, we beseech Thee, Thy mercy, that he (she), who prayed that Thy will might be done, may not receive punishment for his (her) misdeeds, but that even as here below the true faith united him (her) to the ranks of the faithful, so in heaven by Thy mercy he (she) may have fellowship with the choirs of angels. Through Christ our Lord. Amen.[57]

The final prayer at the graveside thus makes no mention of the hope of those left behind; it is concerned only with the journey of the individual soul. Moreover, at the outset of the rite where *Ordo XLIX* had the procession at

---

55. Owusu, 363–364.
56. Rowell, *The Liturgy of Christian Burial*, 72.
57. *Saint Andrew Daily Missal*, 1657–1658.

the house form around the signing of Psalm 114, In exitu Israel, with its paschal, baptismal, and joyful overtones, the 1614 ritual now calls for the singing of the penitential Psalm 130 *De Profundis*:

Out of the depths I cry to you, O Lord:
  Lord, hear my cry.
Listen attentively
  to the sound of my pleading!
If you kept a record of our sins,
  Lord, who could stand their ground?
But with you is forgiveness,
  that you may be revered.

I rely, my whole being relies,
  O Lord, on your promise.
My whole being hopes in the Lord,
  more than watchmen for the daybreak;
more than watchmen for daybreak
  let Israel hope in the Lord.
For with the Lord is faithful love,
  with him generous ransom;
and he will ransom Israel
  from all its sins.

Once again, the tenor of the *De Profundis*, like much of the medieval prayer and hymnody, is focused on the individual soul pleading for God's mercy. While Psalm 130 looks forward to the ransoming of Israel as a whole, it does not portray the image of a people journeying together on their pilgrimage to God (as does Psalm 114). Nevertheless, it has been suggested that praying in the "I-mode," in the person of the dead (*in persona defuncti*) serves as a prayer for the grieving and the Church on earth, "as the living lend their voice to the deceased, they identify themselves in a certain way with him or her, and thus anticipate their own fate and the fate of all living beings."[58]

While the Ritual of 1614 successfully trimmed the repetition of prayers, especially at the home and at the graveside, it not only continued the macabre outlook that took over in the Middle Ages, but now the Requiem Mass

---

58. Ansgar Franz, "'Everything Is Worthwhile at the End': Christian Funeral Liturgy amidst Ecclesial Tradition and Secular Rites," *Studia Liturgica* 32 (2002): 56.

was embellished by overly dramatic Baroque architecture and music. The opulence of Baroque architecture, which helped to set the stage for liturgy based on theatrics, went hand in hand with music that needed to be grand enough to complement the space. Thus, composers such as Mozart, Verdi, and Salieri were commissioned to write grand musical compositions to undergird the Requiem Mass. The wealthy could even hire a composer to write a musical repertoire for their future death. With this rise in drama at the funeral liturgy, death gains a certain sense of beauty in the sixteenth and seventeenth centuries, and mourning becomes a public spectacle in the eighteenth and nineteenth centuries.[59] "Beginning with the eighteenth century," writes Ariès, "man in western societies tended to give death a new meaning. He exalted it, dramatized it, and thought of it as disquieting and greedy."[60] As a result, burial groups began to arise in the eighteenth century to challenge much of the pomp and circumstance that accompanied the burial of the dead and to ensure that the poor were provided with dignified Christian burial.[61] Regarding the "pagan-like" grandeur that began to accompany Christian funerals at this time, the poetic words of Anglican hymn writer John Mason Neale provide a fitting image of the individualization of burial:

> Take hence the heathen trappings, take hence the Pagan show,
> the misery, the heartlessness, the unbelief of woe;
> the nodding plumes, the painted staves, the mutes in black array,
> that get their hard-won earnings by so much grief per day:
> the steeds and scarves and crowds that gaze with half-suspended breath
> as if, of all things terrible, most terrible was death.[62]

Even though the prayers of the Catholic funeral liturgy continued to highlight the soul's depravity and need for God's gracious forgiveness, the society at large in the second half of the second millennium began to see

---

59. See Ariès, *Western Attitudes toward Death*, 67.

60. Ariès, 55–56.

61. See Geoffrey Rowell, "Nineteenth-Century Attitudes and Practices," in *Dying, Death and Disposal*, ed. Gilbert Cope (London: SPCK, 1970), 51. Here Rowell identifies the journal called the *Ecclesiologist* tackling the issue of the wealthy and the dead being buried very differently. He writes: "The 'Christian funerals' the *Ecclesiologist* wished to see would be chanted, with no difference in ceremony between rich and poor. Coffins would be straight-sided and gabled with a cross on the top; palls and mourning cloaks would be provided for the poor; coffins would be carried on biers, not on the shoulders, and where a hearse was used it would be in the approved Gothic style with a gabled roof. White would be employed for the funerals of the young and burial clubs with a religious bias would be encouraged."

62. Text taken from Rowel, "Nineteenth-Century Attitudes and Practices," 50.

death as an opportunity to celebrate the individual. Thus, funerals were not so much about fear of death as a celebration of one's uniqueness and individuality. This outlook is exacerbated in large part due to the creation and growth of the funeral industry. To put it simply, by the time the Second Vatican Council was convened in the fall of 1962, the renewal of the Christian funeral liturgy would be a challenge that ran far deeper than redrafting prayers. Instead, this renewal would demand a restoration of the early Christian vision of death by which all members of Christ are on their pilgrim way to share equally and fully in God's divinity. In Christ, there can be no true individualization of life or death.

Conclusion

Fear has always been one of the primary enemies of the Gospel message. In one of his final farewell discourses to his chosen disciples in the Gospel of John, Jesus reassures them that he will not leave them abandoned but will return to gather them again. The Lord states, "Do not let your hearts be troubled. You trust in God, trust also in me. . . . I am going now to pre-pare a place for you, and after I have gone and prepared you a place, I shall return to take you to myself" (John 14:1, 2b–3a). After his resurrection, the Lord appeared to the women at the tomb with the words "Do not be afraid" (Matthew 28:10). Jesus expects his disciples to minister with courage in his absence; fear is not a suitable response to the call of the Lord.

When Jesus did not return quickly, the temptation to succumb to fear was great for the early Church. Such anxiety is detectable in the Christian community at Thessalonica, for whom Paul writes: "About the times and dates, brothers, there is no need to write to you for you are well aware in any case that the Day of the Lord is going to come upon you like a thief in the night" (1 Thessalonians 5:1–2). Nevertheless, the early Christians, in the midst of doubt and persecution, maintained a genuine hopefulness in the resurrection of the dead. The trust that they had in the Lord's prom-ise that he would call them to himself far overshadowed the nagging fears that God could have other plans for the dead. The longer they waited, how-ever, the greater grew the suspicion that perhaps God's judgment would not be a welcome at an open door.

With the explosion of Christianity in the fourth century and the for-malization of liturgies, doctrines, and creeds, there began to creep into the religion a growing sense of personal unworthiness on the part of the faithful. More and more, Christianity became a penitential religion, whereby followers marked their spiritual progress by self-sacrifice and humility. Added to this was the development of the doctrine of Original Sin, which taught that humans were born sinful and that the body would continue to be the locus of perversion and uncleanliness throughout life. Life and the afterlife would become a battlefield upon which individual disciples were to fight against the Enemy in order to merit God's good graces. Thus, even the sacraments of the Church, instead of being intimate encounters with the Risen Lord meant for the revelation of his presence to the world, now became gauges by which Christians marked progress (and therefore personal merit) along the spiritual path.

It is no wonder that, with the individualization of the Christian journey, the Christian view on death would shift from a celebration of the Church on its pilgrim way to heaven to the feared moment that put the individual soul on trial for all that life entailed, both the good and the bad. The duty of those Christians who remained behind after the death of a loved one soon became that of attempting to pray them out of purgatory. Although the first witness to the Roman liturgy for burial, *Ordo XVIX*, exhibits the tone of paschal hope, subsequent liturgies that appear in Gallican missals predominantly have a theme of fear. Louis van Tongeren sums up this change in his article "Individualizing Ritual: The Personal Dimension in Funeral liturgy":

> The paschal character of the funeral moved to the background during the Middle Ages, when the accent was more on the judgment to which the deceased were subject. Initially it was believed that death brought a better life in God's presence, but gradually death became a source of fear. To be able to appear before the face of God, a person had to be cleansed of transgressions. In light of the doctrines regarding purgatory, death became the moment of judgment and the beginning of a hard process of purification. Anxiety regarding judgment gained the upper hand and death was surrounded by devotional rituals which were to influence this judgment in a positive manner. By having Masses said for a deceased person, or by repeating specific prayers, or by acquiring certain indulgences, the fearsome ordeal could be mollified. In this way

people hoped to be able to die a blessed death and alleviate the situation of those who had already died.[63]

Even after the Protestant reformers tried to summon the Church to move away from what appeared to be the ability to buy one's way into heaven, the Requiem Mass grew in splendor and incorporated absolution of the soul as its essential objective. In the centuries that witnessed the rapid explosion of modernization around the world as well as the breakdown of community life (with the population of cities), death became increasingly an individualistic affair. The rituals themselves began to slide toward celebrating the accomplishments one achieved in this life rather than enacting remembrance of the oneness of Christ's Body on earth and in heaven. It would be the work of the liturgical reform instituted by the Second Vatican Council to restore the paschal, and therefore the ecclesial, spirit of the death of a Christian.

63. Louis van Tongeren, "Individualizing Ritual: The Personal Dimension in Funeral Liturgy," *Worship* 78 (2004): 118–119.

CHAPTER FOUR

Restoring the Ecclesial Spirit in the
Order of Christian Funerals

At the funeral rites, especially at the celebration of the Eucharistic Sacrifice, the Christian community affirms and expresses the union of the Church on earth with the Church in heaven in the one great communion of Saints. Though separated from the living, the dead are still at one with the community of believers on earth and benefit from their prayers and intercession. At the rite of final commendation and farewell, the community acknowledges the reality of separation and commends the deceased to God. In this way it recognizes the spiritual bond that still exists between the living and the dead and proclaims its belief that all the faithful will be raised up and reunited in the new heavens and a new earth, where death will be no more.[1]

The Constitution on the Sacred Liturgy laid out an agenda for the reform of the Eucharist in its second chapter and then in chapter 3, "The Other Sacraments and the Sacramentals," turned to the reform of the celebration of the six remaining sacraments as well as other liturgical rites, among them funerals. In paragraphs 81 and 82, the Council Fathers call for the renewal of funerals to center around three topics: (1) the restoration of the paschal nature of funerals, (2) the integral connection of regional customs, and (3) the provision of rites for the death of infants. As with all liturgical reform, the Council mandates that the guiding principle for drafting new rites must be "that all the faithful be led to that full, conscious, and active participation in liturgical celebrations called for by the very nature of the liturgy."[2] Mandating the execution of "full, conscious, and active participation" in the various components of funeral liturgies—gathering around the body at death, keeping vigil with the dead, processing with the body,

---

1. OCF, 6.
2. SC, 14.

celebrating the funeral Mass, and participating in the rite of committal—
becomes an even more imposing challenge for assemblies of mixed faiths
and for people preoccupied with time constraints and responsibilities
thrust upon them by secular society.

As was seen in chapter 2, the earliest sources of the Christian tradition
suggest that believers had a very hopeful stance toward death. The Lord Jesus
had promised that upon his return he would gather the nations to himself,
and Christians held this promise as imminent. They made important life
choices, such as how to include Gentiles into their fold as well as whether to
remain celibate for the Kingdom, based on the promise that they would share
in a better life in the new world to come. Thus, they treated the dead as active
members of the Body of Christ. Although the dead would no longer contribute to the Body by works of the flesh, they would now participate in the
Church by praying and guiding all to heaven. The Preface for the Solemnity
of All Saints (November 1) expresses this vision:

> For today by your gift we celebrate the festival of your city,
> the heavenly Jerusalem, our mother,
> where the great array of our brothers and sisters
> already gives you eternal praise.
>
> Towards her, we eagerly hasten as pilgrims advancing by faith,
> rejoicing in the glory bestowed upon those exalted members
>   of the Church
> through whom you give us, in our frailty, both strength and
>   good example.

This prayer beautifully expresses the dynamism of the pilgrim Church
"advancing by faith"; it is a community of "exalted" members and those
who still experience the trials of earthly existence in "our frailty." Those
baptized into Christ are one with him forever, and thus, the Christians of
the first several centuries believed that they had a duty to care for the dead
with great reverence, for the sake of both pastoral concern for those grieving and for the expression to the surrounding society of the strength of
Christian hope. Coming together as one around death, Christians performed difficult tasks as a community.

This positive vision of death, by which the Church makes its way together
into divine life, started to unravel as Christianity began to consume itself

with sin. As we saw in chapter 3, beginning with St. Augustine and the formation of the doctrine of Original Sin in the late fourth century and heightened extensively by Gregory the Great in the sixth century, the Church would become intensely preoccupied with the individual soul. Death for the Christian was transformed from the joyful occasion of a blessed sleep, or a *Migratio ad Dominum*, or one's birthday itself to the fear of eternal damnation or unending purgation. The Church of the living no longer saw its obligation as prayerfully caring for their dead who continue on in the Body of Christ. Rather, it understood its duty as praying the dead out of purgatory. Anniversary Masses for the dead were no longer for consolation and refreshment purposes; they were now the means of reparation to pay the weighty debt of human sin committed by the dead.

When the Catholic reformers after the Council of Trent labored to put into force the sacramental rituals that would endure for the next four hundred years, little attempt was made to restore the paschal nature of funerals. Furthermore, Trent served to systematically accentuate a universal Roman liturgy at the expense of local cultural considerations. To add to this, a liturgy that had long been stripped from the people's hands became even more so the specialized work of clerics; the faithful simply filled the pews and the priests went about their work, using a language largely foreign to most in attendance. As is stated in *Guide for Celebrating Funerals*:

> The decrees of the Council of Trent had sought to counter the Protestant
> Reformation's rejection of this theology of Church and sacraments
> centered on the propitiatory (atoning) power of priests that the
> reformers said rendered the wider body of the baptized (the laity)
> passive observers of sacred rites. Thus did the content and style of the
> funeral in the 1614 Roman Ritual open into three and a half centuries
> of a centralized, rigid, clerical order of service driven by didactic
> concepts (souls, sins, judgment, expiation, purgation, and so on), while
> the laity practiced local customs of prayer (such as reciting the Rosary),
> expressions of loss and grief, and solidarity with the bereaved (such as
> "the Irish wake").[3]

Cultural forces likewise played a role in the increasingly individualization of death. As the industrialization of Western societies brought with it

---

3. Joseph DeGrocco, Bruce Morrill, and Richard Rutherford, *Guide for Celebrating Funerals* (Chicago: Liturgy Training Publications, 2017), 9.

alienation from one's work (at the expense of personal creativity) as well as the self-sufficiency of one's household (at the expense of participation in community), so too did death disappear from the public realm. In the twentieth century, it became common for people to die in hospitals rather than in homes. "Death in the hospital," writes Ariès, "is no longer the occasion of a ritual ceremony, over which the dying person presides amidst his assembled relatives and friends."[4] At the same time, the funeral industry took over where the family left off to provide care for the dead with a "dignity" expressed in extensive embalming practices, caskets exuding comfort, and processions complete with limousines and police escorts. All of this served to disguise the grim reality of death's ugliness, simultaneously making the expression of faith in the resurrection increasingly more concealed. Even the monuments that mark the place of burial would become a means lauding the individual accomplishments made by the deceased here on earth; graves became places of differentiation rather than communion.[5]

The 1969 *Ordo exsequiarum* and Its English Translations

If all of Christian liturgy is meant to be a participation in the Paschal Mystery, then there is no doubt that funerals were ripe for reform in the late 1960s. Not only would the Consilium charged with the duty of drafting revised or new liturgies have to take into consideration a high degree of passivity on the part of the faithful (who were not truly catechized on the meaning and nature of liturgical prayer), but it would have to contend with cultural dynamics that were quite often at odds with Christian virtues (that is, death as something to be avoided rather than death as entrance into a new way of being in Christ). One of the liturgical scholars responsible for the reform of the funeral liturgy after the Second Vatican Council, Pierre-Marie Gy, writes:

---

4. Ariès, *Western Attitudes toward Death from the Middle Ages to the Present*, 88.

5. See Charles Brown, "The Environment of Disposal: The Exterior," in *Dying, Death, and Disposal*, ed. Gilbert Cope (London: SPCK, 1970), 109. Brown writes: "In the medieval age the parish graveyard was merely a grassed enclosure dominated by a free standing cross, where individual marking of the graves was probably not customary at all, and from which periodically all the bones were removed and stored in a charnel house. In later times, inscribed stones marked the place of burial, and the virtues and merits of the life of wealthy individuals were often commemorated."

Since the seventeenth century, the funeral liturgy has been affected by two sorts of change: firstly, those resulting from the developments in city-dwelling, and secondly, changes in popular attitudes towards death. On the grounds that cemeteries constituted a threat to health, the eighteenth century placed them at a distance from the churches, on the boundaries of the towns and villages. Again, the general development of the urban style of life and the advent of motor traffic led to the disappearance in the towns of the funeral procession. . . . Furthermore, attitudes have also changed. There has grown up, even in the Christian milieu, a sort of taboo with regard to death; one which has come to demand considerable discretion both in preaching and in formulating liturgical prayers in the vernacular. In many cases, the language of the traditional prayers on the subject of hell, judgment or the sins of the deceased would strike us today as unbearably cruel, had they not been softened down or adapted when the ritual was reformed or in the course of translation.[6]

When the Council Fathers set forth the agenda for liturgical renewal and proclaimed in the introduction to the Constitution on the Sacred Liturgy that "the rites be revised carefully in the light of sound tradition, and that they be given new vigor to meet the circumstances and needs of modern times,"[7] they were laying the foundation for a monumental task indeed!

Thus, on August 15, 1969, nearly four years after the close of the Second Vatican Council and almost six years after it had promulgated *Sacrosanctum Concilium*, the Congregation for Divine Worship released the *editio typica* (the official Latin text) of the *Ordo exsequiarum*.[8] One of the major contributions of the work of the Consilium committee that was to study and revise the rite of funerals, *Coetus* XXIII, was their broad understanding of ritualizing death. It would be their conviction that the Church needed to recapture a broader sense of pastoral care surrounding death that had been predominant in the early Church: "The name itself, *Ordo exsequiarum* (the *Rite of Funerals*), suggests a broader understanding of *exsequiae* to include all the rituals with which human death is surrounded from the time of

---

6. Pierre-Marie Gy, "The Liturgy of Death: The Funeral Rite of the New Roman Ritual," *The Way* 11 (1970): 63.

7. SC, 4.

8. See Annibale Bugnini, *The Reform of the Liturgy 1948–1975*, trans. Matthew J. O'Connell (Collegeville, MN: Liturgical Press, 1990), 771–773. Here Bugnini lays out the history of the Consilium and the preparation of an experimental rite.

death itself until the burial."[9] Instead of focusing solely on the funeral Mass as the principle prayer for the reparation of one's sins committed in this life, the pattern suggested by the rite is one of passage, of walking through death together in order to experience the promise of new life. As the prefect to the Congregation for Divine Worship in 1969, Cardinal Benno Gut, writes in the "Decree" for the *Ordo exsequiarum*: "By means of the funeral rites it has been the practice of the Church, as a tender mother, not simply to commend the dead to God but also to raise high the hope of its children and to give witness to its own faith in the future resurrection of the baptized with Christ."[10]

After the publication of the official Latin text of the funeral rites in late 1969, the first English translation was prepared by the International Committee on English in the Liturgy (ICEL) in 1970 (printed in 1971) with a second translation to follow in 1989. The 1971 *Rite of Funerals* contains an introduction that sets forth the paschal nature of the complex of rituals that comprises Christian burial. Annibale Bugnini summarizes the overall changes to the rite that the introduction attempts to explain theologically:

> [T]he Introduction emphasizes the point that a Christian funeral is a celebration of the paschal mystery of Christ as accomplished in his faithful followers. . . . To this end they (the reformers) drew from the treasury of the euchological tradition texts that would best express this aspect of funerals. At the same time, they got rid of texts that smacked of a negative spirituality inherited from the Middle Ages. Thus they removed such familiar and even beloved texts as the *Libera me, Domine*, the *Dies irae*, and others that overemphasized judgment, fear, and despair. These they replaced with texts urging Christian hope and giving more effective expression to faith in the resurrection.

> These changes explain the closer and more organic connection between the funeral and the Eucharistic celebration in the new rite, the restoration of the Alleluia, and the abandonment of the color black for another which, in the judgment of the episcopal conferences, will inspire a calmer approach to sorrow and suggest a hope that is illumined by the Paschal Mystery. The same perspective is at work in the directive that the Paschal candle be placed near the coffin. Finally, in accordance with

---

9. Owusu, "Funeral Rites in Rome and the Non-Roman West," 365.

10. "Decree," *Order of Christian Funerals*, xi.

the general principles governing the reform, the rite urges the participation not only of the family, friends, and relatives of the deceased but of the entire community. The community thus shares the lot of each brother or sister and gives witness, as a community, to its faith in the resurrection.[11]

As will be seen with the introduction to the 1989 second English translation of the *Ordo exsequiarum*, the theological and pastoral instruction that opens the *Rite of Funerals* presents a renewed outlook on the nature of death. The contents of the rest of the book suggest a thorough renewal of the rite. Chapter 1 of the 1971 *Rite of Funerals* contains the texts for a vigil for the deceased. The 1614 ritual made no mention of a wake or vigil service, but "the new rite recognizes the pastoral value of the prayer vigil and makes it part of the present-day funerals."[12] Next, the rite contains three plans with various stations for the celebration of funerary rites: Plan 1 has three stations—namely, in the house, in the church (with the celebration of Mass), and at the cemetery; Plan 2 has two stations, in a chapel (with the celebration of God's Word and a final farewell) and at the graveside; Plan 3 is located entirely in the house of the deceased (with the placing of the body in the casket, the celebration of God's Word, and a final farewell). All three plans contain a rite of final commendation, which replaces the former absolution at the end of Mass. "It is not a rite of purification but a true and proper 'farewell' or *valedictio* in which the Christian community confides one of its members to the heavenly Church at the moment of interment."[13] The remaining four chapters of the 1971 *Rite of Funerals* are devoted to funerals for children, various texts for funerals of adults, and various texts for funerals of both baptized and unbaptized children.

By and large, this first English edition of the *Ordo exsequiarum* was well received in the United States. Writing fifteen years after its first liturgical use, Robert Hovda offered a two-installment evaluation of the *Rite of Funerals* in his "Amen Corner" in the journal *Worship*.[14] He begins with a glowing assessment of the rite:

---

11. Bugnini, *The Reform of the Liturgy*, 773–774.

12. Bugnini, 774.

13. Bugnini, 776.

14. See Robert W. Hovda, "Reclaiming for the Church the Death of a Christian," *Worship* 59 (1985): 148–154, and Robert W. Hovda, "Reclaiming for the Church the Death of a Christian II," *Worship* 59 (1985): 251–261.

The Catholic funeral liturgy as published in 1969 for local adaptation is so beautiful yet strong, so reserved yet compassionate, so full of faith and hope yet so straightforwardly accepting of our natural sister death, that it is very difficult to understand how American funerals got to be so pretentious and ostentatious, as phony and unreal and camouflaged, as destructive of the economic well-being of low-to-moderate income families as they have become.[15]

Hovda notes that the major problem for the renewal of the funeral liturgy is not the liturgy itself but rather the influence of cultural practices and the neglect of parishes to educate the faithful on the meaning of Christian death. He writes: "The funeral liturgy's strength and paschal character are undeniable, and the recent reform of the rites has served this character well. But we must seek to change the surrounding customs and practices, both in the parish and in society at large, which dominate the consciousness and experience of the bereaved in particular and the faith community in general."[16]

Writing a decade after the introduction of the *Rite of Funerals*, Robert J. Hoeffner, then the director of liturgy for the Diocese of Orlando, Florida, both praises the restored funeral liturgy and raises what he considers to be a major flaw. At the outset of his article "A Pastoral Evaluation of the Rite of Funerals," Hoeffner raises his basic concern: "After ten years of official use of the new *Rite of Funerals* (1969), American Catholics do not seem to be handling death any better than before."[17] While Catholic funerals have successfully been transformed from the "morbidity" of the pre-conciliar rite into a "hope-filled" celebration, Hoeffner argues that the attitudes of Christians towards death remain unchanged.[18] The author suggests the following as the root of the problem:

---

15. Hovda, 148–149. He continues to suggest that the liturgy is beautiful, while our culture is problematic: "Wake, reception at the church door, funeral Mass, rite of final commendation and farewell, committal, with the reverent carrying and prominent locations of relics (in urn) or body (in casket)—the liturgy itself is part of the solution, not part of the problem. But the rites of the church are being smothered, dominated, thrown back into the shadows by a combination of cultural practices that militate against the healthy and spiritual values of simplicity, honesty and prudent economy."

16. Hovda, 151–152.

17. Robert J. Hoeffner, "A Pastoral Evaluation of the Rite of Funerals," *Worship* (1981): 482.

18. Hoeffner, 482. Hoeffner writes: "Surely it must be admitted that American Catholic funerals have lost the morbidity that characterized their prayers before the council. The resurrectional motif with paschal alleluias give them a positive, hope-filled emphasis and tone unknown for many centuries. Water, incense, white palls, paschal candles, white vestments, bright banners, and even 'snappy' music have completely transformed the celebrations of funerals . . . But we still allow the same death-denial practices in funerary care that plague the general society."

My suspicion is that the central difficulty in the American Catholic approach to death, funeral ritual and care is a deficiency or void in establishing a relationship between the living and the dead. As Americans we are part of a culture that tries to conceal the death reality. We no longer personally prepare our dead for burial, or even bury them. We are seldom in the presence of a dying person. If we are to care for our dead, we must have a reason for so doing, that is, a relationship and consequent responsibility. This communion of living and dead is essential to the formation of good funeral ritual, and allows for relationships of respect and care. Remembering, based on present as well as past relationship, is central to the care of the dead, as well as the center of prayer for the dead. Relationship is the basis for funeral ritual as rite of passage, which seems to be a universal reality in cultures which believe in any kind of afterlife.[19]

Thus, Hoeffner echoes the theme that is at the heart of this present work, namely, that the relationship established in Baptism with Christ and his Church does not come to an end at death, but rather, that relationship is reordered. As hospitals have sanitized the ugliness of dying, and as the funeral industry wishes to satisfy families with every mode of convenience, the hard work of understanding relationship anew is mitigated.[20] Consequently, just as there is a rush to return to normalcy, there is also a rush to move the dead into the final resurrection. As with everything in a society of immediate gratification, the state of waiting for the fullness of the resurrection is eliminated. "The white vestments and alleluias, while speaking emphatically of resurrection and hope, have moved too much to resurrection as accomplished fact."[21] Thus, Hoeffner maintains that more emphasis on treating the *Rite of Funerals* as an extended rite of passage to be enacted fully and richly in each of its stages—separation, transition, incorporation—is necessary for the reform to truly take hold.

---

19. Hoeffner, 482–483.

20. Hoeffner, 491. Hoeffner writes: "In America, where happiness was the core and substance, the *raison d'être* of society, death threatened the very fiber of social structure. It must therefore be hidden, covered up, denied. After a period of uncontrolled mourning in the face of utter meaninglessness and loss, there is an attempt in America to completely remove death from the realm of reality. In the twentieth century dying has been systematically moved into hospitals, and defined as a cessation of care; funerary care has moved out of the home and into professional 'homes' which try in every way to conceal death. Mourning and grief are considered socially unacceptable and threatening, and are passed through with the help of the professional as quickly as possible, if at all."

21. Hoeffner, 493–494.

Moving briefly to the second generation of translations (the contents of which will be employed throughout the rest of this chapter) the 1989 *Order of Christian Funerals* is expanded with the addition of the Office for the Dead as well as additional prayer texts for the dead and moments of prayer centered around keeping watch with the dead. It is important to note that the OCF is supplemented by the additional appendix released in the United States in 1997 on cremation, which contains rubrics specific to the presence of cremated remains in the church as well as several adaptations to texts. Instead of the three "plans" for the funeral liturgy, the OCF structures the funeral rites according to the three principle moments of prayer for the gathered Christian community: (1) the vigil, (2) the funeral Mass or funeral liturgy outside of Mass, and (3) the rite of committal. Significantly, the 1989 translation unites these three stations in part 1 of the OCF, "Funeral Rites," and intends for the ritual moments to be one continuous liturgical event. "Within the dynamic movement of the rituals, Christians are carried through the days of mourning until the final farewell at burial. Each ritual does not really begin as a separate ritual but resumes the prayer from the previous gathering. . . . The rites are stational liturgies—a ritual journey with those who grieve through the various periods of mourning."[22] Thus, this second translation of the *Ordo exsequiarum*, with the inclusion of the Office for the Dead and additional prayers for critical moments in the grieving process, is an attempt to fill out or symbolically strengthen the ritual process of death.

Ecclesiological Advances in the *Order of Christian Funerals*

At the conclusion of chapter 1 of this work, an attempt was made to summarize baptismal ecclesiology according to the five headings: (1) A United People (Christians are one in the Body of Christ), (2) A Pilgrim People (baptismal life is a process of becoming), (3) A Self-Giving People (Baptism demands a letting go of self), (4) A Priestly People (Baptism is discipleship and entails service), and (5) A Holy People (sanctity is a result of attachment to Christ). While these five headings do not exhaust either the mystery of Baptism nor the mystery of the Church, they point to the serious

---

22. DeGrocco, Morrill, and Rutherford, *Guide for Celebrating Funerals*, 37.

responsibility of those baptized into Christ. Baptism is not meant to produce passive or disinterested Christians, guaranteed the security of heaven in the next life; it is meant to be a way of life lived here and now with conviction and courage. Thus, these five headings will be used to organize this present evaluation of the post–Vatican II reform of Christian funerals. Not only will the merits of this renewal come to light, but also ways in which the rituals might be more revelatory of the Church's participation in the Paschal Mystery will surface.

A United People

As has been continually pressed throughout, the vision of the early Church regarding the death of a Christian was one that flowed out of a corporate worldview. Because Christians were one in Christ in this life, they would be one in the next as well. Furthermore, that oneness transcended mortal life and death; the living and the dead comprise one Church destined for the fullness of life in God. In other words, there are not two churches, with one in heaven and one on earth; there is but one Church. This corporate understanding of death had a relatively short life in the history of the Church and was replaced as early as the middle of the first millennium by a pessimistic theology of death based on judgment and fear. Because so much of this dread around God's wrath was based upon individual sin, the image of the unified Body of Christ would dwindle and nearly fade out of the Christian imagination.

However, the *Order of Christian Funerals* decidedly returns the Church to a corporate understanding of death. The General Introduction to the OCF is filled with references to death as a communal event for the Christian family. Here are a few examples:

In the Eucharistic Sacrifice, the Church's celebration of Christ's Passover from death to life, the faith of the baptized in the Paschal Mystery is renewed and nourished. Their union with Christ and with each other is strengthened: "Because there is one bread, we who are many, are one body; for we all partake of the one bread" (1 Corinthians 10:17). (3)

At the death of a Christian, whose life of faith was begun in the waters of Baptism and strengthened at the Eucharistic table, the Church intercedes on behalf of the deceased because of its confident belief that death is not the end nor does it break the bonds forged in life. (4)

"If one member suffers in the body of Christ which is the Church, all
the members suffer with that member" (1 Corinthians 12:26). For this
reason, those who are baptized into Christ and nourished at the same
table of the Lord are responsible for one another . . . The Church
calls each member of Christ's Body—Priest, Deacon, layperson—
to participate in the ministry of consolation: to care for the dying,
to pray for the dead, to comfort those who mourn. (8)

These are just a few of the many references to the oneness of the Body of
Christ and the responsibility that each Christian has for the fruition of the
Church. Owusu writes: "An essential legacy that the Roman funeral tradition has left us is that death is not only very personal but also highly com-
munitarian."[23] Although the burgeoning of the medical profession and
work of hospitals lures society into the illusion that death is a very individualistic experience, the Christian ideal is something very different. Death
unites the community even deeper in its bonds forged in Christ.

As mentioned earlier, the OCF envisions the three principle moments
for gathering as a community—the vigil, the funeral liturgy, and the
committal—as one seamless liturgy. In the medieval world, these rites were
understood as prayer for the absolution of the individual soul. However,
as Richard Rutherford is fond of saying: the vigil, as well as the entirety of
the *Order of Christian Funerals* is "of the Church, by the Church, and for
the Church."[24] The Invitation to Prayer at the vigil clearly expresses the
unity of God's People:

My brothers and sisters, we believe that all the ties of friendship and
affection which knit us as one throughout our lives do not unravel
with death.

Confident that God always remembers the good we have done and
forgives our sins, let us pray, asking God to gather N. to himself.[25]

The theme of the "ties of friendship and affection which knit us as one
throughout our lives" and that endure into life eternal is echoed in the vigil's
Opening Prayer that follows after a period of silent prayer:

---

23. Owusu, "Funeral Rites in Rome and the Non-Roman West," 373.
24. See DeGrocco, Morrill, and Rutherford, *Guide for Celebrating Funerals*, 20.
25. OCF, 71.

Lord our God,
the death of our brother (sister) N.
recalls our human condition
and the brevity of our lives on earth.
But for those who believe in your love
death is not the end,
nor does it destroy the bonds
that you forge in our lives.
We share the faith of your Son's disciples
and the hope of the children of God.
Bring the light of Christ's Resurrection
to this time of testing and pain
as we pray for N. and for those who love him (her).
Through Christ our Lord.
Amen.[26]

As was seen in chapter 2, the early Church believed that it needed to keep watch with the body from the moment of death until the body's final burial. The Opening Prayer at the Vigil for the Deceased does not shield the community from the harsh reality of death nor the pain of mourning but puts death into a perspective of ongoing life in the Body of Christ: "death is not the end, nor does it destroy the bonds that you forge in our lives." Such a faith expresses the unity that cannot be torn apart by power or prestige; death is a reminder that our Baptism serves as a social leveler. Nevertheless, Margaret Smith asks in *Facing Death Together*: "Do we really believe that in death there are no distinctions and that no one group within the baptized community is privileged?"[27]

The Vigil service has had an ambivalent reception at best on the part of the Catholic community. In many places, the tradition of reciting a Rosary for the deceased (a form of private devotion) continues to be the preferred form of prayer in the context of the wake. It is also not uncommon for family members to do away with the wake entirely or to compress the time of viewing and to combine it with the funeral liturgy. *Guide for Celebrating Funerals* states:

---

26. OCF, 72.

27. Margaret Smith, *Facing Death Together: Parish Funerals*, (Chicago: Liturgy Training Publications, 1998), 52.

There are many challenges to celebrating the Vigil in the way the OCF intended. It is not surprising that in some parts of our nation, mostly in the West but also in pockets across the country, Catholics are requesting both a more telescoped, simplified pattern and more personalized rites. Within Catholic communities, it is not the Funeral Mass that falls victim to simplification, it is the Vigil. For reasons of time, money, age, illness, demographics, cultural and religious differences in extended families, and the like, a time of wake or vigil with the body and mourners is becoming telescoped more and more into the time set for the Funeral Liturgy or into the liturgy itself. . . . Such telescoping can shift the emphasis of the Funeral Liturgy itself from a celebration in thanks and praise for what God has done through the Paschal Mystery of Christ's Death and Resurrection and continues to do in the life and death of this Christian and the Church into a framework for personal expressions of mourning in song, poetry, favorite memorabilia, eulogies, and the like.[28]

It must be asked whether these options allow the Christian community to enact its duty of keeping watch around the body of one of its members, focusing on what Christ has accomplished for the world through his death and Resurrection. Unfortunately, the time of visitation often lacks the seriousness of prayer entailed by vigiling and becomes yet another form of family gathering.

The second opportunity for the assembling of the Christian community is the funeral liturgy, with the clearest expression of the Paschal Mystery being the celebration of the Eucharist. As the General Introduction to the funeral liturgy states:

At the funeral liturgy the community gathers with the family and friends of the deceased to give praise and thanks to God for Christ's victory over sin and death, to commend the deceased to God's tender mercy and compassion, and to seek strength in the proclamation of the Paschal Mystery. Through the Holy Spirit the community is joined together in faith as one Body in Christ to reaffirm in sign and symbol, word and gesture that each believer through Baptism shares in Christ's Death and Resurrection and can look to the day when all the elect will be raised up and united in the kingdom of light and peace. (129)

---

28. DeGrocco, Morrill, and Rutherford, *Guide for Celebrating Funerals*, 18–19.

Since the church is the place where the community of faith assembles for worship, the rite of reception of the body at the church has great significance. The church is the place where the Christian life is begotten in Baptism, nourished in the Eucharist, and where the community gathers to commend one of its deceased members to the Father. The church is at once a symbol of the community and of the heavenly liturgy that the celebration of the liturgy anticipates. In the act of receiving the body, the members of the community acknowledge the deceased as one of their own, as one who was welcomed in Baptism and who held a place in the assembly. Through the use of various baptismal symbols the community shows the reverence due to the body, the temple of the Spirit, and in this way prepares for the funeral liturgy in which it asks for a share in the heavenly banquet promised to the deceased and to all who have been washed in the waters of rebirth and marked with the sign of faith. (131)

As these instructions imply, there is no greater symbol of the Paschal Mystery than Christians assembling for the Eucharist, in gathering to perform what they have been trained to do week after week, in recollecting together with all of the wounds and warts that comprise human life. In the funeral liturgy, this symbol is particularly acute as the hope for new life is revealed in the dead body (a symbol perhaps diminished in the presence of cremated remains instead of the body).

Therefore, the oneness of the Body of Christ is meant to be abundantly clear at the threshold of the church. It is important to note that the OCF has limited the amount of words said as the body of the deceased is welcomed into the church. The symbol of the assembly, along with symbols of Christian faith speak for themselves. "As the community assembles to welcome the deceased into its midst for the last time," writes Smith, "it does so in the way the deceased in baptism began his or her journey of faith—with candle, water, cross, word, white garment and community."[29] After the greeting by the presider, the only words officially used at the door of the church are attached to the sprinkling of the casket with holy water: "In the waters of Baptism / N. died with Christ and rose with him to new life. / May he (she) now share with him eternal glory."[30] The pall is then placed on the casket,

---

29. Smith, *Facing Death Together*, 62. She continues: "Death for the Christian is a culmination of the pilgrimage of paschal faith that began in baptism."

30. OCF, 160.

followed by the entrance procession and the placing of Christian symbols on the casket when it has reached the foot of the altar.[31]

The absence of words as the body is brought into the church, marked with the waters of Baptism and clothed with a white garment symbolizing baptismal purity, is new in the 1989 OCF. In the 1971 *Rite of Funerals*, words accompanied both the sprinkling of the casket and the covering of it with a white pall. The decision to delete the words was made in accordance with the Council's call for "noble simplicity" in the reformed liturgies: "The rites should be marked by a noble simplicity; . . . they should be within the people's powers of comprehension and as a rule not require much explanation."[32] Nevertheless, notice the richness of the words that accompanied these gestures in 1971:

> I bless the body of N., with the holy water that recalls his (her) baptism of which Saint Paul writes: All of us who were baptized into Christ Jesus were baptized into his death. By baptism into his death we were buried together with him, so that just as Christ was raised from the dead by the glory of the Father, we too might live a new life. For if we have been united with him by likeness to his death, so shall we be united with him by likeness to his resurrection.

> and

> On the day of his (her) baptism, N. put on Christ. In the day of Christ's coming, may he (she) be clothed with glory.[33]

Furthermore, the 1971 text included a rubric for the inclusion of the Paschal candle in the procession: "It is appropriate that the paschal candle be carried in the entrance procession."[34] However, the Congregation for Divine Worship demanded that this instruction be omitted in the 1989 ritual. It may be argued that the absence of explanatory words in conjunction with the sprinkling of the casket and the placing of the pall, as well as the absence of the Paschal candle in the procession, make it quite difficult for

---

31. OCF, 161–163.
32. SC, 34.
33. *Rite of Funerals*, 38.
34. *Rite of Funerals*, 37.

the assembly to make the symbolic connections with Baptism.[35] This could be a missed opportunity to strengthen baptismal bonds.

The symbols at the threshold of the church are powerful and are designed to draw all into contemplation of the seriousness of their baptismal commitment. Take, for example, the white pall. A bulletin insert describes it as follows: "The pall, the long, white cloth that covers the casket at funerals, is another baptismal symbol. During the baptismal rite, a white gown, a symbol of new life in Christ, is worn. The placement of the pall recognizes that the deceased person is clothed with Christ."[36] This is a fine description of the pall. Being "clothed with Christ" shows forth the equality of those baptized into Christ. The funeral industry sells a wide range of caskets, from the least-expensive pressed-board box to the Cadillac models that may be covered in gold. However, in Christ, none of that matters. The funeral pall serves as a leveler. No matter what the casket may convey about wealth or social status, the pall reveals the deeper reality that no member of the Body of Christ is worth any more or any less than any other member. For this reason, the instructions to the funeral liturgy mandate the removal from the casket, at the church doors, national flags or insignia of clubs or associations to which the deceased belonged.[37] In Christ, there is no Canadian or Mexican, no Knight of Columbus or member of an altar and rosary society; all are clothed in Christ.

A Pilgrim People

One of the primary means of symbolizing the Church in the first few Christian centuries was the image of the ship. The Christian voyage begins at Baptism and continues until the day of the Lord's return. The success of this voyage depends upon all of the members of Christ's Body taking up their appointed tasks. No individual Christian would arrive at their destiny ahead of the entire Church. Hoeffner describes the symbol of the ship:

---

35. See Joseph Cunningham, "Chronicle: Revised *Order of Christian Funerals*," *Worship* 65 (1991): 60–64. Cunningham writes: "The Funeral Mass in the revised Order of Christian Funerals is pastorally flawed. Although the new prayers for various occasions are a welcome addition, the directives on symbols and their usage and the absence of familiar texts are a sore point with pastors" (60).

36. Kristopher W. Seaman, "Baptismal Symbols at Funerals," *Pastoral Liturgy*® 46, no. 5 (2015): 16a, www.pastoralliturgy.org/resources/BaptismalSymbolsatFunerals.pdf.

37. OCF, 38. "Only Christian symbols may rest on or be placed near the coffin during the funeral liturgy. Any other symbols, for example, national flags, or flags of insignia of associations, have no place in the funeral liturgy."

One of the most interesting aspects of this image is the fact that the dead and the living are all aboard the same ship. They constitute different ranks, represented by ladders, riggings and passengers; but all are tied together in the love of Christ. It is one Church. None arrive in the kingdom until all arrive in the kingdom. There is a unity, a communion, a relationship between the living and the dead, a common expectancy and hope, a common goal. There existed in the early church a communal or corporate eschatology.[38]

As has been seen, this corporate eschatology did not have a long staying power in the Church. The triumph of a theology of death centered on the fear of God's judgment and the sinfulness of the human person made Christians less desirous to complete the pilgrimage here on earth to continue it in the next life. They could not occupy themselves with the concern and well-being of others when so much attention needed to be paid to their individual soul.

However, true pilgrimage necessitates the abandonment of self-focus and a willingness to live in the moment. A pilgrim is one who lives in a sort of in-between space—neither here nor there—seeing life as always something more. Pilgrims are less concerned about controlling life than they are living life.[39] As one pilgrim writes: "Life's difficult passages, sorrows, crosses, even deaths necessarily lead to new life in all kinds of surprising and glorious ways. Keeping an eye peeled for grace ahead guards us from despair. . . . We fall, we fail, we harm one another. Then we rise, we reconcile, we heal, and we continue down the road."[40] The pilgrim way embraces life as an ongoing process. Even when the pilgrim reaches the so-called endpoint, his or her pilgrimage is not over; it has really just begun. So it is with our baptismal life. Each day is a choice to live as a disciple of Christ—to pick up, to heal, and to start anew.

The *Order of Christian Funerals*, in keeping with the Council's desire to reform the rite to "express more clearly the paschal character of Christian

---

38. Hoeffner, "A Pastoral Evaluation of the Rite of Funerals," 483–484.

39. See Edward Fischer, "Aging as Worship," *Worship* 52 (1978): 98–108. Similar to pilgrims who must surrender the need to control in order to complete the journey, the process of aging can be a seen as a vocation that gives praise to God by virtue of the forced acceptance of one's limits. Fischer writes: "By the time you grow old you should have learned to 'allow.' In youth you are no good at 'allowing'; you want to force everything right here and now. But as time passes you can learn to allow for less resiliency and above all learn to allow God to enter your life" (107).

40. Kevin A. Codd, "'I Am a Pilgrim on the Earth': The Pilgrim Way," *Worship* 84 (2010): 169.

death,"[41] demonstrates well the pilgrimage that is the life of the Christian community. The following passages from the General Introduction to the OCF make clear the journey and the destiny that comprise Christian faith:

> In the face of death, the Church confidently proclaims that God has created each person for eternal life and that Jesus, the Son of God, by his Death and Resurrection, has broken the chains of sin and death that bound humanity. (1)

> The proclamation of Jesus Christ "who was put to death for our sins and raised to life to justify us" (Romans 4:25) is at the center of the Church's life. The mystery of the Lord's death and resurrection gives power to all of the Church's activity. . . . The Church's liturgical and sacramental life and proclamation of the Gospel make this mystery present in the life of the faithful. (2)

> Since in Baptism the body was marked with the seal of the Trinity and became the temple of the Holy Spirit, Christians respect and honor the bodies of the dead and the places where they rest. Any customs associated with the preparation of the body of the deceased should always be marked with dignity and reverence and never with the despair of those who have no hope. (19)

> Processions, especially when accompanied with music and singing, can strengthen the bond of communion in the assembly. (41)

> Processions continue to have special significance in funeral celebrations, as in Christian Rome where funeral rites consisted of three "stages" or "stations" joined by two processions. Christians accompanied the body on its last journey. From the home of the deceased the Christian community proceeded to the church singing psalms. When the service in the church concluded, the body was carried in solemn procession to the grave or tomb. During the final procession the congregation sang Psalms praising the God of mercy and redemption and antiphons entrusting the deceased to the care of the Angels and Saints. The funeral liturgy mirrored the journey of human life, the Christian pilgrimage to the heavenly Jerusalem. (42)

It is important to restate that Baptism into Christ is a process. One never completes Christian initiation because there is always more growth that

---

41. SC, 81.

will take place in the Body of Christ. The funeral liturgy of the Middle Ages that led to the Requiem Mass was also based on the processual nature of life and death, but it placed too great an emphasis on the need to pray the dead out of purgatory. Rather than the "sleep" that was death in the early Church, the time of purification before sanctification was feared and considered something to be moved through as quickly as possible.

The OCF is designed so as to honor the passage of life into death as a process for the pilgrim Church. It intends for the Christian community to gather at the time of death, to keep vigil with the body, to console and walk with those most stricken by grief, to pray for the dead, and to bury the body "in the sure and certain hope"[42] that all will rise together in Christ. As the second part of the first station, with the vigil being the first, the OCF includes a section entitled "Related Rites and Prayers," comprised of "Prayers after Death," "Gathering in the Presence of the Body," and "Transfer of the Body to the Church or to the Place of Committal." The OCF states:

> These rites are signs of concern of the Christian community for the family and close friends of the deceased. The compassionate presence of the minister and others and the familiar elements of these simple rites can have the effect of reassuring the mourners and of providing a consoling and hopeful situation in which to pray and to express their grief.[43]

These three moments for prayer, in addition to the three standard services—vigil, funeral, committal—clearly demonstrate that walking through death is a process. It takes time to grieve and to heal, and the Christian community sets out to be companions with the bereaved on this journey. It takes time and ritual to acknowledge and understand the new role that the deceased has taken on in the Body of Christ.

Taking each of these rites sequentially, the "Prayers after Death" represents the Church's initial display of comfort for the mourners.[44] The invitation to prayer at the outset offers praise to the Father for the gift of his consolation, and the three choices of readings that follow all focus on the strength that is granted in prayer and the need for faith in the resurrection. After the reading, the Lord's Prayer is recited, and then the presider utters

---

42. OCF, 202.
43. OCF, 99.
44. OCF, 103.

two prayers (one for the deceased person and one for the mourners). The prayer for the deceased centers around an optimistic passage to "a place of refreshment, light, and peace":

Holy Lord, almighty and eternal God,
hear our prayers for your servant N.,
whom you have summoned out of this world.
Forgive his (her) sins and failings
and grant him (her) a place of refreshment, light, and peace.
Let him (her) pass unharmed through the gates of death
to dwell with the blessed in light,
as you promised to Abraham and his children for ever.
Accept N. into your safekeeping
and on the great day of judgment
raise him (her) up with all the Saints
to inherit your eternal Kingdom.
Through Christ our Lord.[45]

Absent from this prayer is any sort of fear or negativity about the dead person passing "though the gates of death." The "great day of judgment" is the joyful goal for which the Church lives out its daily journey in this life. This journey with the dead is emphasized even more in the prayer for the mourners that follows:

Father of mercies and God of all consolation,
you pursue us with untiring love
and dispel the shadow of death
with the bright dawn of life.

[Comfort your family in their loss and sorrow.
Be our refuge and our strength, O Lord,
and lift us from the depths of grief
into the peace and light of your presence.]

Your Son, our Lord Jesus Christ,
by dying has destroyed our death,
and by rising, restored our life.
Enable us therefore to press on toward him,
so that, after our earthly course is run,

45. OCF, 107.

he may reunite us with those we love,
when every tear will be wiped away.
Through Christ our Lord.[46]

This prayer uses the beautiful image of God "pursuing" us with love and opening for us the way to "the bright dawn of life." We "press on" toward Christ, hoping that the day will come when "every tear will be wiped away." The presider then prays the bold faith statement from Revelation 14:13: "Blessed are those who have died in the Lord; let them rest from their labors for their good deeds go with them," leads the community in the *Requiem aeternum*, and imparts a final blessing.[47] Once again, the clear and certain evidence of this rite points to a theology of death that is thoroughly paschal; the emphasis is on healing and newness of life.

A second moment on the passage through death, begun at the bedside of the dying person, is the "Gathering in the Presence of the Body." In a culture that denies death, contact with a dead body is generally avoided or to be feared. The OCF, therefore, includes a time for allowing mourners to face head on the reality and messiness of death. The rubrics governing the rite state:

> This rite provides a model of prayer that may be used when the family first gathers in the presence of the body, when the body is to be prepared for burial, or after it has been prepared. The family members, in assembling in the presence of the body, confront in the most immediate way the fact of their loss and the mystery of death.[48]

Often a minister may lead the immediate family in this rite as they gather for the public viewing. However, this misses the pastoral intention of the rite, which is intended to help mourners address the truth that death cannot be disguised. *Guide for Celebrating Funerals* states: "The ritual for Gathering in the Presence of the Body provides the family with the stark reality of their loss and causes them to come face-to-face with the mystery of death."[49] Therefore, the nature of this rite invites consideration of how some of the ancient rituals of preparing the body in the home might be reclaimed. While it is true that family members are not particularly eager

---

46. OCF, 107.
47. OCF, 108.
48. OCF, 109.
49. DeGrocco, Morrill, and Rutherford, *Guide for Celebrating Funerals*, 37.

to linger around the place of death, especially when the person dies in a hospital, Christians need to consider anew how to restore the display of reverence for the body of the deceased.

As with the prayers after death, the Gathering in the Presence of the Body is optimistic in nature and takes on the joyful sense of paschal passage. It begins with the Sign of the Cross and the reading of one of two brief Scripture verses, both of which focus on faith as lifting a burden.[50] The first ritual gesture around the body is the act of sprinkling it with holy water, accompanied by one of three formularies. The third formulary is the most expansive: "The Lord God lives in his holy temple yet abides in our midst. / Since in Baptism N. became God's temple / and since the Spirit of God lived in him (her), / with reverence we bless his (her) mortal body."[51] The reference here to baptismal dignity that continues to pervade the body of the deceased is clear. Furthermore, just as the singing of psalms and hymns accompanied the preparation of the body in the early Church, so does this rite intend for the singing or recitation of a psalm (either 130 or 115 and 116). Psalm 130 is both a profession of hope in God's loving mercy and kindness and a statement of "waiting for the Lord" (that is, the outlook of pilgrims):

> Out of the depths I cry to you, O Lord;
> Lord, hear my voice!
> Let your ears be attentive
> to my voice in supplication.
>
> If you, O Lord, mark iniquities,
> Lord, who can stand?
> But with you is forgiveness,
> that you may be revered.
>
> I trust in the Lord;
> my soul trusts in his word.
> My soul waits for the Lord
> more than sentinels wait for the dawn.
>
> For with the Lord is kindness
> and with him is plenteous redemption;

---

50. OCF, 112–113.

51. OCF, 114.

And he will redeem Israel
   from all their iniquities.[52]

Psalm 130 is clearly a prayer of patient waiting. This is followed by the praying
of the Lord's Prayer and the choice of two concluding prayers. Both prayers
ask the Lord to "welcome" the pilgrim safely home from his or her journey:

A:
God of faithfulness,
in your wisdom you have called your servant N.
out of this world;
release him (her) from the bonds of sin,
and welcome him (her) into your presence,
so that he (she) may enjoy eternal light and peace
and be raised up in glory with all your Saints.
Through Christ our Lord.

B:
Into your hands, O Lord,
we humbly entrust our brother (sister) N.
In this life you embraced him (her) with your tender love;
deliver him (her) now from every evil
and bid him (her) enter eternal rest.
The old order has passed away:
welcome him (her) then into paradise,
where there will be no sorrow, no weeping nor pain,
but the fullness of peace and joy
with your Son and the Holy Spirit
for ever and ever.[53]

Neither of these prayers offers much insight as to what the journey will look
like, but the welcoming into paradise is replete with "eternal light and
peace" and the "fullness of peace and joy." The rite concludes in exactly the
same way as the Prayers after Death: the statement from Revelation 14:13
is made, the Requiem aeternum is prayed, and a final blessing is imparted
by the presider.[54]

---

52. OCF, 115.
53. OCF, 117.
54. OCF, 118.

The third of the "Related Rites and Prayers" conjoined with the vigil section of the *Order of Christian Funerals* is entitled "Transfer of the Body to the Church or to the Place of Committal." This rite provides for the procession of the body. It is extremely simple and is meant to be a model "for the adaptation by the minister according to the circumstances."[55] However, as we discovered from the early Christian sources, the procession itself is a very important part of reordering the Church and a time for the public proclamation of faith in the resurrection. The instructions for this rite state:

> The procession to the church is a rite of initial separation of the mourners from the deceased; the procession to the place of committal is the journey to the place of final separation of the mourners from the deceased. Because the transfer of the body may be an occasion of great emotion for the mourners, the minister and other members of the community should make every effort to be present to support them. Reverent celebration of the rite can help reassure the mourners and create an atmosphere of calm preparation before the procession.[56]

The rite begins with an invitation by the minister that acknowledges that this assembly has gathered to both pray for "everlasting peace and rest" for the deceased and to gain hope in "the promise of eternal life."[57] A Scripture verse (either Colossians 3:3–4 or Romans 6:8–9) is read followed by a "litany" of praise directed to Christ for the many blessings that his Resurrection has bestowed upon the faithful departed.[58] For example, the first trope of the litany praises Christ for participation in eternal life through Baptism: "Word of God, Creator of the earth to which N. now returns: In Baptism you called him (her) to eternal life to praise your Father for ever: Lord, have mercy."[59] The praying of the Lord's Prayer follows, after which one of three concluding prayers is prayed by the presider. The first two refer to the mourners' grief and to the soul's transition to the "eternal Kingdom," to "your kingdom of light and peace," while the third option is solely for the strengthening of faith for those who grieve.[60] The minister invites those gathered to join in the procession: "The Lord guards our coming in and

---

55. OCF, 119.
56. OCF, 120.
57. OCF, 121.
58. OCF, 122–123.
59. OCF, 123.
60. OCF, 124–125.

our going out. / May God be with us today / as we make this last journey with our brother (sister)."[61] The rite then concludes with the procession and the singing (or reciting) of Psalm 122 with the antiphon "Let us go rejoicing to the house of the Lord" or other psalms or hymns.[62]

In our culture, in which the church or the place of burial are often some distance from the starting point of the body's transfer, the funeral procession has lost much of its symbolic value. The procession is considered more of a necessary movement to arrive at the next step in the ritual process. However, the journey itself is critical. With the body reverently cared for at the front of the procession, the Body of Christ moves together to allow itself to be gradually reformed anew.[63] Although it be only minutes in duration, the procession provides the stage for healing to take place. This procession is a corporate movement different from waiting in line for concert tickets or entrance into a civic arena; this is a people moving toward their final destiny. With weight on their feet, these Christians sing together in hope: "I rejoiced because they said to me, 'We will go up to the house of the Lord.' And now we have set foot within your gates, O Jerusalem."

While it may be difficult to form a procession of the entire Christian community to the church in preparation for the funeral liturgy, parish communities may do well to contemplate anew the symbolic and corporate value of the procession to the place of committal. This final movement of farewell is particularly important for all of the members of the Body of Christ to share. The instructions for the procession to the place of committal state:

> At the conclusion of the funeral liturgy, the procession is formed and the body is accompanied to the place of committal. This final procession

---

61. OCF, 126.

62. OCF, 127.

63. See Long, *Accompany Them with Singing*, 157. Although Long is writing here of the greeting of the body at the outset of the funeral liturgy, his description of the body's function with the assembled people applies to funeral processions in general. He writes: "In a funeral, the deceased is, in a sense, one of the worshipers, a member of the praying congregation in the way that he or she has always been. In another sense, though, the deceased person is obviously not just another worshiper. The death of this Christian is a main reason and context for this service. This is the last time this saint will be present in the body in this place of worship, and this is in part a service of farewell. God will be worshipped here and the Gospel proclaimed as always, but today this worship and proclamation will be done in the light of this particular person's life and death. Taken together, this means that the deceased should assume a both/and position—both as one among the congregation, and also as one this day prominent and visible."

of the funeral rite mirrors the journey of human life as a pilgrimage to God's Kingdom of peace and light, the new and eternal Jerusalem. (148)

Especially when accompanied with music and singing, the procession can help to reinforce the bond of communion between the participants. Whenever possible, Psalms or songs may accompany the entire procession from the church to the place of committal. In situations where a solemn procession on foot from the church to the place of committal is not possible, an antiphon or song may be sung as the body is being taken to the entrance of the church. Psalms, hymns, or liturgical songs may also be sung by participants as they gather at the place of committal. (149)

There should be no mistaking the pilgrim nature of these rubrics. The Church is not sent forth into the world after any Eucharistic liturgy as isolated individuals but rather as the Body of Christ, renewed in its bonds and confident of its faith. Thus, the funeral procession to the place of committal is an act of evangelization, as it reveals to the world our share in the resurrected life in Christ even (or perhaps most especially) in the face of death. As Owusu states: "The Church rejoices when it is able to hand over one of its members to the community of the saints. . . . The antiphon *In Paradisum* (Oe 69), which accompanies the procession to the burial place, more than being an intercessory invocation of the saints is a triumphant convocation."[64]

A Self-Giving People

The word *sacrifice* is not popular in a culture and age that thrives on the stockpiling of material possessions. Nor is it easy to talk about surrender of the self when the rights of the individual are considered sacrosanct. Yet Baptism into Christ is self-sacrifice. One is called upon to shed the self to live freely in Christ. As Paul writes: "I have been crucified with Christ and yet I am alive; yet it is no longer I, but Christ living in me" (Galatians 2:20). We live in a culture that celebrates individualism, and yet Christianity abides by another attitude: self-sacrifice for the other.

The early Church made the connection between sacrifice and death. At the moment of death, the community as a whole understood its responsibility for the other members. Whether it was through providing food for mourners, gathering for prayer and keeping vigil with the deceased, or

---

64. Owusu, "Funeral Rites in Rome and the Non-Roman West," 373.

celebrating a memorial meal at the graveside on anniversaries of the burial, the Christian community identified the bonds of its members as far more central to its existence than individual gifts and talents alone. As Christians in the Middle Ages increasingly developed fear as the major motif of death, it became more and more necessary to accentuate the individual merits and personal successes of the deceased in order to, perhaps, lessen the blow of God's punishment. The wealthy could afford to pay composers to write a beautiful Requiem Mass sure to delight the heavenly powers, but what about the poor? Funerals grew to be a form of social separation rather than a celebration of cohesion, just as Baptism became a sacrament of individual justification rather than a seal of corporate responsibility.

The means by which Christians are called to give of the self in the crisis of the death of one of their members are many. What is celebrated in death is the final and truest stripping of oneself; in death, any remaining vestiges of self-reliance are removed. "But in the end there is death," writes Mark Searle, "where we lose everything we have left to lose."[65] Thus, even in death, the dead person plays a role in the Body's self-offering to God. The General Introduction to the *Order of Christian Funerals* offers hints as to how the Christian community is called to sacrifice in the hour of death:

> Christians celebrate the funeral rites to offer worship, praise, and thanksgiving to God for the gift of life which has now been returned to God, the author of life and the hope of the just. The Mass, the memorial of Christ's Death and Resurrection, is the principal celebration of the Christian funeral. (5)

> Members of the community should console the mourners with words of faith and support and with acts of kindness, for example, assisting them with some of the routine tasks of daily living. Such assistance may allow members of the family to devote time to planning the funeral rites with the Priest and other ministers and may give the family time for prayer and mutual comfort. (10)

> The community's principal involvement in the ministry of consolation is expressed in its active participation in the celebration of the funeral rites, particularly the vigil for the deceased, the funeral liturgy, and the rite of

---

65. Mark Searle, *Called to Participate: Theological, Ritual, and Social Perspectives*, ed. Barbara Searle and Anne Y. Koester (Collegeville, MN: Liturgical Press, 2006), 40.

committal. For this reason these rites should be scheduled at times that permit as many of the community as possible to be present. (11)

Since liturgical celebration involves the whole person, it requires attentiveness to all that affects the senses. The readings and prayers, Psalms and songs should be proclaimed or sung with understanding, conviction, and reverence. Music for the assembly should be truly expressive of the texts and at the same time simple and easily sung. The ritual gestures, processions, and postures should express and foster an attitude of reverence and reflectiveness in those taking part in the funeral rites. (21)

A brief homily based on the readings is always given after the Gospel reading at the funeral liturgy and may also be given after the readings at the vigil service; but there is never to be a eulogy. (27)

These excerpts from the General Introduction suggest that the liturgies that surround death and burial require hard work, attentiveness, and great pastoral care. People are invited to take part in liturgical prayer in such a way that they surrender their preoccupations with self, and instead, contemplate the work of healing that Christ himself accomplishes within his Body.[66] The grace and noble simplicity in which symbols used in the funeral rites, such as the Paschal candle, the holy water, incense, or the bread and wine, are employed will aid the assembly in sacrificing the self in order to be immersed in the Paschal Mystery.

When a family loses a loved one, right away questions arise regarding how to best memorialize the dead. What suit would dad want to be wearing in the casket? What photos for a collage can be collected that best represent mom's life? Who should be granted the honor of being pallbearers, readers, and servers? These questions, while necessary, do not get at the central question for the death of a Christian—namely, how did the deceased let go of himself or herself in order to live anew in Christ? This question is, of course, much more difficult to answer than those that usually surface in the planning that goes into the funeral. However, this is the question to which the family and the community at large should ultimately be led to consider in the days of preparation, gathering for visitation and prayer, and

---

66. See Stephen S. Wilbricht, "Gesturing for an Epiphany: Renewing the Unspoken Language of Worship," *Pastoral Liturgy* 42, no. 5 (2011): 4–8.

ultimately, the question that lingers with us after the body is committed to its final place of rest.

The way in which the OCF treats God's Word demonstrates that the funeral liturgy is to be a sign that death is the final sacrifice of self. What is the purpose of the proclamation of the Word and what is the nature of the homily that is to follow? Families will often resent being told that it is not permissible to read a poem in place of one of the Scripture readings at the funeral Mass, and they bristle even more when they feel that the homily does not contain enough biographical information about their deceased loved one. However, the Church's wisdom needs to be appreciated here. Neither the reading of God's Word nor the liturgical homily are occasions for isolating a particular Christian, but rather, they are for unifying the Body of Christ. As stated in the introductory material for the funeral liturgy:

> The reading of the word of God is an essential element of the celebration of the funeral liturgy. The readings proclaim the Paschal Mystery, teach remembrance of the dead, convey the hope of being gathered together again in God's Kingdom, and encourage the witness of Christian life. Above all, the readings tell of God's design for a world in which suffering and death will relinquish their hold on all whom God has called his own.[67]

Thus, the readings for the funeral are not chosen based upon what they say about the dead, but rather about what they say about God working in the lives of all his faithful, living and dead. Participation in the readings at the funeral Mass ought to be a time of discovery, when members of the assembly recognize that the way in which they have been looking at the world is not necessarily the way in which God does. Hearing God's Word in the context of the funeral requires contemplating the question: how is God making all things new in this very moment, in this time of pain and suffering? This question, in and of itself, is expressive of a Christian attitude of sacrifice.

But even more letting go is required in the homily. Again, the introductory rubrics put forth the aim of the funeral homily:

> A brief homily based on the readings should always be given at the funeral liturgy, but never any kind of eulogy. The homilist should dwell

---

67. OCF, 137.

on God's compassionate love and on the Paschal Mystery of the Lord as proclaimed in the Scripture readings. Through the Homily, the community should receive the consolation and strength to face the death of one of its members with a hope that has been nourished by the proclamation of the saving word of God.[68]

Paragraph 27 of the praenotanda states that "there is never to be eulogy," and in paragraph 141, the same instruction is reinforced that the homily must never be "any kind of eulogy." The OCF does not specify precisely the reasons behind this mandate, but it is certainly that eulogizing about a person's achievements or history distracts the community from focusing on the Paschal Mystery, which is its grounds for hope. As John Melloh acknowledges: "Real tension exists between the eulogy and the homily . . . ; many people feel a need for the eulogy and many eulogies are regularly preached at funerals."[69]

Liturgists and pastors have wrestled for years with this instruction, recognizing the problem of a form of preaching at funerals that devolves into eulogizing, sometimes even functioning to "canonize" the deceased. Instead of the storyline being that of Christ, the story becomes that of the deceased. Yet the objective of every Christian funeral is to witness to God's victory over sin and death; the homilist tells how God has done this in the life of the person who has died. As Robert A. Krieg contends: "The funeral homily is not a eulogy. That is, it is not a speech in praise of a person's virtues and accomplishments. The funeral homily is a testimony. It attests to God's mysterious overtures among us and also to one person's response in his or her living and dying."[70] Krieg suggests that every life involves a narrative of God's invitation and a particular individual's human response, and that the objective of the funeral homily is to try to parallel that narrative to the drama of God's gift and Jesus' response of selfless love.[71] Krieg concludes:

> The homily should stress the readings in such a way that God's wondrous deeds are proclaimed, the deceased is honored, family and friends receive encouragement, and the hope of reunion is renewed. . . .

---

68. OCF, 141.

69. John Allyn Melloh, "Homily or Eulogy? The Dilemma of Funeral Preaching," *Worship* 67 (1993): 503.

70. Robert A. Krieg, "The Funeral Homily: A Theological View," *Worship* 58 (1984): 223.

71. Krieg, 234.

In this view the funeral homily is not a eulogy. It does not narrow its focus to one individual. It is a testimony about God's invitations and the response of one member of the human community. Therefore, the homily consists of a dialectic between the revelation of God in Jesus Christ and the unfolding of a human life. Through the interplay of these two sets of stories God is praised, the deceased is shown respect, and the congregation is drawn more deeply into the paschal mystery.[72]

While Krieg's argument is that the homily is not a eulogy because it is principally about the narrative of God's invitation made in human history, another argument may be made that preaching that turns to eulogy tends to be death-denying and self-indulgent. For example, in his article "The Unavoidable Discomforts of Preaching about Death," Richard Dillon contends that funeral preaching must center around the "obedience of death."[73] By this, the author means that Christians must be aided in seeing death as a pervasive part of life; death does not occur just at the end of life, it is something lived as an everyday reality. Learning to die is thus self-sacrificial. Dillon writes:

> Insofar as one yields the pursuit of personal interests and the aggrandizement of self in loving service of others, one already tastes the privation of death, especially because it is the death of Christ which provides both example and energy. When the ordinarily insatiable human ego is forced from center stage by the rule of Christ, it is quite accurate for the "wounded" to cry: "With Christ I have been crucified. Now it is not I who live, but Christ lives in me" (Gal 2:19). Such a union is not mystical rapture, but the self-sacrificial harmony of wills in the hard, down-to-earth business of everyday life. . . . One who has learned from the Lord's example to lay down one's life in others' service does not then face death at the end as an unwilling victim. . . . Dying is less alien, less shattering, to lives which were sacrificed in others' service all along.[74]

Death is always outside one's control (except in the case of suicide), and thus, life is all about the practice of relinquishing control. Dillon maintains

---

72. Krieg, 239.

73. See Richard J. Dillon, "The Unavoidable Discomforts of Preaching About Death," *Worship* 57 (1983): 486–496.

74. Dillon, 494.

that talking about death as "obedience to God's rule" is to be the nature of the funeral homily as a whole.[75] By dying in the flesh, the person has surrendered to the paradox of God's will; there can be no human accomplishment made on earth that is as great as this sacrifice of self. In fact, liturgy as a whole can be understood as a regular and repeated attempt to put on death, for as Mark Searle writes: "The 'sting' and 'victory' of death lie in death's ability to take our life against our will and hence to defeat us. If, on the other hand, we were to learn from the celebration of the paschal mystery to surrender our lives totally to God in Christ, the death of the Christian would be but the further and final rehearsal of a pattern learnt in life and practiced over and over again in a lifetime of liturgical participation."[76]

A Priestly People

The self-giving nature of the Church is very much tied to the understanding of the People of God as a nation of "priests." Baptism is rooted in discipleship; it entails service not only to one's brothers and sisters in faith but also to the world at large awaiting the coming of God's Kingdom. Ultimately, there is only one priest, Jesus the Christ, whose perfect sacrifice of obedient love on the cross won salvation for all. Those baptized into his name are called to participate in Christ's priestly ministry, a ministry of healing, reconciliation, and awakening hearts to God's rule. The Second Vatican Council's Decree on the Ministry and Life of Priests (*Presbyterorum ordinis*) states:

> The Lord Jesus "whom the Father consecrated and sent into the world" (Jn 10:36) gave his whole mystical body a share in the anointing of the Spirit with which he was anointed (see Mt 3:16; Lk 4:18; Acts 4:27; 10:38). In that body all the faithful are made a holy and kingly priesthood, they offer spiritual sacrifices to God through Jesus Christ, and they proclaim the mighty acts of him who has called them out of darkness into his admirable light (see 1 Pet 2:5, 9). Therefore there is no such thing as a member who does not have a share in the mission of the whole body.

---

75. Dillon, 495.

76. Mark Searle, "On Death and Dying," *Assembly* 5, no. 5 (1979): 49. He concludes this editorial with the following: "The liturgy does not instruct us about themes; it rather shapes and disciples us in a style of life, that of conformity to the dead and risen Christ."

Rather, all of the members ought to reverence Jesus in their hearts
(see 1 Pet 3:15) and by the spirit of prophecy give testimony to Jesus.[77]

All Christians, by virtue of their baptismal membership in the Body
of Christ, have a priestly vocation. While not necessarily called to the ministerial priesthood, theirs is to be a life of offering prayer and praise to God
for the salvation of the whole world and of enacting works of justice, love,
and mercy for all in need. The priestly work of Christians is not limited to
participation in the Eucharist but extends into the world in every way that
the saving power of Christ is given witness.

In terms of the funeral liturgy, the early Church, even though it often
suffered for its public manifestations of faith, would not hide its conviction
that with death comes hope. Instead of mourning with dirges of despair,
Christians publicly processed with psalms of joy and gladness. Instead of
gathering at the grave with gifts of food and drink for fear that the shadow
of the dead might curse the living, the early Church celebrated at the grave
as a way to mark the deceased's *dies natalis*, or true day of birth. But the
Church, from its conception, believed in the need to pray, not simply in the
company of the dead, but for the dead as well. Just as the dead could play
a role in guiding the Church on earth, so could the living continue to
strengthen their bonds with the dead through prayer.

Unfortunately, the individualization of death brought with it the gradual demise of witnessing to death as a graced opportunity for joy and celebration as well as the concomitant transformation of prayer for the dead
coming to mean prayer for the purgation of the soul. The absolution that
was inserted at the end of the funeral liturgy in the Middle Ages suggests
that the soul was to be presented to God for judgment rather than as a gift
of the continuing perseverance and self-sacrifice of the Church on its way
to heaven. The priestly role of the faithful would be limited to witnessing
to the power of rosaries and indulgences prayed with the intention to free
the dead from the possible descent into hell.

The *Order of Christian Funerals*, with its clearly established paschal overtones, helps to redefine the priestly ministry of Christians as it involves
dying, death, and hope in the resurrection of the dead. The following are a

---

77. *Presbyterorum ordinis*, 2.

few of the expressions the General Introduction provides of the priestly duty that all Christians are called to undertake when a fellow Christian dies:

> The celebration of the Christian funeral brings hope and consolation to the living. While proclaiming the Gospel of Jesus Christ and witnessing to Christian hope in the resurrection, the funeral rites also recall to all who take part in them God's mercy and judgment and meet the human need to turn always to God in times of crisis. (7)

> The responsibility for the ministry of consolation rests with the believing community, which heeds the words and example of the Lord Jesus: "Blessed are they who mourn; they shall be consoled" (Matthew 5:3). Each Christian shares in this ministry according to the gifts and offices in the Church. (9)

> In the celebration of the funeral rites laymen and laywomen may serve as readers, musicians, ushers, pallbearers, and according to existing norms, as extraordinary ministers of Holy Communion. Pastors and other Priests should instill in these ministers an appreciation of how much the reverent exercise of their ministries contributes to the celebration of the funeral rites. Family members should be encouraged to take an active part in these ministries, but they should not be asked to assume any role that their grief or sense of loss may make too burdensome. (15)

> Having heard the word of God proclaimed and preached, the assembly responds at the vigil and at the funeral liturgy with prayers of intercession for the deceased and for all the dead, for the family and all who mourn, and for all in the assembly. The holy people of God, confident in their belief in the communion of Saints, exercise their royal Priesthood by joining together in this prayer for all those who have died. (29)

Outside of their liturgical ministries, the Christian people exercise their priesthood in a myriad of ways by offering support to the grieving. Consolation can be as simple as the exchange of an embrace, the clutch of a hand, or the assistance given in wiping away a tear. "When a Christian dies," Smith writes, "the church offers its consolation in a variety of ways, giving attention to the spiritual needs of the bereaved as well as to their human psychological needs."[78] The OCF leaves the organization of most

---

78. Smith, *Facing Death Together*, 10.

forms of Christian consolation in the hands of individuals and communities, but it provides the contents of ritual that is intended to be executed as consolation.

Thus, it is helpful to look at several moments of prayer and what these convey regarding the ministry of the Christian community as a whole. To begin with, the several options for the opening Collect of the funeral Mass reveal the Church's conviction that it has the duty to pray for the dead. The first Collect from B. "Outside Easter Time" states:

> O God, who are mercy for sinners
> and the happiness of your Saints,
> give, we pray, to your servant N.,
> for whom (today) we perform the fraternal offices of burial,
> a share with your chosen ones in the blessedness you give,
> so that on the day of resurrection,
> freed from the bonds of mortality,
> he (she) may come before your face.
> Through our Lord Jesus Christ, your Son,
> who lives and reigns with you in the unity of the Holy Spirit,
> one God, for ever and ever.[79]

In this prayer at the outset of the liturgy, the Church acknowledges its duty to prayerfully bury the dead. The prayers that are uttered over the gifts prior to the Eucharistic Prayer are generally even more specific about the community's ministry being one of making offering for the purpose of reconciling the dead with God. The Prayer over the Offerings from A. "Outside Easter Time" reads:

> As we humbly present to you
> these sacrificial offerings, O Lord,
> for the salvation of your servant N.,
> we beseech your mercy,
> that he (she), who did not doubt your Son
> to be a loving Savior,
> may find in him a merciful Judge.
> Who lives and reigns for ever and ever.[80]

---

79. *The Roman Missal*, Masses for the Dead.
80. *The Roman Missal*, Masses for the Dead.

Likewise, the Prayer over the Offerings from Collection B "Outside Easter Time":

> Be near, O Lord, we pray, to your servant N.,
> on whose funeral day
> we offer you this sacrifice of conciliation,
> so that, should any stain of sin have clung to him (her)
> or any human fault may have affected him (her),
> it may, by your loving gift, be forgiven and wiped away.
> Through Christ our Lord.[81]

These prayers for the salvation of the deceased are prayed in hope. They are meant to express the Church's belief that a share in eternal life is a gift from God that cannot be won by individual merit. Thus, the ministry of prayer on the part of the Church is essential to the baptismal commitment of each of its members.

As with the orations at the opening of the funeral liturgy and over the gifts as the altar has been prepared, the intercessions in the Universal Prayer that conclude the Liturgy of the Word manifest the Church's belief that it has an obligation to pray for the dead as well as the living. These prayers are voiced in faith that God will transform creation according to his will; these prayers come from the heart of a priestly people.[82] The instructions for the funeral Mass state: "In the Universal Prayer (Prayer of the Faithful), the community responds to the proclamation of the word of God by prayer for the deceased and all the dead, for the bereaved and all who mourn, and for all in the assembly."[83] The *Order of Christian Funerals* contains two sets of intercessions that are meant to apply to the immediate circumstances and therefore may be rewritten for the particular occasion.[84] The pattern of the two sets of prayers each contains two intercessions for the deceased individual, for deceased relatives and friends, for those who have died in war, for those who have died and whose faith is known only to God, for the family and friends of the deceased, and for the faith of the entire assembly. The following intercessions from set A demonstrate the Church's ministry

---

81. *The Roman Missal, Masses for the Dead.*

82. See my "The History, Theology, and Practice of the Prayers of the Faithful," *Pastoral Liturgy*ª 41, no. 6 (2010): 4–8 (reprinted in Michael S. Driscoll and J. Michael Joncas, *The Order of Mass: A Roman Missal Study Edition and Workbook* (Chicago: Liturgy Training Publications, 2011), 327–339).

83. OCF, 142.

84. OCF, 167.

to pray for both the living and the dead who await the fullness of the resurrection:

> In Baptism N. received the light of Christ. Scatter the darkness now and lead him (her) over the waters of death.
> Lord, in your mercy:
> R. Hear our prayer.

> Our brother (sister) N. was nourished at the table of the Savior. Welcome him (her) into the halls of the heavenly banquet.
> Lord, in your mercy:
> R. Hear our prayer.

> Many people die by violence, war, and famine each day. Show your mercy to those who suffer so unjustly these sins against your love, and gather them to the eternal kingdom of peace.
> Lord, in your mercy:
> R. Hear our prayer.

> We are assembled here in faith and confidence to pray for our brother (sister) N. Strengthen our hope so that we may live in the expectation of your Son's coming.
> Lord, in your mercy:
> R. Hear our prayer.

These four examples point to the process that is death; not only does the Church pray for the dead to be ushered in to the "halls of the heavenly banquet," but it prays that the Church may "live in the expectation" of Christ's coming in glory. In other words, the death of a Christian jolts the Church into a certain reawakening, in which it sees beyond the veil of death into the joy of the Kingdom.

Furthermore, it is important to highlight that both sets of intercessions in the OCF contain collects to the Universal Prayer that are about the communion of all the souls who have died. Rather than being a prayer for the absolution of the particular deceased in whose memory the funeral liturgy is being celebrated, the collects pray for the oneness of all the dead. Both prayers are reproduced here:

Option A:
Lord God,
giver of peace and healer of souls,
hear the prayers of the Redeemer, Jesus Christ,
and the voices of your people,
whose lives were purchased by the blood of the Lamb.
Forgive the sins of all who sleep in Christ
and grant them a place in the Kingdom.
Through Christ our Lord.

Option B:
May the prayer of those who cry to you,
benefit the souls of your servants, O Lord:
free them, we pray, from all their sins
and make them sharers in your redemption.
Through Christ our Lord.

It is not uncommon to hear presiders change these orations to the Universal Prayer in such a way as to avoid mentioning the reality of sin. Note, however, that it is the forgiveness of the sin of all the dead that is the plea in these prayers. Overall, the Universal Prayer manifests clearly that death invites the Christian community to exercise a ministry of praying for the healing of the Body of Christ and the world as a whole. Just as every time the Church gathers to celebrate the Eucharist by opening with an attitude of contrition—"Brethren [brothers and sisters], let us acknowledge our sins, and so prepare ourselves to celebrate the sacred mysteries"—so too does the funeral liturgy allow Christians to exercise their priesthood in Jesus Christ by praying for the mercy of God for all who have died.

Finally, it is helpful to examine together the phraseology used in the Missal's five prefaces for the dead that the priest prays at the altar in union with those who have "lifted up their hearts to the Lord." The prefaces can be heard together as one giant testimony to the Christian hope in the resurrection of the dead, the hope that undergirds the mission of Christianity in general:

Preface I for the Dead: The hope of resurrection in Christ
In him the hope of blessed resurrection has dawned,
that those saddened by the certainty of dying
might be consoled by the promise of immortality to come.

Indeed for your faithful, Lord,
life is changed not ended,
and, when this earthly dwelling turns to dust,
an eternal dwelling is made ready for them in heaven.[85]

Preface II for the Dead: Christ died so that we might live
For as one alone he accepted death,
so that we might all escape from dying;
as one man he chose to die,
so that in your sight we all might live for ever.[86]

Preface III for the Dead: Christ, the salvation and the life
For he is the salvation of the world,
the life of the human race,
the resurrection of the dead.[87]

Preface IV for the Dead: From earthly life to heavenly glory
For it is at your summons that we come to birth,
by your will that we are governed,
and at your command that we return,
on account of sin,
to that earth from which we came.
And when you give the sign,
we who have been redeemed by the Death of your Son,
shall be raised up to the glory of his Resurrection.[88]

Preface V for the Dead: Our resurrection through the victory of Christ
For even though by our own fault we perish,
yet by your compassion and your grace,
when seized by death according to our sins,
we are redeemed through Christ's great victory,
and with him called back to life.[89]

These five prefaces bear no trace of a theology that is fearful of God's wrath; instead, they underscore God's compassion and the perpetuation of life after death in Jesus Christ. The powerful phrase from Preface I, "indeed for

---

85. *The Roman Missal*, The Order of Mass, 78.
86. *The Roman Missal*, The Order of Mass, 79.
87. *The Roman Missal*, The Order of Mass, 80.
88. *The Roman Missal*, The Order of Mass, 81.
89. *The Roman Missal*, The Order of Mass, 82.

your faithful, Lord, life is changed not ended," sums up belief in the Paschal Mystery. Likewise, rather than suggesting judgment as the end toward which human sinfulness leads, Preface IV contends that the death of an individual points to the day of corporate resurrection: "And when you give the sign, we who have been redeemed by the Death of your Son, shall be raised up to the glory of his Resurrection." All in all, these five prefaces to the Eucharistic Prayer for the funeral Mass reveal the priestly work of the Christian community—namely, that of proclaiming the power of Christ's Resurrection and the Church's participation in it. Work for the salvation of the world is being accomplished here, for the community "having been spiritually renewed at the table of God's word, turns for spiritual nourishment to the table of the Eucharist. The community with the Priest offers to the Father the sacrifice of the New Covenant and shares in the one bread and the one cup."[90]

A Holy People

In the fifth chapter of *Lumen gentium*, "The Universal Call to Holiness," the Council Fathers mandate that "all Christians in whatever state or walk in life are called to the fullness of Christian life and to the perfection of charity."[91] The history of Christian burial practices, however, demonstrates that as the Church became more organized along hierarchical lines, people began to distinguish holiness according to degrees. In the Middle Ages, people often sought to be buried in the disguise of a monk or a nun in the hopes that they would be seen as a holy person. Over the centuries, as religious life grew and spread throughout the world, and as the separation between the lay and clerical states became greater, holiness as a way of life was left up to those who chose a particular lifelong religious vocation. The Constitution on the Church upholds a different vision:

> The forms and tasks of life are many but there is one holiness, which is cultivated by all who are led by God's Spirit and, obeying the Father's voice and adoring God the Father in spirit and in truth, follow Christ, poor and humble in carrying his cross, that they may deserve to be sharers in his glory. All, however, according to their own gifts and

---

90. OCF, 143.
91. LG, 40.

duties must steadfastly advance along the way of a living faith, which arouses hope and works through love.[92]

Just as there is but one priest, Jesus Christ, there is also only one holiness that is distributed throughout the members of Christ's Body. When Christ breathed the Spirit upon the Apostles on the first day of the week (John 20:19–23), it was a universal charism that he was imparting to the Church. In the very same way, the funeral liturgy is a celebration of the one holiness that is ours. While recognizing the gifts each member offers the Church, the celebration of one's entrance into a new dimension of life in Christ is about the communion that all share.

While the Catholic Church celebrates a solemnity on November 1 for all the saints officially recognized and canonized, it understands the setting apart of particular holy men and women as a prelude to how all will be in the resurrection of the dead. The Constitution on the Sacred Liturgy states:

> In the earthly liturgy we take part in a foretaste of that heavenly liturgy celebrated in the holy city of Jerusalem toward which we journey as pilgrims, where Christ is sitting at the right hand of God, minister of the sanctuary and of the true tabernacle (see Rv 21:2; Col 3:1; Heb 8:2); we sing a hymn to the Lord's glory with the whole company of heaven; venerating the memory of the saints, we hope for some part and fellowship with them; we eagerly await the Savior, our Lord Jesus Christ, until he, our life, shall appear and we too will appear with him in glory (Phil 3:20; Col 3:4).[93]

Therefore, whether in heaven or on earth, the "saints" of God are meant to be one in their praise and adoration of the Almighty. The liturgy that is celebrated in time here in this world is meant to prepare us for the perfection of relationships as they were intended to be before God.[94] Where the human eye sees difference and separation, God is able to see communion. Ours is the vision contained in revelation: "These are the ones who have survived the time of great distress; they have washed their robes and made them white in the blood of the Lamb. / 'For this reason they stand

---

92. LG, 41.

93. SC, 8.

94. See Stephen S. Wilbricht, *Rehearsing God's Just Kingdom: The Eucharistic Vision of Mark Searle* (Collegeville, MN: Liturgical Press, 2013). This book examines the four major parts of the Roman Catholic Mass in terms of how they rehearse the baptized in embracing the worldview of Christ and, therefore, the practice of just relationships.

before God's throne / and worship him day and night in his temple'"
(Revelation 7:14–15).

Thus, the whole point of sanctity and growing together as a holy people is not to separate from or to avoid the "ugliness" and sin of this world
but rather to be able to see God's unifying grace in all things. The General
Introduction to the *Order of Christian Funerals* hints at this vision of holiness in several places:

> At the funeral rites, especially at the celebration of the Eucharistic
> Sacrifice, the Christian community affirms and expresses the union
> of the Church on earth with the Church in heaven in the one great
> communion of Saints. Though separated from the living, the dead are
> still at one with the community of believers on earth and benefit from
> their prayers and intercession. (6)

> Music is integral to the funeral rites. It allows the community to
> express convictions and feelings that words alone may fail to convey.
> It has the power to console and uplift the mourners and to strengthen
> the unity of the assembly in faith and love. (30)

> Prayerful silence is an element important to the celebration of the
> funeral rites. Intervals of silence should be observed, for example,
> after each reading and during the final commendation and farewell,
> to permit the assembly to reflect upon the word of God and the
> meaning of the celebration. (34)

While the OCF does not specifically spell out how "music" and "prayerful
silence" are related to the awakening of the assembly to God's vision of right
relationships, it is clear that both serve unifying purposes in the enactment
of liturgical prayer. Neither is meant to simply fill a void; rather, both are
meant to allow worshippers to experience their connectedness with others
in the assembly at a deeper level.

There is no doubt that the moment within the liturgy whereby attention is called to the participation of the dead in the Communion of the
Saints is at the final commendation. The instructions for the funeral Mass
contain the following description of the final commendation:

> The final commendation is the final farewell by the members of the
> community, an act of respect for one of their members, whom they
> entrust to the tender and merciful embrace of God. This act of farewell

also acknowledges the reality of separation and affirms that the community and the deceased, baptized into the one Body, share the same destiny, resurrection on the last day. On that day the one Shepherd will call each by name and gather the faithful together in the new and eternal Jerusalem. (146)

Whereas in the medieval sacramentaries this portion of the liturgy turned to prayers of absolution for the dead person's soul, the renewed ritual emphasizes the bonds that endure between the living and the dead. The final commendation begins with the presiding minister inviting the community to prayer. Both forms of this invitation express the desire for healing and for hope, and thus necessarily for the reordering of relationships in the Body of Christ:

Option A:
Before we go our separate ways, let us take leave of our brother (sister). May our farewell express our affection for him (her); may it ease our sadness and strengthen our hope. One day we shall joyfully greet him (her) again when the love of Christ, which conquers all things, destroys even death itself.

Option B:
Trusting in God, we have prayed together for N. and now we come to the last farewell. There is sadness in parting, but we take comfort in the hope that one day we shall see N. again and enjoy his (her) friendship. Although this congregation will disperse in sorrow, the mercy of God will gather us together again in the joy of his Kingdom. Therefore let us console one another in the faith of Jesus Christ.[95]

In both cases, the assembly is propelled into the future when there will be a reunion of friendship in heaven. It is interesting to note that the 1971 *Rite of Funerals* contains five options for the invitation to prayer at the final commendation, with Options D and E most closely resembling the prayers just cited; the 1989 translation has placed 1, 2, and 3 in chapter 20 (the last chapter of the ritual book).[96] Unlike the present invitations listed in the main body of the commendation liturgy, the first three of the 1971 rite

---

95. OCF, 171.
96. OCF, 402.

focus on the dead, justifying why God should have mercy on his/her soul. For example, Option A from the 1970 rite reads:

> With faith in Jesus Christ,
> we reverently bring the body of our brother (sister)
> to be buried in its human imperfection.
>
> Let us pray with confidence to God,
> who gives life to all things,
> that he will raise up this mortal body
> to the perfection and the company of the saints.
>
> May God give him (her) a merciful judgment
> and forgive all his (her) sins.
> May Christ, the Good Shepherd,
> lead him (her) safely home
> to be at peace with God our Father.
> And may he (she) be happy for ever
> with all the saints
> in the presence of the eternal King.[97]

While it could be argued that this invitation to prayer more specifically includes the deceased among the Communion of Saints, it fails to make reference to the destiny of the entire Church on its pilgrim way toward "the presence of the eternal king." The two invitations in the 1989 rite emphasize the healing of the whole Church. In them, the images of "greeting" the deceased as well as "seeing" them and "enjoying" their friendship call the Christian community to contemplate the purifying fire of God's love that reveals more of relationship than what we can ever experience on earth. Thus, how do we approach so great a mystery? With the silence mandated by the next rubric in the commendation liturgy.[98]

After the period of silence, which is to convey both farewell and respect, signs of farewell generally take place, such as the sprinkling of the casket with holy water (usually omitted so as not to suggest a repetition of the

---

97. *Rite of Funerals*, 46.

98. OCF, 172. See also paragraph 147, which states: "The pause for silence allows the bereaved and all present to relate their own feelings of loss and grief to the mystery of Christian hope in God's abundant mercy and his promise of eternal life."

greeting of the casket at the church doors) or honoring it with incense.[99] "Incense is a striking gesture," Joseph Cunningham maintains, "which should not be over-used or needlessly duplicated."[100] While the United States' version of the OCF expects that these gestures be accompanied by silence, the Canadian translation of the *Ordo exsequiarum* offers two spoken texts to clarify the use of water and incense at this point in the liturgy. First, if the sign of farewell is to be the sprinkling of the casket with holy water, the Canadian OCF includes this instruction for the assembly: "In baptism, N. shared in the death and resurrection of Christ. May he/she be welcomed into the glory of eternal life."[101] If, instead, incense is employed as a sign of farewell, the Canadian version provides these words for catechesis: "As a sign of respect for our brother/sister, N. we let this incense rise to God, who has called him/her to share in his glory."[102] Some would argue that eliminating such words of instruction is detrimental to the assembly's participation; however, what is more important is the way in which these symbols convey reverence and respect. As Smith contends: "The assembly needs to see and smell clouds of incense. . . . The incensing must be done thoroughly and mindfully, to make clear the sense of circling the deceased in a touching gesture of respect and honor."[103]

The honor paid to a holy life through the incensation is echoed in the hopeful song of farewell that follows.[104] The text provided in the OCF is the familiar "Saints of God," which may be sung to a variety of tunes. This text is hopeful, as it is a joyful song of reception for the soul in heaven. At the same time, it is expressive of the union among the saints of God in heaven and the saints of God who plod through life on earth:

> Saints of God, come to his (her) aid!
> Hasten to meet him (her), angels of the Lord!
> R. Receive his (her) soul and present (him) her to God the Most High.

---

99. OCF, 173. See also Smith, *Facing Death Together*, 77. She writes: "The rite is brief and poignant, inviting the assembly to bid its farewell in both sign and song and to commend the deceased to the care of God and the company of saints. This rite can easily be misunderstood, particularly since water and incense are used as signs of farewell, whereas at the same point in our old funeral rites they were signs of purification and absolution."

100. Cunningham, "Revised *Order of Christian Funerals*," 64.

101. *Order of Christian Funerals*, Canadian Conference of Catholic Bishops, © International Committee on English in the Liturgy, Inc., 1985, 342.

102. OCF (Canada), 342.

103. Smith, *Facing Death Together*, 78.

104. OCF, 174.

May Christ, who called you, take you to himself;
may angels lead you to the bosom of Abraham.
R. Receive his/her soul and present him (her) to God the Most High.

Eternal rest grant unto him (her), O Lord,
and let perpetual light shine upon him (her).
R. Receive his (her) soul and present him (her) to God the Most High.

The song of farewell, in which the assembly is invited to envision the angels and saints hastening to embrace the newly arrived soul into paradise, is the confident expression of hope in the resurrection of the dead. It affirms the transition of the deceased into the "perpetual light" of God and consoles those who remain with the assurance of God's grace and mercy toward the dead. The OCF states: "The song of farewell, which should affirm hope and trust in the Paschal Mystery, is the climax of the rite of final commendation. It should be sung to a melody simple enough for all to sing."[105] All are meant to participate in the singing of this song because the communion it heralds is the communion that is to be the living sign of the Church: the Body of Christ is one!

The next component component of the final commendation is the prayer of commendation itself.[106] The rite offers the choice between two prayers, both quite similar to the prayers in the 1971 translation. Option B limits the commendation to the soul of the deceased, while Option A more fully includes a thanksgiving for the blessings of the person's life and a plea for the ongoing consolation of family and friends. The point of this latter prayer is clear: commendation of the faithful departed entails ongoing thanksgiving and transformation, just as does participation in the Paschal Mystery of Christ demand gratitude and a willingness to be converted anew each day. The text of this prayer is as follows:

Into your hands, Father of mercies,
we commend our brother (sister) N.
in the sure and certain hope
that, together with all who have died in Christ,
he (she) will rise with him on the last day.

---

105. OCF, 147.
106. OCF, 175.

[We give you thanks for the blessings
which you bestowed upon N. in this life:
they are signs to us of your goodness
and of our fellowship with the Saints in Christ.]

Merciful Lord,
turn toward us and listen to our prayers:
open the gates of paradise to your servant
and help us who remain
to comfort one another with assurances of faith,
until we all meet in Christ
and are with you and with our brother (sister) for ever.
Through Christ our Lord.

Abundantly clear in this prayer of commendation, and in the overall liturgical action of farewell, is the absence of a tone of absolution. Recall the final prayer of absolution at the end of the funeral Mass prior to the 1969 revisions:

O God, whose property is ever to have mercy and to spare, we humbly beseech Thee on behalf of the soul of Thy servant N., which Thou has this day called out of this world, that Thou wouldst not deliver him (her) into the hands of the enemy, nor forget him (her) for ever, but command that he (she) be taken up by Thy holy angels and borne to our home in paradise, that having put his (her) hope and trust in Thee, he (she) may not suffer the pains of hell, but may come to the possession of eternal joys.[107]

This prayer is a direct pleading of the faithful on behalf of the deceased for the liberation of the soul from the "hands of the enemy" and the "pains of hell." The new prayer, however, offers images of "fellowship with the saints of Christ" and the hope that God will "open the gates of paradise" to the deceased. The phrase "in the sure and certain hope" could be used in preaching and catechesis on the Christian attitude toward death; our hope in the resurrection of the dead is forever sure.

The last ritual element of the final commendation is the procession to the place of committal. It begins with the deacon or priest offering the

---

107. *Saint Andrew Daily Missal*, 1654.

invitation: "In peace let us take our brother (sister) to his (her) place of rest."[108] The 1997 appendix on cremation offers an alternate form of dismissal if the committal is delayed or if the body is to be cremated before interment: "In the sure hope of the resurrection, / we take leave of our brother (sister): / let us go in peace."[109] The procession then begins, accompanied by music and song. Of all the ritual processions in the complex of funeral rites, this is the most important. As the rubrics for the funeral Mass state: "This final procession of the funeral rite mirrors the journey of human life as a pilgrimage to God's Kingdom of peace and light, the new and eternal Jerusalem."[110] However, such seriousness is rarely given today to the ritual enactment of the procession. The assembly exits through the church doors and either lingers to chatter or scatters as quickly as possible to avoid traffic congestion. Herein lies a most prophetic way that the Church can express its belief in the resurrection—brothers and sisters, united in Christ, walking as one and singing with conviction: "May the angels lead you into paradise; may the martyrs come to welcome you and take you to the holy city, the new and eternal Jerusalem."[111] This is the Church that is not ashamed to demonstrate her holiness.

Conclusion

As this chapter comes to an end, there should be no doubt in the reader's mind that the 1969 *Ordo exsequiarum* and its translations have proven to be successful in restoring the paschal nature of the funeral liturgy. Gone is the fear that predominated the 1614 ritual, as well as many of its forerunners, and duly established is the conviction that the funeral liturgy is a celebration of life. Smith writes:

> Since the OCF sees death as part of a movement from life to life, or from baptism to baptism, there is much that is baptismal about its rites. The sacrament of baptism is an anticipation of death, ushering the new Christian into the journey that will culminate in death. Death then is celebrated in a baptismal way. The cluster of symbols by which the new Christian was welcomed in baptism—the assembly gathered around

---

108. OCF, 176.
109. OCF, 437.
110. OCF, 148.
111. OCF, 176.

the paschal candle, the sign of the cross, the water bath, the white garment—these same symbols find a natural home in those rites with which the Christian is given farewell.[112]

Even in the face of life ended tragically, the OCF promotes an environment of hope and joy, whereby the Christian community is invited into deeper contemplation of the mystery of Christ's sorrowful death and glorious Resurrection. The 1971 *Rite of Funerals* and its 1989 successor, the *Order of Christian Funerals*, demonstrate the Christian belief that the dead are part of an established "order" of the Church, that they have entered into a time of eschatological waiting that is at the core of the Church's nature; "the deceased passes with the farewell prayers of the community of believers into the welcoming company of those who need faith no longer but see God face to face."[113] The funeral rites point to a Church that is based on baptismal unity. *Lumen gentium* concludes its first chapter with this beautiful image: "The church, 'like a stranger in a foreign land, presses forward amid the persecution of the world and the consolations of God,' announcing the cross and death of the Lord until he comes (see 1 Cor 11:26)."[114] The dead remind us that patient waiting for the Kingdom of God that is already-but-not-yet is our life, our identity, and our mission on earth and in heaven. John P. Meier writes: "The deceased is a member of the church. And the church still looks forward to Christ's Parousia, to the resurrection of the dead, to what Paul describes as the handing over of the kingdom to the Father, when God will be all in all."[115]

At this point, the reader might wonder why no attention has been given to the third station of the funeral rites, the rite of committal. Like the vigil and the funeral liturgy, the rite of committal has been reformed to "express more clearly the paschal character of Christian death."[116] However, of the three stations, it is probably the least effective for moving the grieving process toward appropriate resolution and leading the Church to a reestablished sense of incorporation in Christ. At the grave, or at another place of interment, death continues to be disguised and does not ritually support

112. Smith, *Facing Death Together*, 22–23.
113. OCF, 206.
114. LG, 8.
115. John P. Meier, "Catholic Funerals in the Light of Scripture," *Worship* 48 (1974): 214.
116. SC, 81.

transition into the last stage of passage, that of reintegration. More and more, the burial of the dead is being delayed or has become a private affair for the family, failing to allow for the liturgical participation of the community as a whole. Thus, the final section of the last chapter will explore how the rite of committal might be more a liturgical celebration of the Paschal Mystery, whereby those at the place of interment are led to look deeply into the reality of death and be even more convinced of the promise of resurrection.

What remains to be asked is the following: although the funeral rites have been successfully renewed so as to reclaim the paschal joy that surrounded death in the early Church, have they truly restored the ecclesial nature of death that so undergirded the development of burial rites at the outset of Christianity? Is it not the case that funerals, regarded mostly as "celebrations of life," magnify the life accomplishments and the unique qualities of the deceased rather than honor how the deceased's individual gifts and talents contributed to a profound union with the Body of Christ, a union more important than any personal achievement one might make? Furthermore, are not so many decisions surrounding death made to provide comfort and convenience and privacy for families at the expense of the believing community's need to fulfill its obligations to reorder the Church and to faithfully celebrate the transition of the dead to a new status within Christ's Body? The reality is that while the liturgy of death has been thoroughly reformed, the attitudes of the surrounding culture generally win the day and overshadow the Church's faith. We turn to these and other daunting conundrums in the last chapter.

CHAPTER FIVE

Contemporary Conundrums and Pastoral Possibilities

Death itself, we should remember, holds an important place in the mystery of Christian life; the death of any one Christian is a community, ecclesial affair. It places demands on the entire community, requiring the Church's immediate attention to the needs of the deceased and the living.[1]

The primary principle for the reform of the liturgy that was established by the Second Vatican Council is the promotion of participation on the part of all engaged in worship. *Sacrosanctum Concilium*, 14, mandates that "in the reform and promotion of the liturgy, this full and active participation by all the people is the aim to be considered before all else." When each member of the assembly is fully participating in the corporate prayer of the Church, witness is given to the oneness that is the Body of Christ. Our baptismal life becomes both tangible and palpable. The liturgy itself is thus a means of evangelization. The Constitution on the Sacred Liturgy states:

> Liturgical services are not private functions, but are celebrations belonging to the Church, which is "the sacrament of unity," namely, the holy people united and ordered under their bishops.

> Therefore liturgical services have to do with the whole Body of the Church; they manifest it and have effects upon it; but they also concern the individual members of the Church in different ways, according to their different orders, offices, and actual participation.[2]

The very nature of the liturgy, whether it be the celebration of Mass or the execution of a sacrament or a sacramental (such as a blessing), is to manifest the unity of the Body, thereby revealing the unity that is ours in Christ. *Sacrosanctum Concilium* goes on to say that this sacramental oneness is

---

1. Rutherford, *The Death of a Christian*, 131.
2. SC, 26.

best achieved when "when each one, minister or lay person, who has an office to perform, should do all of, but only, those parts which pertain to that office by nature of the rite and the principles of liturgy."[3]

Therefore, at the outset of this final chapter, the questions considered are the following: Although the funeral liturgy in its three stational rites of vigil, funeral liturgy proper, and committal have been renewed to manifest death as a communal matter that leads to a newly ordered Church, has there been an embrace of "full, conscious, and active participation" in all that these rites truly entail? Or do the structure and the fullness of the rites give way to cultural demands and family concerns, such as time constraints, social fears, economic worries, and even traditional piety, preventing the community from enacting its responsibility "to care for the dying, to pray for the dead, to comfort those who mourn"?[4] For example, the *Order of Christian Funerals* states that the vigil service for the deceased may either take the form of a Liturgy of the Word or a portion of the Office for the Dead, yet in many places, the vigil never takes place or the praying of the Rosary continues to be the preferred form of communal prayer at the time of visitation.[5] Praying the Rosary may seem less formal for families or more in accord with the tradition of past generations (that is, "something that grandma liked to do"). However, this means that devotional prayer substitutes for the living Word of God, a word specifically chosen for the community's instruction and consolation.[6] Thus, have Christians been educated on the importance of the vigil liturgy, and do parish communities see that their assembling for this form of corporate prayer is the work of manifesting the oneness of Christ's Body for the healing and consolation of all who mourn?

Most likely, the answer to these questions reveals a universal disappointment: death continues to be experienced in an individualistic way in

---

3. SC, 28.

4. OCF, 8.

5. OCF, 54.

6. See DeGrocco, Morrill, and Rutherford, *Guide for Celebrating Funerals*, 133. The authors write: "The liturgical rites of the Church should be the family's priority for the wake. However, the pastoral approach considers how to appropriately incorporate the family's requests. Certainly the official rites of the Church—actions of the Body of Christ—take precedence over devotional prayers like the Rosary. Therefore, the Funeral Rites should not be replaced or eliminated—the Vigil Liturgy should be the main form of prayer at a wake or visitation. However, perhaps another time can be found for the Rosary; for example, if the Vigil Liturgy is going to be conducted in the evening, then the Rosary can be prayed in the afternoon."

our Christian communities. The liturgical rites are published and in place to handle death as a communal process, but so often these rites are discarded or short-circuited. The symbols and gestures of the Paschal Mystery are replaced by photos and memorabilia of the dead. Liturgical music that speaks of the resurrection and the Communion of Saints is trumped by the contemporary twangs that the dead heard on the radio and hummed in the shower. Families are usually well intentioned in their desire to redesign the liturgy. They wish to replace or omit certain aspects of the funeral rites to create an environment of greater intimacy in which the uniqueness and personal attributes of the deceased might be on center stage. However, stimulating the imagination to try to keep alive the memory of the deceased in this life is too limited in scope. Christians need to remember the promise of the life yet to come. Eternal life is the antithesis of anything individualistic; it is the life of perfect unity in Christ.

Therefore, both the "contemporary conundrums" and the "pastoral possibilities" that are highlighted in this final chapter center around the building up of the Body of Christ. While pastors and funeral planners must be sensitive to the wishes of the family, respecting their need for privacy, the funeral rites are, first and foremost, a celebration of the Church. In other words, pastoral sensitivity must accompany a deep concern for the participation of the parish community. Ansgar Franz, who calls the Christian community the "bearer" of the Christian burial liturgy, writes:

> In contrast to the clear tendencies of the secular obsequies to privatization and familiarization on the one hand and to the centering on the speaker on the other, the Christian burial liturgy is a celebration that is borne by the community. This is not only a theological necessity that comes from baptism, but also a practical necessity. The realization of the form of ritual participation requires participants who actively carry the ceremony; and those immediately affected by the death are by themselves not in a condition to do this. This is very much the case with the singing, and it is of fundamental importance to break into song against death. It will be necessary to strengthen the consciousness in the communities more clearly than we have in the past, that therein lies a genuine task of Christian ministry.[7]

---

7. Franz, "Everything is Worthwhile at the End," 67.

There is no question that the funeral industry today makes it possible for families to execute so many aspects of the disposal of the dead in private. Often the need that the community has to ritualize the passage from death to new life of one of its members is totally forgotten. If the Catholic faith is going to continue to hold firm to the belief that the dead belong to the Communion of Saints and that the Church of the baptized are together making a journey into the fullness of God's Kingdom, then the death of a Christian must once again become an ecclesial affair, one by which the death of an individual is a faithful step forward on the Church's pilgrimage toward the heavenly banquet. The poetic words of Mark Searle are particularly appropriate for this corporate understanding of death: "The pilgrimage of faith is not a journey in a straight line, with death waiting at the end, but a kind of spiral through which progress is made only in successively deeper experiences of death and rebirth."[8] Thus, the Christian community must be truly invested in every aspect of dying, death, and burial, for "deeper experiences of death and rebirth" is its very nature.

Society's Denial and Disguise of Death

A major part of renewing the funeral rites in order to make them more paschal, and therefore more about the Body of Christ, is the healthy acceptance of death. In fact, a fundamental component of the Paschal Mystery is that Jesus selflessly embraced the suffering of the cross that would be born as a perfect sacrifice for the Father. It is this approach to suffering and death that Christians claim to rehearse each time they celebrate the Eucharist, for here the self is offered together with the entire Body of Christ to be returned to the Father. Even when death is not put into the framework of paschal living, there is no escaping it. Greg Lehmen calls death "life's quiet companion," and he writes: "Death for us is not the musket shot or the hangman's noose. It is not the high-powered rifle of the mass murderer. Death is part of the spirit of our existence: an event which moves and changes us."[9] Death is a part of each person's life.

---

8. Mark Searle, *Christening: The Making of Christians,* cited in Wilbricht, *Rehearsing God's Just Kingdom,* 203.

9. Greg Lehmen, "Life's Quiet Companion," in *The Penguin Book of Death,* ed. Gabrielle Carey and Rosemary Sorensen (Ringwood, Vic., Australia: Penguin, 1997), 224.

However, such an approach toward death is no longer a societal norm. Ariès contends that "the modern attitude toward death, that is to say the interdiction of death in order to preserve happiness, was born in the United States around the beginning of the twentieth century."[10] So many facets of culture in the United States work to keep death at bay. From the huge array of commercials for medications of every sort touted to help a person live better and longer, to injections that will eliminate wrinkles and signs of aging, to the building of senior living centers that ensure one stays active and alert, we do everything we can to prolong life. In the words of J. M. Cameron, "Now we have the impression that death is something that can be postponed almost indefinitely through surgery and the use of antibiotics."[11] Even after one has died, every effort is taken by the funeral industry to disguise death: the embalmed body is carefully made to appear lifelike, the casket looks as comfortable as a couch, the grave is covered with artificial grass, making the bare earth invisible. Ariès states:

> Thus during the wakes or farewell "visitations" which have been preserved, the visitors come without shame or repugnance. This is because in reality they are not visiting a dead person, as they traditionally have, but an almost-living one who, thanks to embalming, is still present, as if he were awaiting you to greet you or to take you off on a walk. The definitive nature of the rupture has been blurred. Sadness and mourning have been banished from this calming reunion.[12]

Hospitals have served the same function in our society. They have relocated the drama of dying into a sanitized arena that promotes contemplation of the science of medicine rather than of the mystery of suffering and death. All of this has led to the mindset that death can be controlled rather than confronted.

Beyond the highly sophisticated funeral business and the commercialized medical world, the liturgy itself can foster the disguise of death and the fears associated with it. If the liturgy bends too much in the direction of a joyful celebration of life, the stinging bite of death often goes unaddressed. John Meier writes: "There is a danger that the so-called 'Mass of the Resurrection' (a designation apparently quite popular with funeral

---

10. Ariès, *Western Attitudes toward Death*, 94.
11. J. M. Cameron, "On Death and Human Existence," *Worship* 50 (1976): 259.
12. Ariès, *Western Attitudes toward Death*, 101–102.

directors) can become a votive mass in honor of Saint Pollyanna. It is insipid and insensitive to speak only of joy and triumph when the mourners in the pews are trying to grapple with the real mysteries of pain, suffering and sometimes tragedy."[13] Thus, while the prevailing Christian outlook toward death must always lead to hope, the liturgy must help promote authentic grieving and must acknowledge the truth of real separation. The funeral liturgy underscores the already-but-not-yet reality of Christ's victory. Meier writes: "And so the church, while rejoicing in Christ's triumph, still prays that at some future date she and all her departed may share fully in that triumph."[14]

With the critique that the *Order of Christian Funerals* has not served as an ally in combating the denial of death that is pervasive in today's society,[15] the truth is that communities struggle to employ the rite in its fullness. The addition of the section "Related Rites and Prayers" to the 1989 OCF is evidence that the Church provides public rituals to accompany the process of bereavement. "These rites are signs of the concern of the Christian community for the family and close friends of the deceased. The compassionate presence of the minister and others and the familiar elements of these simple rites can have the effect of reassuring mourners and of providing a consoling and hopeful situation in which to pray and to express their grief."[16] The three rites of this section—"Prayers after Death," "Gathering in the Presence of the Body," and "Transfer of the Body to the Church or to the Place of Committal"—"provide opportunities to express grief and emotions in a faith context."[17] They allow those closest to the deceased the opportunity to face death head on with all its ugliness and pain, and to put this suffering into a faith perspective. The OCF states: "The

---

13. Meier, "Catholic Funerals in the Light of Scripture," 209.

14. Meier, 214.

15. See Robert Sparkes and Richard Rutherford, "The Order of Christian Funerals: A Study in Bereavement and Lament," *Worship* (1986): 499. Regarding this critique the authors write: "The mandate of the Constitution on the Liturgy that the funeral rites be revised to express more fully the paschal mystery was aptly met in the Rite's emphasis on the Lord's victory over death. Yet where the Rite has failed to fulfill that same mandate has been the source of the principal criticism leveled against the revision. The cross as instrument of victory is still the cross—death by crucifixion—death in all its harsh, faith-challenging reality. Calvary touched by Easter remains Calvary. Without due emphasis on *pascha passio* in Paul and the Fourth Gospel, the New testament profession of pascha transitus would have been a half truth. From this perspective, where the *Rite of Funerals* has failed to fulfill expectations is in its apparent inability to express sufficiently the pain and suffering of human loss in the face of death."

16. OCF, 99.

17. Sparkes and Rutherford, "The Order of Christian Funerals," 507.

family members, in assembling in the presence of the body, confront in the most immediate way the fact of their loss and the mystery of death."[18]

Although the process of washing the body and preparing it for burial has long been turned over to funeral directors, and would undoubtedly be largely undesirable to retrieve as a Christian tradition, interaction with the body is important in facing the reality of death.[19] Hoeffner comments: "[S]ome simplified version, even a ritual washing of hands and face, some signs of respect and separation must be observed if the reality of death is to be grasped by the living, and if the human foundation for establishing a new relationship is to be called to mind at the moment of death."[20] In the ritual "Gathering in the Presence of the Body," the minister has the option of sprinkling the body with holy water.[21] It is possible for the presider to mention that this water was blessed in the context of the praying community, who participates in this prayer through the bonds of Baptism. Furthermore, family members and friends might be invited to mark the body with the water and then to trace the Sign of the Cross upon the body at the time of the final blessing.[22] The family might also consider the possibility of placing a small cross or crucifix or the rosary in the hands of the deceased before the body is taken away for final preparation. One of the goals of these rites is to help the mourners to accept the reality of death, letting go of fears and resisting the desire to shirk it. Sparkes and Rutherford comment: "Like lament these rites offer a faith-filled space to express emotions and suffering and to reaffirm our bonds with God and the deceased."[23]

Given the fact that these moments of prayers are generally quasi-private in nature, how does the Christian community as a whole participate in them? The reality is that they are indeed designed to be intimate occasions of prayer for the immediate family and closest friends. This is where parishes might discover the praying of the Office for the Dead as a valuable treasure. It is here that the Christian community may realize its baptismal

---

18. OCF, 109.

19. It is worth noting that Orthodox Jews continue to maintain a ritual washing of the body to this day. One source states: "Jewish laws mandate the proper preparation and interment of the deceased's body. Before the body is buried, it is washed with warm water by devoted members of the Jewish community. The body is washed completely, but never left to rest face down." Taken from https://www.funeralwise.com/customs/jewish/orthodox/ (accessed February 25, 2018).

20. Hoeffner, "A Pastoral Evaluation of the Rite of Funerals," 495.

21. OCF, 114.

22. OCF, 108 and 118.

23. Sparkes and Rutherford, "The Order of Christian Funerals," 507–508.

identity as a priestly people, offering prayer specifically for the deceased and the family. The *Order of Christian Funerals* states:

> In the celebration of the Office for the Dead members of the Christian community gather to offer praise and thanks to God especially for the gifts of redemption and resurrection, to intercede for the dead, and to find strength in Christ's victory over death. When the community celebrates the hours, Christ the Mediator and High Priest is truly present through his Spirit in the gathered assembly, in the proclamation of God's Word, and in the prayer and song of the Church. The community's celebration of the hours acknowledges that spiritual bond that links the Church on earth with the Church in heaven, for it is in union with the whole Church that this prayer is offered on behalf of the deceased.[24]

Even though the family may be unaware that the Church offers this prayer for them, a great bond of unity is shared, as the rubric just cited suggests. In fact, this is one of the ways in which the dead minister to the Church: because of their death, the Christian community assembles and recognizes its oneness in Christ once again. It is also a way that the community works to puts its grief into the framework of the Paschal Mystery; it confronts its sorrow in order to strengthen its hope in God's promise that we have won redemption.

The renewed baptismal identity of the Christian community is beautifully communicated in the rubric that describes the function of the psalmody within the office for the dead:

> In praying the Psalms of the Office for the Dead, the assembly offers God praise and intercedes for the deceased person and the mourners in the words of prayer that Jesus himself used during his life on earth. Through the Psalms the assembly prays in the voice of Christ, who intercedes on its behalf before the Father. In the psalms of petition and lament it expresses its sorrow and its firm hope in the redemption won by Christ. In the Psalms of praise the assembly has a foretaste of the destiny of its deceased member and its own destiny, participation in

---

24. OCF, 349. See also OCF 350 and 351, which state respectively: "The celebration of Morning Prayer from the Office for the Dead relates the death of the Christian to Christ's victory over death and affirms the hope that those who have received the light of Christ at Baptism will share in that victory." "Through Evening Prayer from the Office for the Dead the community gives thanks to God for the gift of life received by the deceased and praises the Father for the redemption brought about by the sacrifice of his Son, who is the joy-giving light and the true source of hope."

the liturgy of heaven, where every tear will be wiped away and the Lord's victory over death will be complete.[25]

Whether or not a community is accustomed to gathering for daily Morning or Evening Prayer, the death of one of its members is an appropriate occasion to call the members together as one. Thus, catechesis on the Office for the Dead might lead parish communities to embrace this form of prayer as a principal component of their ministry to the dead and those who are grieving. The OCF instructs that pastors and other ministers should "encourage members of the parish community to participate in the celebration as an effective means of prayer for the deceased, as a sign of their concern and support for the family and close friends, and as a sign of faith and hope in the Paschal Mystery."[26]

The *Order of Christian Funerals*, like the *Rite of Christian Initiation of Adults*, is designed to be an elongated process of conversion that is marked by successive public steps expressive of the growth in faith. Just as the RCIA is designed to be an encounter with the living Christ that is experienced in daily life and celebrated within the context of the Christian community, so the *Order of Christian Funerals* is meant to celebrate a deepening of faith and hope in the Risen Lord. It does not expect that grief will be overturned in an instant, but rather, the rituals are designed to help the community discover insight along the journey toward burial. The Church must work to challenge society as a whole to strip away all that shields her from encountering and accepting the brutal reality of death.

Honoring the Process of Bereavement

Beyond working to ensure that the rituals that the OCF prescribes are neither eliminated nor minimized, the Body of Christ needs to be catechized on a Christian theology of death and educated on how it might assist in the bereavement process. While the funeral liturgy, in all its stational aspects, is to help the community reorder itself, complete with a renewed worldview on the Paschal Mystery, the participation of the community in bereavement ministry is a primary way it enacts its identity as a holy people. Sparkes and Rutherford describe the bereavement process as follows:

---

25. OCF, 355.
26. OCF, 368.

The bereavement process comprises a series of emotional and cognitive states leading to adaptation to the loss. They have no fixed order. One state of bereavement, once experienced, may recur and it is possible for the bereaved to become stuck in one or other state. Ordinarily the first response of a person to the news of a death is one of shock, numbness, and disbelief. The bereaved experience a sense of unreality and denial, particularly when the news is unexpected. These initial reactions help the bereaved to deal with the death gradually. Feelings of anger and/or distress appear when the bereaved begins to face the reality of the news. He or she may continue to deny the reality and seek escape by way of fantasies associated with death.[27]

The grieving process is both private and public. Mourning can lead to the seeking out of companionship, but it often points in the direction of isolation. Denial is best supported when one does not have the input of other voices. This is precisely where the ministry of the Christian community can be of preeminent value. In reaching out toward those most immediate to death in simple ways, such as preparing and delivering food to the family, performing the daily chores that belonged to the deceased, and in simply being present to the family, the Christian community enacts a ministry of bereavement. The acceptance of individualism as a guiding attitude in our society and the fear of invading the privacy of others often prevent us from reaching out in such simple ways. Our baptismal commitment ought to keep us from following this social pattern.

There are programmatic ways in which the local parish might help guide and support bereavement as a process. First, the Christian community does not need to wait until the death of one of its members to reflect on the meaning of death. Death education, which would include studying a Christian theology of death, talking about how the surrounding society is at odds with Christian values on death, and creating strategies on how to confront death as a community when it occurs, is possible for all parishes. Ernest Morgan writes in *Dealing Creatively with Death: A Manual of Death Education and Simple Burial*:

Death education is for everyone, because it relates not just to death but to our feelings about ourselves and nature and the universe we live in. A prime function of death education is to help us think and feel deeply

---

27. Sparkes and Rutherford, "The Order of Christian Funerals," 501.

about the meaning of life in its many relationships—to help mature our values. . . . Confronting death imaginatively through experience, reading, thinking, lectures, and discussions often has the paradoxical effect of enriching life.[28]

For instance, a local community could easily read and discuss a classic work on bereavement, such as C. S. Lewis' *A Grief Observed*, or it could process together a more contemporary study on grieving, such as Sandra Gilbert's 2006 work *Death's Door: Modern Dying and the Way We Grieve*.[29] It might also be helpful to invite local morticians to talk to the community about the process of planning funerals, the options that are possible for burial, and the financial costs that are associated with cremation and embalming.

However, the ministry most needed in parish communities is that which follows up with mourners long after the funeral rites have concluded. This is a time that is particularly critical in the bereavement process. As Sparkes and Rutherford write: "After the funeral, the dominant experience is the pain of separation. The dead person is absent, yet the survivor's home and environment contain constant reminders of the deceased. It is a period of grieving with intense distress, yearning, pining and longing."[30] Turning to the model embodied in the *Rite of Christian Initiation of Adults*, the final period of formation called "mystagogy" might be adapted for use at this stage in the bereavement process. Mystagogy is the time devoted to post-baptismal reflection on the sacraments of initiation and the first steps of Christian life as they have thus far been experienced by newly made Christians, the neophytes. For instance, during the period of mystagogy, the newly baptized share with each other what they experienced during the Easter Vigil, what they heard, what they saw, what they smelled, what they touched, and how they felt. The experience of one person sparks the imagination of another, and new insight is generated. Of this time of formation, Kathleen Hughes writes, "[C]ommunal reflection such as this is a healthy antidote to a privatized religion and a tendency on the part of North

28. Ernest Morgan, *Dealing Creatively with Death: A Manual of Death Education and Simple Burial* (Hinesburg, VT: Upper Access, 2001), 1.

29. See C. S. Lewis, *A Grief Observed* (New York: Harper and Row, 1961) and Sandra Gilbert, *Death's Door: Modern Dying and the Way We Grieve* (New York: W.W. Norton, 2006).

30.Sparkes and Rutherford, "The Order of Christian Funerals," 502.

Americans to rugged individualism, especially when it comes to communicating deeply held religious insights and convictions."[31]

In the case of a parish bereavement process, those who have experienced the death of a family member or close friend could be invited to gather to discuss what they experienced in the celebration of the funeral liturgy as well as in the subsequent days and weeks. Did any of the symbols used in the funeral help them to make the connection with Christ's death and Resurrection? Did the participation of the community help the family to grieve appropriately? How has the experience of the Sunday Eucharist since the funeral been a source of healing and consolation? One of the most important aspects of mystagogy in the initiation process, and likewise in the bereavement process, is the value it places on the individual's experience. Hughes writes:

> The key to mystagogical reflection is that it is subjective rather than objective; it is about my experience and your experience of an encounter with God through the sacramental celebration. The mystagogical task is to enable the newly baptized to reflect on their personal experience of celebration and what it triggered in their inner world, to move from a vague awareness of the mystery dimension of their lives to a greater conceptual and affective clarity. And to find a proper way to continue to allow experience and expression to inform one another. Only through a pooling of our experiences will we have anything even approaching a full sense of the presence and power of God active in those who believe.[32]

No two people experience death in the same way. With representatives of the local community to guide the discussion—men and women who have gone through some training in death education—the various perspectives shared on death and the emergence of new life will surely serve the faith development of mourners and members of the Body of Christ alike. Furthermore, establishing such a program as a year-round facet of the parish allows everyone to see that encountering death, just like living a baptismal commitment, is a process that never ends.

Besides parish programs for bereavement, the Body of Christ might also be actively engaged in rituals of healing throughout the year. Rituals

---

31. Kathleen Hughes, *Saying Amen: A Mystagogy of Sacrament* (Chicago: Liturgy Training Publications, 1999), 13.

32. Hughes, 15.

may be designed that are outside the realm of the Church's official liturgy but are designed to be a form of corporate prayer to assist in the grieving process. Of such rites, Susan Marie Smith writes, "[F]or there to be new resurrected life, there must be *real death*. In order for there to be forgiveness, there must be *honestly acknowledged sin*. In order for there to be a healing ritual, there must be willingness and readiness to grow, to change, to embrace new life—and thus for the truth to be neither denied, nor avoided, nor minimized."[33] An example of such a healing ritual that could easily be employed in the parish, even without the direct involvement of ordained clergy, is a "Consolation Candle Service" that both gives thanks for blessings and intercedes for greater faith and trust. Easily adaptable with song and movement, this service is reproduced here in full:

Consolation Candle Service[34]

Seven candles are placed on a stand, a platform, an altar, or any other space that allows the candles to be seen by all. Seven individuals light each of the candles in turn. Appropriate instrumental music plays as a background to the ritual, and a single voice, perhaps alternating female and male voices, reads each of the seven sections.

We light a candle for love:
for the love that we have shared with those who are precious to us;
for the love that flows deep within us that will never end;
for the love that has lived through changing times and events;
for the love that grew from small seeds into great oak trees within us;
for the love that lifts up our spirits and our hearts.

We light a candle for joy:
for the joy that gave birth to so many positive moments,
days and years;
for the joy that our loved ones experienced during their
time here on earth;
for the joy and smiles those near to our hearts gave and received;

33. Susan Marie Smith, "Rites of Healing Along the Baptismal Journey: An Example and Several Principles," *Liturgy* 22 (2007): 55–56.

34. Attributed to the Reverend Christopher J. Heller, an adaptation of "Holiday Helps Candle Service," Annual Ministry of Consolation Program, St. Gerard Majella Church, Port Jefferson Station, New York, 1999 and 2000. Service found in Abigale Rian Evans, *Healing Liturgies for the Seasons of Life* (Louisville, KY: Westminster John Knox Press, 2004), 312–314.

for the joy that flowed from the accomplishments our loved ones
performed and witnessed;
for the joy that gave encouragement to those who would follow in
their footsteps.

We light a candle for memories:
for the memories of gathering, holidays and unrepeatable
special occasions;
for the memories of smells and sounds and meals together that
satisfied far more than our appetites;
for the memories of times together that reminded us of what it
means to be human;
for the memories of faces and voices that are records of our journey
together with others;
for the memories of the people who not only gave us gifts, but who
truly were gifts to us.

We light a candle for tears:
for the tears that flow from our eyes and down our chins at
a moment's notice;
for the silent tears that arrive for no apparent reason, and those
that no one else sees or hears;
for the tears of joy as we remember jokes and stories we have shared
with our loved ones;
for the tears that point us toward our true feelings, and root us in
time and eternity's deepest truths;
for tears that signal an inner release, a new freedom, a relief shared
with those we mourn.

We light a candle for hope:
for the hopes and dreams and plans we shared with those precious
to us;
for the hope and trust we place in the power to continue loving those
whom we have lost in death;
for the hopes our loved ones carried within their hearts and spirits;
for the hope that brings forth in us a confidence to love others now
without regrets;
for the hope and desire to look forward to the next stage of loving
anew those who are close to us.

We light a candle for peace:
>for the peace that we want for our loved ones and for ourselves;
>for the peace that is even deeper than our words and feelings
>>can express;
>for the peace that focuses us for now, and helps us to claim our place
>>in the world;
>for the peace that joins time and eternity in an eternal song of love;
>for the peace that helps to heal the distance that separates us one
>>from another.

We light a candle for strength:
>for the strength that comes from deep within me and sustains me;
>for the strength that empowers me to live each moment and each
>>day to the fullest;
>for the strength that encourages me to live one day at a time
>>without regrets;
>for the strength that allows forgiveness to heal the unfinished parts
>>of our relationships;
>for the strength that allows us to remember those who have left their
>>imprint on our hearts.

This healing service, which employs the sensory symbol of light mixed with intercession and blessing, is just one creative ritual response to the grieving process. Certainly, this prayer could be adapted to incorporate communal singing, the proclamation of the Word, and a brief homily. Parish communities must find ways of being innovative in their attempts to create ritual around bereavement.

Another service for the purposes of bereavement may be found in the resource *Changes: Prayers and Services Honoring Rites of Passage*.[35] The Episcopalian service, "Remembering a Departed Soul," opens with an appropriate gathering song, a greeting, and an opening collect.[36] The congregation is then invited to listen to the Word of God as well as excerpts from poems or other readings. After a brief homily, the assembly professes the Apostles' Creed. The service concludes with the prayers of the people, which express both petition and thanksgiving.[37] These prayers, listed here,

---

35. *Changes: Prayers and Services Honoring Rites of Passage*, (New York: Church Publishing Incorporated, 2007).

36. *Changes* , 75–76.

37. *Changes* , 77–78.

testify to the belief that grieving is an ongoing process, just as is the journey of Baptism:

> Lord Jesus Christ, you are Resurrection and Life: Hear our prayers on behalf of our brother, N.; (for N. and N.), for this whole community, and all who continue to mourn his departing. Even as we grieve, we also give thanks for the fullness of joy in which he lives with you now, and toward which we faithfully travel in healing and hope. We speak N's name in assurance of his eternal life with you, and ask your healing help for our wounded hearts.
> We pray to you, Jesus.
>
> We thank you for the way he lived, and for the love he gave us, rejoicing in the knowledge that he has returned to your paradise where there is no sorrow or sighing, but eternal joy in your presence.
> We pray to you, Jesus.
>
> We lay our grief before you, for you also grieved at the grave of your friend, Lazarus. Give us courage to open our hearts to others, and to weep tears that still need to fall.
> We pray to you, Jesus.
>
> We thank you for all relationships, for those whose love brings us joy; help us testify to your presence in this broken world.
> We pray to you, Jesus.
>
> We ask you to help us live our faith, to take up our work, to correct our course when we stray from you, to give and forgive, and to seek your face in all that we do, so that when we, too, come to die, we will surely have known the fullness of life.
> We pray to you, Jesus.
>
> We thank you, Jesus, for those who have gone before us. Through their lives you helped us learn that in every season of life and death you are near us, standing firm when we falter. We long for the time when your own hand will dry all our tears. Be our Companion this day, our path on the way, and our door to life eternal, as we place ourselves in your love, O Christ, who, with our Father and the Holy Spirit, live in glory everlasting. Amen.

Notice that these prayers, while very much attentive to the joy the deceased soul experiences in God's presence, are largely for the mission of the

Church, in which the "opening" of hearts and the "weeping" of tears is for the good of others. These prayers seek God's help to reveal his presence "in this broken world," to "give and forgive," and to follow Christ "our path on the way." The mystery of death and the work of bereavement are to be contemplated in the framework of Baptism.

The early Christian community attended to the grave as a place of bereavement. Gathering there to celebrate the dead on such occasions as the third, the seventh, and the thirtieth day after death as well as on the annual anniversary of death, was a way that the community continued to maintain a relationship with those who were farther along in the journey toward the Last Day. Today visits to the graveside are typically a private affair. Placing flowers at the grave is done individually. There are simple ways that the local church might address this. Most parishes maintain the tradition of inviting parishioners, in exchange for a small stipend, to identify the names of the deceased to be remembered at daily or weekend Masses. These Mass requests are generally identified in the bulletin. However, more corporate work needs to take place. For example, one Mass each month or every few months might be designated as a time to remember all of the recently deceased in the life of a parish. The names of the dead could be read aloud, and the Mass could even conclude with a communal visit to the cemetery. Here is an example of a prayer for the community one month after a death that could be prayed at the burial place:

> Gracious God, we have lived a month without N. Even in our deepest grief, the work has begun to fill the gaps left by her death. You have sent us consolation through the precious offerings of friends. Yet we continue to need your comfort and help in the work of mourning and healing. We commend N. to your care, as she grows daily in your presence. We pray through Jesus, the Christ, in whom we too look forward to the joys of heaven, and with whom in the Spirit we pray. Amen.[38]

Another corporate gesture of assisting in the bereavement process might be to appoint grief counselors who could be publicly blessed by the Sunday assembly and sent forth to visit and console those who are mourning. So often this work falls to the parish priest; the parish as a whole needs

---

38. *Changes*, 72. See also Janet S. Peterman, *Speaking to Silence: New Rites for Christian Worship and Healing*, 158–163. Here the author offers personal testimony about the importance of making an annual visit to the grave, and she provides an outline of how a communal worship at the grave might unfold.

to be invested in this corporal work of mercy. Finally, public display of *The Book of the Names of the Dead*, with the names of the parish's deceased inscribed within, is a beautiful way of reminding the faithful that the dead are not forgotten but are with us still.[39] While the possibilities for compassionate outreach to the grieving are endless, the ultimate concern is that the community as a whole ought to be actively engaged in it, and, at the very least, must be aware that care is being offered in its name and on its behalf.

Funerals Planned for Convenience, Not for Community

The *Order of Christian Funerals* calls for involving the family in the preparation process for the funeral rites: "Whenever possible, ministers should involve the family in planning the funeral rites: in the choice of texts and rites provided in the ritual, in the selection of music for the rites, and in the designation of liturgical ministers."[40] It also suggests that, if pastorally appropriate, this planning take place prior to death so that the dying Christian might better "face the reality of death with Christian hope."[41] Making plans for the funeral rites may also serve as a valuable time of catechesis, in which the minister of care might be able to discuss the Paschal Mystery in light of the present circumstance of death. However, because of the reality of denial as well as the emotional stress at the time of death, funeral planning often centers on what can be done to spotlight the uniqueness of the deceased (rather than the deceased's participation in the Body of Christ and the Paschal Mystery) as well as how to limit the inconvenience and/or avoid the fears of those closest to the dead. In other words, consideration of the community's need to celebrate the Lord's victory over sin and death in the life of this particular Christian is forgotten.

The foundation of catechesis on the death of a Christian is the recognition that the rituals that celebrate the transition from death in this world

---

39. See DeGrocco, Morrill, and Rutherford, *Guide for Celebrating Funerals*, 142. The authors write: "*The Book of the Names of the Dead* was inspired by the ancient practice of recording the dates of the deaths of loved ones in a necrology, a public record or registry of death. This practice provides the living with an opportunity for healing and consolation in the face of grief. . . . Some parishes place *The Book of the Names of the Dead* near the vestibule or gathering space. Others display the book near the baptismal font with the lighted Paschal candle nearby, symbolizing the deceased have shared in the waters of Baptism, dying with Christ and rising to now share in Christ's Resurrection."

40. OCF, 17.

41. OCF, 17.

to new life in the next are designed to herald Christ. They are designed to sound the transitus of Christ as the pattern of life for the entire community. All facets of planning funeral rites ought to return to the work of proclaiming Christ in his Body. An example of attention to this basic detail can be found in a funeral planning source by Bryan Wolfmueller, *Final Victory: Contemplating the Death and Funeral of a Christian.*[42] Representing the Lutheran tradition, Wolfmueller writes:

> The funeral service is a public service of the Church. It is a public confession of the faith concerning death, burial, resurrection, and the life hereafter. The baptismal theme of death and resurrection with Christ is most prominent (Romans 6:1–11). The funeral service, then, is the public proclamation of the marvelous and gracious works of our great God and Savior, Jesus, applied to this specific situation. In the service, we join the saints and angels, the Church in heaven and on earth, in giving thanks to the Lord Jesus for the gifts He has won and delivered to us in His death and for the comfort Christians find in the resurrection.[43]

The final chapter of this resource, entitled "Confessing Christ with My Funeral," contains a planning worksheet that asks the basic question: "How might I best confess the Lord Jesus to my friends and family?"[44] The objective in funeral planning, whether done by the dying Christian prior to his or her death or by the family after the death of a loved one, is not to choose Scripture or music according to what might be a favorite but according to what might best reveal the Risen Lord.[45] Once again, it is so tempting to make decisions based upon the likes/dislikes of the deceased and family members, but the funeral liturgy is about the Church, and the rites must bear the weight of proclaiming Christ.

Another issue at stake in the preparation process for the funeral liturgy, beyond the selection of music and Scripture that focuses on the Paschal

---

42. Bryan Wolfmueller, *Final Victory: Contemplating the Death and Funeral of a Christian* (St. Louis, MO: Concordia Publishing House, 2009).

43. Wolfmueller, 21.

44. Wolfmueller, 49.

45. Wolfmueller, 49–50. Wolfmueller writes: "When choosing Scripture texts and hymns, people often ask, 'Which one is my favorite?' This is a fine question, and it is a gift from God that we have our favorite texts and songs. When planning our funeral service, though, we want to understand this selection a bit more. Why is this my favorite? What does it say about Jesus? How does it give the promise of forgiveness, the hope of the resurrection?"

Mystery, is the selection of liturgical ministers. The OCF offers the following instruction:

> In the celebration of the funeral rites laymen and laywomen may serve as readers, musicians, ushers, pallbearers, and according to existing norms, as extraordinary ministers of Holy Communion. Pastors and other Priests should instill in these ministers an appreciation of how much the reverent exercise of the ministries contributes to the celebration of the funeral rites. Family members should be encouraged to take an active part in these ministries, but they should not be asked to assume any role that their grief or sense of loss may make too burdensome.[46]

Those who serve as liturgical ministers for the Sunday assembly are expected to be men and women, young and old, who have demonstrated a particular charism for service to the Body of Christ. Readers are commissioned not just to read but to proclaim the Word of God filled with the conviction of faith. Our funeral services deserve the same kind of attention to quality ministry. Much is sacrificed when a family member is asked to serve as a reader and is neither a dynamic reader nor is able to proclaim the Word without being overwhelmed by emotions. The Liturgy of the Word, which leads to a recommitment of faith in the death and Resurrection of Christ and of those who follow him, must be executed gracefully.

A parish that recognizes its baptismal core will organize ministries for the funeral rites and will recommend them for the family's selection. For example, while pallbearers are generally chosen on the basis of a close familial relationship or friendship connection to the deceased, a ministry of serving as a pallbearer for the local community could easily be developed. Imagine a cohort of parishioners who are recognized publicly as caring for the body of the dead as it makes its final procession to the grave. Such a ministry would help to tie in the deceased's life with the parish as a whole. Furthermore, where state law allows, this ministry could be responsible for sharing in the digging of the grave or at least in the burying of the body (depending on state law). Rather than departing from the committal before the body has been lowered into the grave, a parish's team of pallbearers could physically lower the casket into the grave and proceed to cover it with earth. Does this make things more complicated? Indeed it

---

46. OCF, 15.

does. It will take hard work and effort to establish such a ministry, but when it is in place, it could have a huge effect on the symbolic imagination of those participating in the funeral rites. Providing for liturgical ministers, who represent the local church as a whole and not simply a relationship with the deceased, will help to reveal the oneness of the Body of Christ and will serve as a tremendous act of hospitality for those overcome with grief. A parish that is able to demonstrate that we are in this together will have a far greater healing effect for members of the family than will the honoring of friends and family with haphazardly undertaking liturgical ministries with which they are unfamiliar.

In many places, such an emphasis on the fruitful coordination of ministries fulfilled by the members of the Body of Christ will frustrate funeral directors who have taken an active role in filling many of the duties that were once the responsibilities of fellow Christians. Preparing the body for viewing, transporting the body, closing the casket, greeting mourners at the doors of the church, interring the body, as well as a wide array of other customs have largely been transferred to the funeral industry. However, the *Order of Christian Funerals* is clear that Christians bear the primary responsibility of caring for the dead: "[T]hose who are baptized into Christ and nourished at the same table of the Lord are responsible for one another."[47] Margaret Smith contends:

> This is not to suggest that funeral directors do not have the right to offer particular services, nor is it to devalue the genuine service that is offered. Neither does it question the vocation of Catholic funeral directors and their role in the church's ministry, ministry that is its responsibility and privilege to exercise—a ministry that no director or funeral home can replace. It is in the context of the ecclesial community that Christians are made, married, reconciled, healed and gather Sunday after Sunday. It is within that same ecclesial context that the church's ministry of consolation and prayer takes place. The funeral home is not an ecclesial environment.[48]

It might be valuable, therefore, to include funeral directors in the process of organizing public ministry for funeral liturgies. These professional men and women may very well have good insights to share concerning best

---

47. OCF, 8.
48. Smith, *Facing Death Together*, 145.

practices, and including them in a discussion of ministry will help them to understand better the need for the community to perform ministry on behalf of the Body of Christ.

A final suggestion for the fruition of corporate ministry at the time of the death of a member of a parish is the establishment of burial societies.[49] A burial society's chief mission would be to provide for the funeral of a poor person, guaranteeing that poverty has no bearing on the dignity of one's life or death. If there are to be no rich or poor in the Body of Christ, then those who are poor should be treated with the same respect at death as those who are rich. Referring to nineteenth-century England, Rowell suggests that a burial guild works to ensure the equanimity of burial services: "[A] burial guild, frequently with a membership drawn from two or three parishes, would provide a bier, a violet pall with a red cross worked on it, a white pall for the young, and would employ an undertaker or carpenter, who would work to the specifications of the guild. . . . The guiding principle was to deal with death in a devout and real manner, and avoid 'all idle, vain displays of worldly pomp' and 'all trifling and sentimentality.'"[50] If the death of a Christian is meant to be a celebration of reordering the Body of Christ, then burial societies could serve as tangible reminders that funerals are, first and foremost, for the parish community and not only for the family. This may sound harsh, but consider the valuable role that would be played by a group of parishioners working to keep funerals from becoming lavish displays of individualism instead of simple and venerable symbols of a life shed in order to be raised up again in Christ.

Ritualizing Christian Values and Beliefs

In his essay "Towards a Christian Theology of Death," John Hick offers this simple Christian challenge toward society's outlook on death: "Christian faith seeks to match death as the totally unknown with a total trust in the love of God. . . . We can only say that in so far as the trust is real and operative it must take the final sting out of death, the sting of ultimate meaningless and vacuity, and must thereby deprive the grave of its victory over life."[51] There is no doubt that Christianity has a great deal of work to do to

---

49. See Rowell, "Nineteenth-century Attitudes and Practices," 50–53.
50. Rowell, 52.
51. Hick, "Toward a Christian Theology of Death," 24.

embrace this sort of "total trust" for itself and to model such faith to the world. Just as Christian liturgy in general has been greatly affected by cultural attitudes (such as materialism, commercialism, and individualism), so too are decisions in funeral planning often made without regard for core Christian values. If our burial rites are to speak to our faith regarding the resurrection of the dead, it is necessary to recapture some of the ideals of Christianity that once stood in stark opposition to what society cherished the most.

Take, for example, the basic Christian value of simplicity. Christians are men and women, disciples of the Lord, who are called to avoid the allure of material possessions for the sake of God's Kingdom. Even the sacred liturgy of the Church is to exude a "noble simplicity" in all its aspects: "The rites should radiate a noble simplicity. They should be short, clear, and free from useless repetition. They should be within the people's powers of comprehension, and normally should not require much explanation."[52] The same should be true for all that goes into the celebration of the death of a Christian. Consider all of the many options that funeral directors place before their customers: from how the funeral will be advertised, to all of the details regarding the visitation of the deceased, to who will receive the American flag from a military honor guard. The choices held out to a family are vast indeed!

Here are two simple examples. The first concerns the issue of embalming and preparing the body for viewing. A Christian eye for simplicity might insist that the mortician keep the use of cosmetics to a bare minimum in an attempt not to mask the harsh truth of death. Like Baptism, death is a great equalizer. When great lengths are taken to make the body appear just as it did when the person was alive, the emphasis is once again placed upon the individual rather than upon the mystery of death as a transition to eternal life. A Christian simplicity also should guide the selection of a casket or an urn (if the body is cremated). As Ernest Moran writes in *Dealing Creatively with Death: A Manual of Death Education and Simple Burial*, "Simplicity in arrangements can effect great economy, but even more importantly it can help center attention on spiritual values and the life of the person who has died, rather than on material things. It can avoid

---

52. SC, 34.

the appearance of ostentation and extravagance."[53] "Ostentation" and "extravagance" are two worldly desires that Christians are called to shirk. During the funeral liturgy, the white pall serves to neutralize the casket, so that the bodily remains of all Christians appear the same before the altar of God. However, at other moments, such as the vigil and the committal, the casket is in full view. Striving for a noble simplicity in preparing the body for burial, as well as at all other times in the rites of Christian burial, will serve to counter the temptation for extravagance.

Another Christian value that our funeral liturgy invites us to express is the dignity of the body. While our culture spends a tremendous amount of time and money trying to prevent the body from aging and gaining weight, very little is done to promote the body as a "temple of the holy Spirit" (1 Corinthians 6:19). Whether the body after death is interred in the ground or is cremated and returned to ashes, the Church believes that the body is sacred. Since cremation has become a lawful alternative to the burial of a body—"The Church earnestly recommends that the pious custom of burying the bodies of the dead be observed; nevertheless, the Church does not prohibit cremation unless it was chosen for reasons contrary to Christian doctrine"[54]—it is important not to oppose it. However, similar to the issue of sacramental minimalism (Baptism by a few drops of water or reconciliation without real touch), it must be admitted that something important is missing when the body has been reduced to ashes. Richard Rutherford states: "The body that participated integrally in all the other expressions of sacramental life is the primary object of liturgical attention in the traditional funeral liturgy."[55] Moreover, "Humanly speaking as well, the deceased body and cremated human remains do not have the same meaning in the symbolism of death."[56]

Often families will choose to retain the ashes in their homes or to scatter the ashes at a location meaningful to the dead. Today's funeral industry offers a wide variety of attractive vessels to hold the cremated remains, vessels that can too easily become mantle pieces. When the remains of a loved one are held in this fashion, death as an individual reality rather than a

---

53. Morgan, *Dealing Creatively with Death*, 52.

54. *Code of Canon Law*, canon 1176, §3.

55. Richard Rutherford, *Honoring the Dead: Catholics and Cremation Today* (Collegeville, MN: Liturgical Press, 2001), 5.

56. Rutherford, 4.

corporate process is clearly underscored. The same can be said for the scattering of ashes. The ancient Christian practice of burying the body in its entirety testifies to the belief in the resurrection of the body on the last day. The failure to inter the ashes, as well as the decision to scatter the ashes, both move in the direction of an individualistic notion of death and fail to witness to the Christian belief that the souls of the dead are intimately joined as one in the Communion of Saints. Once again, returning to the thought of Rutherford:

> The attitude we are invited to hold in a Catholic practice of cremation places high priority on the long tradition of keeping the memory of our dead, especially in the Catholic cemetery. Prior to cremation it is the body that holds our faithful attention; after cremation it is the grave or niche where the cremated remains rest. [. . .] The appropriate Roman Catholic attitude toward cremation, as noted in the revised funeral liturgy, is rooted in the longstanding Catholic tradition that the death of one of our community is not an isolated event. We bring the body of our deceased loved ones to their final place of rest in a spirit of love and care, and support for those left behind.[57]

When the ashes are kept within the house as a revered artifact, they become a commodity; when they are thrown to the wind at a landmark cherished by the deceased, they are quickly forgotten. Burying the ashes in sacred ground and marking them with a marker or placing them in a columbarium allows for their perpetual remembrance by the community at large. Once again, the temptation with cremation is to handle the ashes in a very privatized way that does not honor the participation of the dead in the wider Christian community.

The rite of committal is the most visible arena in which to display Christian values that are a countersign to those society holds. Because it is usually celebrated outside at the grave—"Whenever possible, the rite of committal is to be celebrated at the site of committal, that is, beside the open grave or place of interment, rather than at a cemetery chapel"[58]—the prayer that accompanies the burial of the body or the interment of ashes is the most public of the rituals contained in the *Order of Christian Funerals*. However, in recent years, it seems as though a large number of those

---

57. Rutherford, 255–256.
58. OCF, 204.

assembled for the funeral liturgy do not accompany the body to its final resting place; the symbolic significance of the procession to the cemetery as well as the responsibility to participate in the burial of the dead has waned tremendously in a society that wants to return to the familiar as quickly as possible. Thus, a word must be said that a restored sense of formal procession to the burial place may speak volumes to society at large. Even in its least orchestrated form, the procession to the place of committal is sure to be noticed.

Furthermore, after the mourners have arrived at the place of committal, a final procession with song to the grave provides a strong image both of the pilgrim journey and Christian faith. The rite of committal offers no suggestion as to the song that might accompany the final procession, but it makes this strong statement about the powerful nature of singing during the overall rite:

> The singing of well-chosen music at the rite of committal can help the mourners as they face the reality of separation. At the rite of committal with final commendation, whenever possible, the song of farewell should be sung. In either form of the committal rite, a hymn or liturgical song that affirms hope in God's mercy and in the resurrection of the dead is desirable at the conclusion of the rite.[59]

Similarly, Thomas Long lauds the practice of singing at the committal:

> The service should have lots of music, and most of it, if not all of it, should be congregational song. Accompany them with singing! It is good for the voices of the community singing praise to be heard above the noisy clamor of death. If there is a soloist or a choir, don't allow them to serenade the congregation. The experience of death cancels all concerts. We have holy work to do, to carry a brother or sister to the grave; so let the choir and the soloists walk along with us. Let them sing *with* the people and on their behalf.[60]

Communal singing is indeed indispensable in the final procession to the grave. Thus, funeral directors could be trained to help mourners gather at a point a short distance from the grave, encouraging them to form a procession behind the casket. Parish cantors and other music ministers could

---

59. OCF, 214.
60. Long, *Accompany Them with Singing*, 172.

be interspersed in the procession to help lead the people in song. Servers with incense, cross, and candles could precede the casket, and the minister, vested "according to local custom,"[61] could lead the entire procession. Restoring the formality of the procession to the grave is an important aspect of the ongoing reform of the burial rite and should not be lost.

For the rite of committal to assume a more challenging role in confronting the values of the American culture, it must be recognized as the third movement of Christian burial, not in any way tangential or separate from all that has taken place before it. The OCF states: "The rite of committal, the conclusion of the funeral rites, is the final act of the community of faith in caring for the body of its deceased member."[62] Once again, the committal service is meant to be about the Church. Far too often families demand that the burial service or the interment of ashes be conducted privately. Perhaps they fear that this will be a very emotional moment and do not wish their manifestation of grief to be viewed publicly. However, the Christian community's faith is extremely important at this time, as the OCF states:

> In committing the body to its resting place, the community expresses the hope that, with all those who have gone before marked with the sign of faith, the deceased awaits the glory of the resurrection. The rite of committal is an expression of the communion that exists between the Church on earth and the Church in heaven: the deceased passes with the farewell prayers of the community of believers into the welcoming company of those who need faith no longer but see God face to face.[63]

The rubrics that govern the rite of committal continue to underscore the participation of the community:

> The community continues to show its concern for the mourners by participating in the rite of committal. The rite marks the separation in this life of the mourners from the deceased, and through it the community assists them as they complete their care for the deceased and lay the body to rest. The act of committal is a stark and powerful expression of this separation. When carried out in the midst of the community of faith, the committal can help the mourners to face the end of one relationship with

---

61. OCF, 215.
62. OCF, 204.
63. OCF, 206.

the deceased and to begin a new one based on prayerful remembrance, gratitude, and the hope of resurrection and reunion.[64]

After the final procession to the grave, the community expresses this Christian hope in the resurrection by the gesture of forming an assembly at the place of interment. Just as faith suggests that a great company of saints gathers in heaven to welcome a new member of Christ's Body into its midst, the Christian community here and now sacramentalizes that heavenly assembly. If celebrated privately, the committal cannot succeed in displaying to the family the significant relationships of disciples who have journeyed with the dead through both the trials and the victories of this chapter of his or her Christian life.

Testifying to the fact that the rite of committal is a prayerful extension of all that has taken place previously in the funeral rite and in the vigil, presiders are not to begin with the traditional Sign of the Cross and greeting. Instead, the rite opens with a beautiful invitation to prayer that portrays the oneness that is the Body of Christ, living and deceased:

> Our brother (sister) N. has gone to his (her) rest in the peace of Christ. May the Lord now welcome him (her) to the table of God's children in heaven. With faith and hope in eternal life, let us assist him (her) with our prayers.
>
> Let us pray to the Lord also for ourselves. May we who mourn be reunited one day with our brother (sister); together may we meet Christ Jesus when he who is our life appears in glory.[65]

Regarding this opening, *Guide to Celebrating Funerals* notes: "The invitation to prayer shifts the mourners' focus to eschatological realities."[66] Gathered around the grave, the faithful are led to contemplate "the table of God's children in heaven" and the great reunion that will take place when Christ will "appear in glory." The eschatological outlook is underscored by the Scripture verse that follows (Matthew 25:34; John 6:39; Philippians 3:20; Revelations 1:5–6).[67] All of these verses look forward to the victory to be

---

64. OCF, 213.
65. OCF, 216.
66. DeGrocco, Morrill, and Rutherford, *Guide for Celebration Funerals*, 73.
67. OCF, 217.

celebrated on the last day: "Our citizenship is in heaven, and from it we also await a savior, the Lord Jesus Christ" (Philippians 3:20).

The attention of the assembly is now turned to the prayer over the place of committal (in the case of ground not previously blessed) and the subsequent committal of the body or of the cremated remains. How countercultural it is to make sacred the ground into which the body will be laid, and yet the Church, as from its very inception, recognizes the grave as a place of rest and peace as the dead await the fullness of light to come. The prayer of blessing reads:

> Lord Jesus Christ,
> by your own three days in the tomb,
> you hallowed the graves of all who believe in you
> and so made the grave a sign of hope
> that promises resurrection
> even as it claims our mortal bodies.
>
> Grant that our brother (sister) may sleep here in peace
> until you awaken him (her) to glory,
> for you are the resurrection and the life.
> Then he (she) will see you face to face
> and in your light will see light
> and know the splendor of God,
> for you live and reign for ever and ever.[68]

One of the most striking aberrations developed by the funeral industry to soften the harsh reality of the grave is the covering of the hole and the barren earth with artificial turf. There is no escaping that the grave "claims our mortal bodies." Christians are meant to peer into the depths of the grave and to recognize the immense contrast between its darkness and the light of the journey into God's splendor. In describing a burial scene in which artificial grass covered every inch of the grave, Smith writes: "Harshness, starkness, the sign of an open grave—all were disguised in a pretense that denied the reality of committal and separation. The grave as a sign of hope was robbed of its power by its sweet-smelling floral mask."[69] Christian burial must not be death-denying; a grave must reveal itself in its raw, cold ugliness.

---

68. OCF, 218.
69. Smith, *Facing Death Together*, 88.

A similar critique may be lodged against the customary way in which the committal of the body (or the ashes) is executed. The *Order of Christian Funerals* provides two formularies (more can be found in the appendix) for the committal.[70] Both make mention of the earth as a place of rest:

A:
Because God has chosen to call our brother (sister) N.
from this life to himself,
we commit his (her) body to the earth
    [or the deep or the elements or its resting place],
for we are dust and unto dust we shall return.

But the Lord Jesus Christ will change our mortal bodies
    to be like his in glory,
for he is risen, the firstborn of the dead.

So let us commend our brother (sister) to the Lord,
that the Lord may embrace him (her) in peace
and raise up his (her) body on the last day.

B:
In sure and certain hope of the resurrection to eternal life
    through our Lord Jesus Christ,
we commend to Almighty God our brother (sister) N.
and we commit his (her) body to the ground
    [or the deep or the elements or its resting place]:
earth to earth, ashes to ashes, dust to dust.

The Lord bless him (her) and keep him (her),
the Lord make his face to shine upon him (her)
    and be gracious to him (her),
the Lord lift up his countenance upon him (her)
    and give him (her) peace.

Notice how the second option makes use of one of the familiar solemn blessings used at the end of the Eucharist. Christians believe that in lowering the body into the earth, they are sending their brother or sister forth upon a great journey. But once again, these words are far less powerful when the grave is disguised and the gathered community is excluded from

---

70. OCF, 219.

the actual burial of the body. Returning to the scene described by Smith in which the mourners were given cold drinks and invited to disperse before the casket was lowered into the ground: "Meanwhile, the thing that the mourners went to the cemetery to do—to commit the body of the deceased to the earth or to the elements—was left to be completed by the anonymous employees of the cemetery. The coffin, suspended over the hole, spoke little of a return to the earth."[71] The OCF is no less direct about the need for the enactment of an actual committal: "The act of committal expresses the full significance of this rite. *Through this act the community of faith proclaims that the grave or place of interment, once a sign of futility and despair, has been transformed by means of Christ's own death and resurrection into a sign of hope and promise.*"[72] The desire on the part of the funeral industry to shield the family from the messiness of the grave must not prevent Christians from burying the dead!

After the committal, the rite concludes relatively quickly, beginning with a set of intercessions that pray for the healing of the mourners and for the eternal life of the deceased: "give to our brother (sister) eternal life," "bring N. to the joys of heaven," "give him (her) fellowship with all your Saints," "grant him (her) a place at the table in your heavenly Kingdom."[73] After the intercessions, the community is invited to pray together the Lord's Prayer, and then the rite comes to a swift end with a concluding prayer and the final blessing.[74] The OCF offers two concluding prayers (as well as several provided in an appendix), with the first focusing solely on God's mercy for the deceased and the second on a hopeful expectation of resurrection for all who have died. The second prayer follows:

Almighty God,
through the Death of your Son on the Cross
you destroyed our death;
through his rest in the tomb
you hallowed the graves of all who believe in you;
and through his rising again
you restored us to eternal life.

---

71. Smith, *Facing Death Together*, 88.
72. OCF, 209. Emphasis mine.
73. OCF, 220.
74. OCF 221–223.

God of the living and the dead,
accept our prayers
for those who have died in Christ
and are buried with him in the hope of rising again.
Since they were true to your name on earth,
let them praise you for ever in the joy of heaven.
Through Christ our Lord.

The final blessing constitutes a plea for the consolation of the living: "Hear your people who cry out to you in their need, and strengthen their hope in your lasting goodness."[75] It also prays for patient understanding: "May the peace of God, which is beyond all understanding, keep your hearts and minds in the knowledge of love of God and of his Son, our Lord Jesus Christ."[76] The people are dismissed with the words: "Go in the peace of Christ."

In many ways the rite of committal feels anticlimactic. Yet often leave-taking is meant to be abrupt. Those who participate regularly in the Eucharist know what this is like when the highpoint of the liturgy celebrated in Communion leads immediately to the dismissal of the assembly. In reality, the act of committing the body to the earth (or another place of rest) is the highpoint of this ritual and moves directly to a contemplative silence, in which the mystery of finality-yet-hoped-for-resurrection produces a stillness of being. The very last rubric of the rite states that "some sign or gesture of leave-taking may be made."[77] Smith writes:

> Some sign or gesture of final leave-taking is encouraged. The practice of throwing a handful of earth into the grave, a vestige of the physical work of filling in the grave, can be a powerful sign that continues the symbolism of burial and expresses the finality of the moment. It also acknowledges the fact that we are people of the earth, and in being returned to the earth the deceased returns to God. [. . .] Death and the act of committal are not respectable or nice, and there seems little sense in this gesture of farewell if the soil is not picked up, touched, handled, felt and allowed to fall—even thud—onto the coffin.[78]

---

75. OCF, 223.
76. OCF, 223.
77. OCF, 223.
78. Smith, *Facing Death Together*, 91–92.

Once again, this action of assisting in the committal of the body has been softened and sanitized in our Western culture. Most often the casket remains suspended above the grave until all the mourners have departed from the graveside, only to be buried by cemetery personnel. Or, if the casket has been lowered, family and friends may be invited to throw flowers into the grave. All of this is much too neat and betrays a sacramental principle that God's grace and the Paschal Mystery are messy business that require of us getting our hands dirty. A culture that wants to keep all things neat and tidy, efficient and convenient, must be countered by the Christian work of burying the dead.

Conclusion

This final chapter has attempted to surface not only a few of the major challenges posed by our cultural attitudes surrounding death and burial, it has tried to present a positive stance toward the possibilities that exist pastorally for the ongoing renewal of our funeral liturgies. It is hoped that the possibilities outweigh the conundrums. In our highly mobile and ever-changing world, it is hard to imagine that the contemplation of the mystery of death will ever spark the Christian imagination once again. And yet, what is contended here is that the recapturing of the celebration of the ecclesial nature of death has much to say about how our day-to-day lives as followers of Christ are lived out. Working to develop the spirit of the OCF in each of its ritual stages has consequences as to how our Baptism is lived. Allowing the ministry of the Body of Christ to flourish and ripen in the face of the death of a Christian helps each member to know his or her worth as a member of Christ who one day will pass over the waters of death on the journey to new life.

This chapter seeks to call parish leaders to understand well the place of the Christian community in the ministry of bereavement and evangelization. The bonds of the community, which are forged in the waters of Baptism and nourished at the Eucharistic table, must be given the time and the space to be reordered. This means that pastors must challenge all members of the community to play an active role in burying the dead. Rutherford writes:

> Parishes where the funeral liturgy is truly communal are, for the most part, parishes where considerable effort has been devoted to remote preparation. This has included parishwide catechesis, especially about

death itself in the 20th century, Catholic faith and contemporary teaching in the face of death, and about the liturgy of death and burial. More than one parish priest has insisted that the best vehicle for such effective funerary catechesis is the funeral liturgy itself. Good, consistent liturgical example demonstrates in practice what is taught in home, school, or parish education classes.[79]

In turn, greater catechesis on the Christian attitude toward death will hopefully lead to creative pastoral solutions that involve not only increased participation on the part of the community in funeral liturgies but also enhanced dialogue with funeral directors and cemetery officials. A theology that links death with baptismal commitment ought not to be threatening to either parishioners or those in the funeral business but ought to pose an opportunity to explore new ways of expressing the relevance of the Christian faith in our modern culture. Therefore, a lacuna acknowledged in this work is empirical research; more discussion needs to take place across the board (among pastors, parishioners, and funeral personnel) to alleviate the contemporary conundrums and to accentuate the pastoral possibilities examined here. For, in reality, these only begin to scratch the surface of the difficult struggle of revealing a courageous faith in the resurrection in a world that lives a gospel other than the one proclaimed by Christ. As members of the one Body, there is much work to be done!

---

79. Rutherford, *The Death of a Christian*, 219.

Conclusion

❦

At the door there to greet us, martyrs, angels, and saints,
And our fam'ly and loved ones, everyone freed from their chains.
We shall feel their acceptance, and the joy of new life.
We shall join in the gathering, reunited in God's love!

We shall rise again on the last day with the faithful, rich and poor.
Coming to the house of Lord Jesus, we will find an open door there,
We will find an open door.[1]

Francis was a fisherman. He spent much of his life navigating the waters of the sea in search of a great catch. Whether calm or turbulent, the ocean was very much his home. With the vast horizon always before him, the journey upon the sea was a never-ending mystery. While the vista of miles and miles of water before him may have appeared much the same from day to day, he never tired of the awesome wonder the ocean presented.

When Francis drew his last breath, surrounded by his faithful wife, his children, and closest friends, the mystery of those waters took on a new dimension, for these were the waters that crossed over from life to death and to the splendor of eternal life. Surely, Francis knew the way and was guided by those saints and loved ones who stood ready to greet him at last.

Francis' funeral attested to the fact that "all the ties of friendship and affection which knit us as one throughout our lives do not unravel with death."[2] In St. Peter the Apostle Church, named for the first among holy fishermen, those assembled around Francis' body knew well the ministry they shared in uniting their hearts with each other and praying for the success of their brother's journey. The care taken in clothing the casket with the white pall, the reverberation of heartfelt song upon the wooden rafters, the faith shared in the proclamation of the Word and in preaching, the procession to communion of those family members and friends whose

---

1. Song text from Jeremy Young, "We Shall Rise Again," verse five and refrain (Chicago: © 1987, GIA Publications Inc.). All rights reserved. Used by permission.
2. OCF, 71.

intersection in life was marked by both joy and pain—this was a community that palpably felt its oneness in Christ.

At the end of the funeral liturgy, when the presider invited the assembly to "take the body of our brother to his place of rest," the crowd of believers followed the casket to the doors of the church building singing the Litany of Saints. When all had assembled in the vestibule, a moment of silence was observed before the funeral personnel removed the pall from the simple wooden casket. The presider once again sprinkled the casket and prayed words found in the procession to the place of committal in the *Order of Christian Funerals*: "May choirs of Angels welcome you and lead you to the bosom of Abraham; and where Lazarus is poor no longer may you find eternal rest."[3] The schola that had led the assembly in song throughout the liturgy organized themselves at the door singing words of hope to all as they departed from the church to their cars to form a procession to the cemetery:

Come to me, all you weary, with your burdens and pain.
Take my yoke on your shoulders and learn from me.
I am gentle and humble, and your soul will find rest,
For my yoke is easy and my burden is light.

Ref. We shall rise again on the last day with the faithful rich and poor.
Coming to the house of Lord Jesus, we will find an open door there,
we will find an open door.

Do not fear death's dominion, look beyond earth and grave.
See the brightness of Jesus shining out to light our way.
Loving Father and Spirit, loving Jesus the Son,
All God's people together, we shall live on as one![4]

Although tears filled the eyes of nearly all the mourners, the community's faith in eternal life far outweighed its fear of death. This was a people who took seriously the call to minister to each other at this moment of pain, as they believed that Francis was ministering to them. While Francis may have crossed the threshold to paradise, the door stood open and beckoned to women and men, young and old, rich and poor, gay and straight, all of

---

3. OCF, 176.
4. Young, "We Shall Rise Again," verses one and four.

whom had journeyed through life together, knowing themselves to be in the same boat. "All God's people together, we shall live on as one."

This project of examining death and the Christian rituals that attend to it has really been a study of the nature of the Church. Baptism into Christ and entrance into eternal life are really two sides of one coin. Both entail the reality of death. Thus, the entirety of the Christian Church is the Paschal Mystery itself—letting go of life, embracing death on a daily basis, and allowing new life to come to fruition. Such is the hallmark of each disciple and is the fundamental characteristic of the Church. It is the way of life that is rehearsed every time Christians gather to celebrate the Eucharist. As the General Introduction to the *Order of Christian Funerals* states: "The mystery of the Lord's Death and Resurrection gives power to all the Church's activity."[5]

What has been designated "baptismal ecclesiology" is a way of looking at the Church that sees that all are in the same boat, crossing through life together on a common pilgrimage through the door that Christ promises to hold open for all. As has been seen, the liturgical rites that concern the Christian community at the time of death—vigil, funeral, and burial—are celebrated for the Church so that the members of the Body of Christ can be reordered once again, seeing their participation in Christ in a new light. This reordering acknowledges that the dead still have a role to play in the Body. Death does not remove a person from the Body of Christ but instead provides them with a new charism, a new worldview in which to see even clearer the glory of God.

The starting point for baptismal ecclesiology is that the Church is never static; it is always in a state of becoming. New members are continually grafted on to the Body of Christ, daily refashioning its charism for ministry. Thus, the Church understands its life on earth to be part of the greater pilgrimage that is the journey into divine life. As stated in the Constitution on the Church:

> The church, to which we are all called in Christ Jesus, and in which by the grace of God, we attain holiness, will receive its perfection only in the glory of heaven, when the time for the renewal of all things will have come (Acts 3:21). At that time, together with the human race, the

---

5. OCF, 2.

universe itself, which is closely related to humanity and which through it attains its destiny, will be perfectly established in Christ (see Eph 1:10; Col 1:20; 2 Pet 3:10–13).[6]

The true mystery of the Church lies in its "perfect establishment" in Christ in the life to come. This demands of Christians the daunting task of realizing anew the unity that exists in Christ's Body today, that in Christ there is no room for division, no justification for lording power one over another, no theological reason for exclusion of any sort. Our pilgrimage on earth toward our heavenly home is meant to be the discovery that we do not make our way to God as individuals but as a holy people.

Baptismal ecclesiology understands the Church to be the domain, the household, of committed disciples who live their lives out of the perspective of a vocation. Baptism is more than just a gift imparted to new members, it is a responsibility to a dedicated and daily following of the Lord's voice. When individual Christians forget the commitment made in Baptism, the Church as a whole grows weaker. Kathleen Cahalan writes:

> Discipleship is not an achievement. It is an identity, a commitment, a way of life, and a response to a call. . . . To be a disciple means to be a follower of Christ, committed to learning his ways; to be a worshiper, joining Christ and the community in praise of God's wonders; to be a witness who proclaims the good news to the world; to be a forgiver by practicing reconciliation, healing and peacemaking; to be a neighbor by living mindfully of others' needs and reaching out to them with compassion; to be a prophet willing to tell the truth about the injustices that harm neighbors; and to be stewards of the creation, the community and the mysteries of the faith. A fully developed understanding of discipleship is yet another way of understanding the church's mission.[7]

Discipleship is no easy task. Neither is that of living as Church in a world that heralds the merits of individualism and resists communal sacrifice. St. Paul reminds us that no power on earth or under the earth is truly able to stifle the Lord's call: "For I am convinced that that neither death, nor life, nor angels, nor principalities, nor present things, nor future things, nor powers, nor height, nor depth, nor any other creature, will be able to

---

6. LG, 48.

7. Cahalan, "Toward a Fundamental Theology of Ministry," 115.

separate us from the love of God, which is in Christ Jesus our Lord" (Romans 8:38–39). Disciples are those who journey as one and allow no worldly attraction or subtle fear to distract them from the destiny of a sharing in divine life.

Not only do our baptismal liturgies describe so eloquently in word and in symbol our participation in Christ, but so too do the liturgies that accompany the death of a Christian. As has been stated many times throughout this work, the Christian work of celebrating death and burial is the liturgy of the Church. It is the responsibility of the Christian community of faith to enact corporate prayer that inserts the death into the framework of Christ's Paschal Mystery. Christian death is communal; a member of Christ's Body makes the transition to new life, but the Body is not severed, merely reordered. Like Baptism, the *Order of Christian Funerals*, in all its ritual expressions, serves to demonstrate the nature of the Church's mystery. Christian funerals show that the Church of earth and of heaven is a *united people* for "we believe that all the ties of friendship and affection which knit us as one throughout our lives do not unravel with death."[8] Both Baptism and death are great levelers that strip away the distinctions that humans use to separate one from another. The Christian prayer for death and burial clearly communicates that the Church is a *pilgrim people*. The Requiem aeternum, which prays for "eternal rest" and "perpetual light" for the individual soul in conjunction with "all the faithful departed" speaks of the journey which is life-into-death. Pilgrims are courageous men and women because they are not solo pioneers.

Furthermore, the death that is necessary in Baptism and that which takes place at the end of life entails the sacrifice of self; thus, the Church is meant to be nothing less than a *self-giving people*. It is in this spirit of self-gift that the Church understands the funeral liturgy to be an arena to celebrate Christ and not to laud the personal achievements of the dead. For this reason, the homily is not a eulogy about the deceased but rather confirmation of "God's compassionate love and on the Paschal Mystery of the Lord."[9] The rite of anointing in the Sacrament of Baptism declares: "As Christ was anointed Priest, Prophet, and King, so may you live always as a member of

---

8. OCF, 71.
9. OCF, 141.

his body, sharing everlasting life."[10] Christians are anointed to be a part of a *priestly people*, who share in the priesthood of Christ, announce the Kingdom of God, and intercede for the salvation of the world. Just so, the entire complex of prayer contained in the *Order of Christian Funerals* is intended to be the world of that people: "Christians celebrate the funeral rites to offer worship, praise and thanksgiving to God."[11] Finally, both baptismal ecclesiology and Christian funerals envision the Church to be a *holy people*. Baptism imparts holiness. Holiness is an immersion into the joys and the sufferings of this world through the adoption of Christ's worldview. A concluding prayer for the rite of committal reads: "God of the living and the dead, accept our prayers for those who have died in Christ and are buried with him in the hope of rising again. Since they were true to your name on earth, let them praise you for ever in the joy of heaven."[12] The Communion of Saints on earth is but a foretaste of the Communion of Saints in heaven.

For far too long, Christians reduced Baptism to the guarantee of eternal life with God. Every effort was made to baptize infants in a timely manner to make sure that they were recipients of God's grace and therefore heirs of heaven. Present also for this same span of history was the growing fear of death, so that the funeral rites focused on the need for God's mercy to shine upon individual souls. Both Baptism and death have suffered in the Christian imagination from the loss of their corporate significance. Both are about active participation in the Body of Christ. More and more work must be done to accentuate Baptism as a committed way of life for serious disciples, while more and more work must be done to regain a sense of the community at work in the celebration of funerals. Both are about the issue of belonging, and therefore the difficult work of relationship. In Baptism, Christians belong to Christ and one another; this belonging does not unravel in death. Restoring the link between Baptism and death will help our imaginations grasp who it is we are called to be in this life as disciples and who we are promised to become in eternal life as saints.

---

10. *Rite of Baptism for Children*, 98
11. OCF, 5.
12. OCF, 222.

BIBLIOGRAPHY

Ariès, Philippe. *Western Attitudes toward Death: From the Middle Ages to the Present*. Translated by Patricia M. Ranum. Baltimore, MD: John Hopkins University Press, 1974.

Augustine. *On Care to Be Had for the Dead*. Edited by Philip Schaff and translated by H. Browne. CreateSpace Independent Publishing Platform, 2015.

Avis, Paul. "Is Baptism 'Complete Sacramental Initiation'?" *Theology* 111 (2008): 163–169.

Baptism, Eucharist and Ministry, Faith and Order Paper No. 111. Geneva: World Council of Churches, 1982.

Batchelder, David B. "Baptismal Renunciations: Making Promises We Do Not Intend to Keep." *Worship* 81 (2007): 409–425.

Bonaiuti, Ernesto and Giorgio La Piana. "The Genesis of St. Augustine's Idea of Original Sin." *Harvard Theological Review* 10 (1917): 159–175.

The Book of Common Prayer and Administration of the Sacraments and Other Rites and Ceremonies of the Church . . . according to the use of the Episcopal Church. New York: Seabury Press, 1979.

Brown, Charles. "The Environment of Disposal: The Exterior." In *Dying, Death, and Disposal*, edited by Gilbert Cope, 108–115. London: SPCK, 1970.

Bugnini, Annibale. *The Reform of the Liturgy 1948–1975*. Translated by Matthew J. O'Connell. Collegeville, MN: Liturgical Press, 1990.

Burt, Donald X. *Augustine's World: An Introduction to His Speculative Philosophy*. Lanham, MD: University Press of America, 1996.

Cahalan, Kathleen A. "Toward a Fundamental Theology of Ministry." *Worship* 80 (2006): 102–120.

Cameron, J. M. "On Death and Human Existence." *Worship* 50 (1976): 246–260.

Changes: Prayers and Services Honoring Rites of Passage, (New York: Church Publishing Incorporated, 2007).

Codd, Kevin A. "'I Am a Pilgrim on the Earth': The Pilgrim Way." *Worship* 84 (2010): 154–170.

Congar, Yves. *Diversity and Communion*. Mystic, CT: Twenty-Third Publications, 1985.

——. "The *Ecclesia* or Christian Community as a Whole Celebrates the Liturgy." In *At the Heart of Christian Worship: Liturgical Essays of Yves Congar*. Translated and edited by Paul Philibert, 15–68. Collegeville, MN: Liturgical Press, 2010.

Covino, Paul F. X. "The Postconciliar Infant Baptism Debate in the American Catholic Church." *Worship* 56 (1982): 240–260.

Crowley, Joann. "Baptism as Eschatological Event." *Worship* 62 (1988): 290–298.

Cunningham, Joseph. "Chronicle: Revised *Order of Christian Funerals*." *Worship* 65 (1991): 60–64.

DeGrocco, Joseph, Bruce Morrill, and Richard Rutherford. *Guide for Celebrating Funerals*. Chicago: Liturgy Training Publications, 2017.

Dillon, Richard J. "The Unavoidable Discomforts of Preaching About Death." *Worship* 57 (1983): 486–496.

Doyle, Dennis M. *The Church Emerging from Vatican II: A Popular Approach to Contemporary Catholicism*. Mystic, CT: Twenty-Third Publications, 1992.

Dulles, Avery. *Models of the Church*. New York: Doubleday, 1974.

Dunning, James B. "The Rite of Christian Initiation of Adults: Model of Adult Growth." *Worship* 53 (1979): 142–153.

Eastman, A. Theodore. *The Baptizing Community: Christian Initiation and the Local Congregation*. 2nd ed. Harrisburg, PA: Morehouse Publishing, 1991.

Evans, Abigail Rian. *Healing Liturgies for the Seasons of Life*. Louisville, KY: Westminster John Knox Press, 2004.

Fahey, Michael A. "Church." In *Systematic Theology: Roman Catholic Perspectives*, vol. 2, edited by Francis Schüssler Fiorenza and John P. Galvin, 4–74. Minneapolis, MN: Fortress Press, 1991.

Farnham, Suzanne G., Joseph P. Gill, R. Taylor McLean, and Susan M. Ward. *Listening Hearts: Discerning Call in Community*. New York: Morehouse Publishing, 1991.

Fischer, Edward. "Aging as Worship." *Worship* 52 (1978): 98–108.

Flannery, Austin, ed. *Vatican Council II: The Basic Sixteen Documents*. Dublin: Dominican Publications, 1996, 2014.

Franz, Ansgar. "'Everything Is Worthwhile at the End'? Christian Funeral Liturgy amidst Ecclesial Tradition and Secular Rites." *Studia Liturgica* 32 (2002): 48–68.

Gaillardetz, Richard R. "In Service of Communion: A Trinitarian Foundation for Christian Ministry." *Worship* 67 (1993): 41–433.

Gibson, Paul. "A Baptismal Ecclesiology—Some Questions." In *Equipping the Saints: Ordination in Anglicanism Today*, edited by Ronald L. Dowling and David R. Holeton, 35–44. Dublin: Columba Press, 2006.

Gilbert, Sandra. *Death's Door: Modern Dying and the Way We Grieve*. New York: W.W. Norton, 2006.

Guerrette, Richard H. "Ecclesiology and Infant Baptism." *Worship* 44 (1970): 433–437.

Gy, Pierre-Marie. "The Liturgy of Death: The Funeral Rite of the New Roman Ritual." *The Way* 11 (1970): 59–75.

Hick, John. "Towards a Christian Theology of Death." In *Dying, Death, and Disposal*, edited by Gilbert Cope, 8–25. London: SPCK, 1970.

Holy Women, Holy Men: Celebrating the Saints. New York: Church Publishing Incorporated, 2010.

Hoeffner, Robert J. "A Pastoral Evaluation of the Rite of Funerals." *Worship* (1981): 482–499.

Hovda, Robert W. "Reclaiming for the Church the Death of a Christian." *Worship* 59 (1985): 148–154.

———. "Reclaiming for the Church the Death of a Christian II." *Worship* 59 (1985): 251–261.

Hughes, Kathleen. *Saying Amen: A Mystagogy of Sacrament*. Chicago: Liturgy Training Publications, 1999.

John Paul II. Apostolic Exhortation, *Pastores dabo vobis*. Rome: Libreria Editrice Vaticana, 1992.

Joslyn-Siemiatkoski, Daniel E. and Ruth A. Meyers. "The Baptismal Ecclesiology of *Holy Women, Holy Men*: Developments in the Theology of Sainthood in the Episcopal Church." *Anglican Theological Review* 94:1 (2012): 27–36.

Kasper, Walter. "Ecclesiological and Ecumenical Implications of Baptism." *Ecumenical Review* 52 (2000): 526–541.

Kavanagh, Aidan. "Christian Initiation of Adults: The Rites." *Worship* 48 (1974): 318–335.

———. "Initiation: Baptism and Confirmation." *Worship* 46 (1972): 263–276.

Kelly, Gerard. "Baptismal Unity in the Divided Church." *Worship* 75 (2001): 511–527.

Klän, Werner. "Reformation Then and Now: Ecclesia Semper Reformanda." *Journal of Lutheran Mission* 3 (2016): 14–22.

Krieg, Robert A. "The Funeral Homily: A Theological View," *Worship* 58 (1984): 222–239.

Lampe, Geoffrey W. H. *The Seal of the Spirit: A Study in the Doctrine of Baptism and Confirmation in the New Testament and the Fathers*. London: Longmans, Green Co., 1951.

Lathrop, Gordon W. *Holy People: A Liturgical Ecclesiology*. Minneapolis, MN: Fortress Press, 1999.

Lawler, Michael G. and Thomas Shanahan. "The Church Is a Graced Communion." *Worship* 67 (1993): 484–501.

Lehmen, Greg. "Life's Quiet Companion." In *The Penguin Book of Death*, edited by Gabrielle Carey and Rosemary Sorensen, 223–231. Ringwood, Vic., Australia: Penguin, 1997.

Levering, Matthew. *The Theology of Augustine: An Introductory Guide to His Most Important Works*. Grand Rapids, MI: Baker Academic, 2013.

Lewis, C. S. *A Grief Observed*. New York: Harper and Row, 1961.

Long, Thomas G. *Accompany Them with Singing: The Christian Funeral*. Louisville, KY: Westminster John Knox Press, 2009.

Long, Thomas G. and Thomas Lynch. *The Good Funeral: Death, Grief, and the Community of Care*. Louisville, KY: Westminster John Knox Press, 2013.

Marx, Paul B. *Virgil Michel and the Liturgical Movement*. Collegeville, MN: Liturgical Press, 1957.

Meier, John P. "Catholic Funerals in the Light of Scripture." *Worship* 48 (1974): 206–216.

Melloh, John Allyn. "Homily or Eulogy? The Dilemma of Funeral Preaching." *Worship* 67 (1993): 502–518.

Meyers, Ruth A. *Continuing the Reformation: Re-Visioning Baptism in the Episcopal Church*. New York: Church Publishing Incorporated, 1997.

Michel, Virgil. "Natural and Supernatural Society." *Orate Fratres* 10 (1936): 243–247, 293–296, 338–342, 394–398, 434–438.

Morgan, Ernest. *Dealing Creatively with Death: A Manual of Death Education and Simple Burial*. Hinesburg, VT: Upper Access, 2001.

Morrill, Bruce. *Divine Worship and Human Healing: Liturgical Theology at the Margins of Life and Death*. Collegeville, MN: Liturgical Press, 2009.

Myers, C. Kilmer. *Baptized into the One Church*. New York: Seabury Press, 1963.

Orr, David. "Educating for the Priesthood of the Faithful." *Worship* 85 (2009): 431–457.

Owusu, Vincent. "Funeral Rites in Rome and the Non-Roman West." In *Sacraments and Sacramentals*, ed. Anscar J. Chupungco, 355–380.

Vol 4 of *Handbook for Liturgical Studies*. Collegeville, MN: Liturgical Press, 2000.

——. *The Roman Funeral Liturgy: History, Celebration and Theology*. Nettetal: Steyler Verlag, 1993.

Paxton, Frederick S. *Christianizing Death: The Creation of a Ritual Process in Early Medieval Europe*. Ithaca, NY: Cornell University Press, 1996.

Peterman, Janet S. *Speaking to Silence: New Rites for Christian Worship and Healing*. Louisville: Westminster John Knox Press, 2007.

Philibert, Paul J. "Human Development and Sacramental Transformation." *Worship* 65 (1991): 522–539.

——. "Reclaiming the Vision of an Apostolic Church." *Worship* 83 (2009): 482–581.

Podmore, Colin. "The Baptismal Revolution in the American Episcopal Church: Baptismal Ecclesiology and the Baptismal Covenant. *Ecclesiology* 6 (2010), 8–38.

Rahner, Karl. *The Church and the Sacraments*. New York: Herder and Herder, 1963.

Rite of Funerals. New York: Catholic Book Publishing Company, 1971.

The Rites of the Catholic Church, volume 1. Collegeville, MN: Liturgical Press, 1990.

Rowell, Geoffrey. *The Liturgy of Christian Burial: An Introductory Survey of the Historical Development of Christian Burial Rites*. London: SPCK, 1977.

——. "Nineteenth-century Attitudes and Practices." In *Dying, Death and Disposal*, edited by Gilbert Cope, 49–56. London: SPCK, 1970.

Rutherford, H. Richard. *Honoring the Dead: Catholics and Cremation Today*. Collegeville, MN: Liturgical Press, 2001.

Rutherford, H. Richard with Tony Barr. *The Death of a Christian: The Order of Christian Funerals*. Revised edition. Collegeville, MN: Liturgical Press, 1990.

Rush, Alfred C. *Death and Burial in Christian Antiquity*. Washington, DC: Catholic University of America Press, 1941.

Scharen, Christian B. "Baptismal Practices and the Formation of Christians: A Critical Liturgical Ethics." *Worship* 76 (2002): 43–66.

Schillebeeckx, Edward. *Christ the Sacrament of the Encounter with God.* New York: Sheed and Ward, 1963.

Seaman, Kristopher W. *Baptismal Symbols at Funerals. Pastoral Liturgy®* 46, no. 5 (2015): 16a. www.pastoralliturgy.org/resources/Baptismal SymbolsatFunerals.pdf.

Searle, Mark. *Called to Participate: Theological, Ritual, and Social Perspectives.* Edited by Barbara Searle and Anne Y. Koester. Collegeville, MN: Liturgical Press, 2006.

———. "On Death and Dying." *Assembly* 5, no.5 (1979): 49.

Sheppy, Paul. "The Dance of Death: Van Gennep and the Paschal Mystery." *Worship* 75 (2001): 553–560.

Smith, Margaret. *Facing Death Together: Parish Funerals.* Chicago: Liturgy Training Publications, 1998.

Smith, Susan Marie. *Christian Ritualizing and the Baptismal Process: Liturgical Explorations toward a Realized Baptismal Ecclesiology.* Eugene, OR: Pickwick Publications, 2012.

———. "Rites of Healing Along the Baptismal Journey: An Example and Several Principles." *Liturgy* 22 (2007): 49–56.

Sparkes, Robert and H. Richard Rutherford. "The Order of Christian Funerals: A Study in Bereavement and Lament." *Worship* 60 (1986): 499–510.

Stevick, Daniel B. *Baptismal Moments; Baptismal Meanings.* New York: Church Hymnal Corporation, 1987.

Tigan, Anne. "By the Rivers of Babylon: Reflections on Pilgrimage, Jerusalem and Funeral Liturgy." *Worship* 72 (1998): 330–344.

Van Gennep, Arnold. *The Rites of Passage.* Chicago: University of Chicago Press, 1960.

Van Tongeren, Louis. "Individualizing Ritual: The Personal Dimension in Funeral Liturgy." *Worship* 78 (2004): 117–138.

Watkins, Keith. "Baptism and Christian Identity: A Presbyterian Approach." *Worship* 60 (1986): 55–63.

Weil, Louis. "Baptismal Ecclesiology: Uncovering a Paradigm." In *Equipping the Saints: Ordination in Anglicanism Today*, edited by Ronald L Dowling and David R. Holeton, 18–34. Dublin: Columba Press, 2006.

Wilbricht, Stephen S. "Gesturing for an Epiphany: Renewing the Unspoken Language of Worship." *Pastoral Liturgy* 42, no. 5 (2011): 4–8.

———. "The History, Theology, and Practice of the Prayers of the Faithful." *Pastoral Liturgy*® 41, no. 6 (2010): 4–8. (Reprinted in *The Order of Mass: A Roman Missal Study Edition and Workbook*, Michael S. Driscoll and J. Michael Joncas, 327–339. Chicago: Liturgy Training Publications, 2011.

———. *Rehearsing God's Just Kingdom: The Eucharistic Vision of Mark Searle.* Collegeville, MN: Liturgical Press, 2013.

Wolfmueller, Bryan. *Final Victory: Contemplating the Death and Funeral of a Christian.* St. Louis, MO: Concordia Publishing House, 2009.

Wood, Susan K. "Conclusion: Convergence Points toward a Theology of Ordered Ministries." In *Ordering the Baptismal Priesthood: Theologies of Lay and Ordained Ministry*, edited by Susan K. Wood, 256–267. Collegeville, MN: Liturgical Press, 2003.

INDEX

Abraham 47, 57, 70, 78–79, 86, 95, 125, 151, 192

absolutio (absolution) 9, 92–93, 96–98, 103, 111, 116, 138, 142, 148, 152

adult catechumenate (see *Rite of Christian Initiation of Adults*)

altar 71, 81, 88, 120, 141, 143, 169, 180

Ambrose 52, 63

angels 13, 39, 50–51, 56–57, 64, 70, 76, 79, 85, 93, 98, 123, 150–153, 175, 191–192, 194

Anglican Church (*see* Episcopal Church)

anniversary of death 51, 107, 173

anxiety 76, 87, 101–102

Apostles 21–22, 50, 70, 146

Apostolic Constitutions 47, 50, 61, 69–70

apostolic succession 16

architecture 3, 100

ashes (*see* also cremains) 5, 68, 87–90, 180

    interment of 181, 183

    scattering of 181

assembly 7, 19, 68, 119, 121, 123, 129, 133–134, 139, 141, 147–148, 150–151, 153, 157, 164, 171, 173, 176, 184–185, 188

attitudes

    Christian 34, 40, 53, 57, 76, 131, 133–134, 143

    of fear (*see* fear)

    of joy 66, 77, 88

    of thanksgiving 71, 74, 88, 151

    surrounding death 41, 45, 53, 77, 81, 109, 112, 153, 161, 189–190

Augustine 35, 59, 61, 78–82, 107

banquet 46–47, 72, 76, 119, 142, 160

Baptism

    as a way of life 4, 21, 24, 26, 37, 40, 119, 122, 137, 157, 172, 194, 196

    as burial 2, 7, 36, 40, 58, 119–120, 153

    as leveler (equalizer) 15, 19–20, 24–25, 40, 43, 117, 179, 195

    corporate nature of 4, 15, 17–19, 24, 28, 31, 38, 40, 154, 163

Baptism, Eucharist and Ministry 17

baptismal

    commitment 7, 9–10, 19, 23–24, 41, 121, 141, 166, 168, 190

    covenant 21–23

    dignity 8, 15, 30, 127

baptismal eschatology 83, 122

baptistery 81

Baroque period 100

bereavement process 10, 162, 165–168, 171, 173, 189

Body of Christ

    reordered 43–44, 72, 75, 148, 178

Book of Common Prayer 20–21, 23–24, 31

Book of the Names of the Dead, The 174

burial

    early Christian 9, 43, 44, 46–48, 58, 60, 63, 65–66, 68–69, 72, 75–76, 91

    garments 58

    groups/societies 65, 100, 178

    rite of 62, 70, 77, 97, 102, 110, 179, 183

    sanitization of 96, 113, 163